PENGUIN PLAYS

PLAYS PLEASANT

BERNARD SHAW

PLAYS PLEASANT

*

ARMS AND THE MAN

CANDIDA

THE MAN OF DESTINY

YOU NEVER CAN TELL

PENGUIN BOOKS

Penguin Books Ltd, Harmondsworth, Middlesex, England
Penguin Books Australia Ltd, Ringwood, Victoria, Australia

—

Plays Pleasant first published 1898
Published in Penguin Books 1946
Reprinted 1949, 1951, 1953 (twice), 1955, 1956, 1958, 1959,
1961 (twice), 1963, 1964, 1965, 1966, 1968, 1970
Copyright © the Estate of Bernard Shaw, 1898
Protected by Copyright in all Berne Convention countries

—

Arms and The Man first produced in London, 1894; in New York, 1894 (the first Shaw
play produced in America)
Candida produced in London (privately) 1900, (publicly) 1904; in New York, 1903; in
Brussels, 1907 (the first performance of a Shaw play in French); in Paris, 1908 (the
first Shaw performance in France)
The Man of Destiny first produced at Croydon, 1897: in London, 1901; in New York,
1899; in Berlin, 1904
You Never Can Tell first produced in London (publicly) and in New York, 1905; in Berlin,
1906; in Paris, 1913

—

Made and printed in Great Britain
by Richard Clay (The Chaucer Press) Ltd,
Bungay, Suffolk
Set in Monotype Baskerville

Contents

PREFACE   7

ARMS AND THE MAN   17
An Anti-romantic Comedy

CANDIDA   91
A Mystery

THE MAN OF DESTINY   161
A Fictitious Paragraph of History

YOU NEVER CAN TELL   209
A Comedy

Preface

(1898)

READERS of the discourse with which the 'Unpleasant' volume commences will remember that I turned my hand to play-writing when a great deal of talk about 'the New Drama', followed by the actual establishment of a 'New Theatre' (the Independent), threatened to end in the humiliating discovery that the New Drama, in England at least, was a figment of the revolutionary imagination. This was not to be endured. I had rashly taken up the case; and rather than let it collapse I manufactured the evidence.

Man is a creature of habit. You cannot write three plays and then stop. Besides, the New movement did not stop. In 1894, Florence Farr, who had already produced Ibsen's Rosmersholm, was placed in command of the Avenue Theatre in London for a season on the new lines of Miss A. E. F. Horniman, who had family reasons for not yet appearing openly as a pioneer-manageress. There were, as available New Dramatists, myself, discovered by the Independent Theatre (at my own suggestion); Dr John Todhunter, who had been discovered before (his play The Black Cat had been one of the Independent's successes); and Mr W. B. Yeats, a genuine discovery. Dr Todhunter supplied A Comedy of Sighs: Mr Yeats, The Land of Heart's Desire. I, having nothing but unpleasant plays in my desk, hastily completed a first attempt at a pleasant one, and called it Arms and The Man, taking the title from the first line of Dryden's Virgil. It passed for a success, the applause on the first night being as promising as could be wished; and it ran from the 21st of April to the 7th of July. To witness it the public paid £1777:5:6, an average of £23:2:5 per representation (including nine matinées). A publisher receiving £1700 for a book would have made a satisfactory profit: experts in West End theatrical management will contemplate that figure with a grim smile.

In the autumn of 1894 I spent a few weeks in Florence, where I occupied myself with the religious art of the Middle Ages and its destruction by the Renascence. From a former visit to Italy on the same business I had hurried back to Birmingham to discharge my duties as musical critic at the Festival there. On that occasion a very remarkable collection of the works of our British 'pre-Raphaelite' painters was on view. I looked at these, and then went into the Birmingham churches to see the windows of William Morris and Burne-Jones. On the whole, Birmingham was more hopeful than the Italian cities; for the art it had to shew me was the work of living men, whereas modern Italy had, as far as I could see, no more connection with Giotto than Port Said has with Ptolemy. Now I am no believer in the worth of any mere taste for art that cannot produce what it professes to appreciate. When my subsequent visit to Italy found me practising the playwright's craft, the time was ripe for a modern pre-Raphaelite play. Religion was alive again, coming back upon men, even upon clergymen, with such power that not the Church of England itself could keep it out. Here my activity as a Socialist had placed me on sure and familiar ground. To me the members of the Guild of St Matthew were no more 'High Church clergymen', Dr Clifford no more 'an eminent Nonconformist divine', than I was to them 'an infidel'. There is only one religion, though there are a hundred versions of it. We all had the same thing to say; and though some of us cleared our throats to say it by singing revolutionary lyrics and republican hymns, we thought nothing of singing them to the music of Sullivan's Onward Christian Soldiers or Haydn's God Preserve the Emperor.

Now unity, however desirable in political agitations, is fatal to drama; for every drama must present a conflict. The end may be reconciliation or destruction; or, as in life itself, there may be no end; but the conflict is indispensable: no conflict, no drama. Certainly it is easy to dramatize the prosaic conflict of Christian Socialism with vulgar Unsocialism: for instance, in Widowers' Houses, the clergyman, who does not appear on the stage at all, is the real antagonist of the slum landlord. But the obvious conflicts of unmistakable good with unmistakable evil can only supply the crude drama of villain and hero, in which some absolute point of view is taken, and the dissentients are treated by the dramatist as enemies to be piously glorified or indignantly vilified. In such cheap wares I do not deal. Even in my unpleasant propagandist plays I have allowed every person his or her own point of view, and have, I hope, to the full extent of my understanding of him, been as sympathetic with Sir George Crofts as with any of the more genial and popular characters in the present volume. To distil the quintessential drama from pre-Raphaelitism, medieval or modern, it must be shewn at its best in conflict with the first broken, nervous, stumbling attempts to formulate its own revolt against itself as it develops into something higher. A coherent explanation of any such revolt, addressed intelligibly and prosaically to the intellect, can only come when the work is done, and indeed *done with*: that is to say, when the development, accomplished, admitted, and assimilated, is a story of yesterday. Long before any such understanding can be reached, the eyes of men begin to turn towards the distant light of the new age. Discernible at first only by the eyes of the man of genius, it must be focussed by him on the speculum of a work of art, and flashed back from that into the eyes of the common man. Nay, the artist himself has no other way of making himself conscious of the ray: it is by a blind instinct that he keeps on building up his masterpieces until their pinnacles catch the glint of the unrisen sun. Ask him to explain himself prosaically, and you find that he 'writes like an angel and talks like poor Poll', and is himself the first to make that epigram at his own expense. John Ruskin has told us clearly enough what is in the pictures of Carpaccio and Bellini: let him explain, if he can, where we shall be when the sun that is caught by the summits of the work of his favorite Tintoretto, of his aversion Rembrandt, of Mozart, of Beethoven and Wagner, of Blake and of Shelley, shall have reached the valleys. Let Ibsen explain, if he can, why the building of churches and happy homes is not the ultimate destiny of Man, and why, to thrill the unsatisfied younger generations, he must mount beyond it to heights that now seem unspeakably giddy and dreadful to him, and from which the first climbers must fall and dash themselves to pieces. He cannot explain it: he can only shew it to you as a vision in the magic glass of his artwork; so that you may catch his presentiment and make what you can of it. And this is the function that raises dramatic art above imposture and pleasure hunting, and enables the playwright to be something more than a skilled liar and pandar.

Here, then, was the higher but vaguer and timider version, the incoherent, mischievous, and even ridiculous unpracticalness, which offered me a dramatic antagonist for the clear, bold, sure, sensible, benevolent, salutarily shortsighted Christian Socialist idealism. I availed myself of it in Candida, the drunken scene in which has been much appreciated, I am told, in Aberdeen. I purposely contrived the play in such a way as to make the expenses of representation insignificant; so that, without pretending that I could appeal to a very wide circle of playgoers, I could reasonably sound a few of our more enlightened managers as to an experiment with half a dozen afternoon performances. They admired the play generously; indeed, I think that if any of them had been young enough to play the poet, my proposal might have been acceded to, in spite of many incidental difficulties. Nay, if only I had made the poet a cripple, or at least blind, so as to combine an easier disguise with a larger claim for sympathy, something might have been done. Richard Mansfield, who had, with apparent ease, made me quite famous in America by his productions of my plays, went so far as to put the play actually into rehearsal before he would confess himself beaten by the physical difficulties of the part. But they did beat him; and Candida did not see the footlights until my old ally the Independent Theatre, making a propagandist tour through the provinces with A Doll's House, added Candida to its repertory, to the great astonishment of its audiences.

In an idle moment in 1895 I began the little scene called The Man of Destiny, which is hardly more than a bravura piece to display the virtuosity of the two principal performers.

In the meantime I had devoted the spare moments of 1896 to the composition of two more plays, only the first of which appears in this volume. You Never Can Tell was an attempt to comply with many requests for a play in which the much paragraphed 'brilliancy' of Arms and The Man should be tempered by some consideration for the requirements of managers in search of fashionable comedies for West End Theatres. I had no difficulty in complying, as I have always cast my plays in the ordinary practical comedy form in use at all the theatres; and far from taking an unsympathetic view of the popular preference for fun, fashionable dresses, a little music, and even an exhibition of eating and drinking by people with an expensive air, attended by an if-possible-comic waiter, I was more than willing to shew that the drama can humanize these things as easily as they, in the wrong hands, can dehumanize the drama. But as often happens it was easier to do this than to persuade those who had asked for it that they had indeed got it. A chapter in Cyril Maude's history of the Haymarket Theatre records how the play was rehearsed there, and why I withdrew it. And so I reached the point at which, as narrated in the preface to the Unpleasant volume, I resolved to avail myself of my literary expertness to put my plays before the public in my own way.

It will be noticed that I have not been driven to this expedient by any hostility on the part of our managers. I will not pretend that the modern actor-manager's talent as player can in the nature of things be often associated with exceptional critical insight. As a rule, by the time a manager has experience enough to make him as safe a judge of plays as a Bond Street dealer is of pictures, he begins to be thrown out in his calculations by the slow but constant change of public taste, and by his own growing conservatism. But his need for new plays is so great, and the few accredited authors are so little able to keep pace with their commissions, that he is always apt to overrate rather than to underrate his discoveries in the way of new pieces by new authors. An original work by a man of genius like Ibsen may, of course, baffle him as it baffles many professed critics; but in the beaten path of drama no unacted works of merit, suitable to his purposes, have been discovered; whereas the production, at great expense, of very faulty plays written by novices (not 'backers') is by no means an unknown event. Indeed, to anyone who can estimate, even vaguely, the complicated trouble, the risk of heavy loss, and the initial expense and thought, involved by the production of a play, the ease with which dramatic authors, known and unknown, get their works performed must needs seem a wonder.

Only, authors must not expect managers to invest many thousands of pounds in plays, however fine (or the reverse), which will clearly not attract perfectly commonplace people. Playwriting and theatrical management, on the present commercial basis, are businesses like other businesses, depending on the patronage of great numbers of very ordinary customers. When the managers and authors study the wants of these customers, they succeed: when they do not, they fail. A public-spirited manager, or an author with a keen artistic conscience, may choose to pursue his business with the minimum of profit and the maximum of social usefulness by keeping as close as he can to the highest marketable limit of quality, and constantly feeling for an extension of that limit through the advance of popular culture. An unscrupulous manager or author may aim simply at the maximum of profit with the minimum of risk. These are the opposite poles of our system, represented in practice by our first rate managements at the one end, and the syndicates which exploit pornographic farces at the other. Between them there is plenty of room for most talents to breathe freely: at all events there is a career, no harder of access than any cognate career, for all qualified playwrights who bring the manager what his customers want and understand, or even enough of it to induce them to swallow at the same time a great deal that they neither want nor understand; for the public is touchingly humble in such matters.

For all that, the commercial limits are too narrow for our social welfare. The theatre is growing in importance as a social organ. Bad theatres are as mischievous as bad schools or bad churches; for modern civilization is rapidly multiplying the class to which the theatre is both school and church. Public and private life become daily more theatrical: the modern Kaiser, Dictator, President or Prime Minister is nothing if not an effective actor; all newspapers are now edited histrionically; and the records of our law courts shew that the stage is affecting personal conduct to an unprecedented extent, and affecting it by no means for the worse, except in so far as the theatrical education of the persons concerned has been romantic: that is, spurious, cheap, and vulgar. The truth is that dramatic invention is the first effort of man to become intellectually conscious. No frontier can be marked between drama and history or religion, or between acting and conduct, nor any distinction made between them that is not also the distinction between the masterpieces of the great dramatic poets and the commonplaces of our theatrical seasons. When this chapter of science is convincingly written, the national importance of the theatre will be as unquestioned as that of the army, the fleet, the Church, the law, and the schools.

For my part, I have no doubt that the commercial limits should be overstepped, and that the highest prestige, with a financial position of reasonable security and comfort, should be attainable in theatrical management by keeping the public in constant touch with the highest achievements of dramatic art. Our managers will not dissent to this: the best of them are so willing to get as near that position as they can without ruining themselves, that they can all point to honorable losses incurred through aiming 'over the heads of the public', and will no doubt risk such loss again, for the sake of their reputation as artists, as soon as a few popular successes enable them to afford it. But even if it were possible for them to educate the nation at their own private cost, why should they be expected to do it? There are much stronger objections to the pauperization of the public by private doles than were ever entertained, even by the Poor Law Commissioners of 1834, to the pauperization of private individuals by public doles. If we want a theatre which shall be to the drama what the National Gallery and British Museum are to painting and literature, we can get it by endowing it in the same way. In the meantime there are many possibilities of local activity. Groups of amateurs can form permanent societies and persevere until they develop into professional companies in established repertory theatres. In big cities it should be feasible to form influential committees, preferably without any actors, critics, or playwrights on them, and with as many persons of title as possible, for the purpose of approaching one of the leading local managers with a proposal that they shall, under a guarantee against loss, undertake a certain number of afternoon performances of the class required by the committee, in addition to their ordinary business. If the committee is influential enough, the offer will be accepted. In that case, the first performance will be the beginning of a classic repertory for the manager and his company which every subsequent performance will extend. The formation of the repertory will go hand in hand with the discovery and habituation of a regular audience for it; and it will eventually become profitable for the manager to multiply the number of performances at his own risk. It might even become worth his while to take a second theatre and establish the repertory permanently in it. In the event of any of his classic productions proving a fashionable success, he could transfer it to his fashionable house and make the most of it there. Such managership would carry a knighthood with it; and such a theatre would be the needed nucleus for municipal or national endowment. I make the suggestion quite disinterestedly; for as I am not an academic person, I should not be welcomed as an unacted classic by such a committee; and cases like mine would still leave forlorn hopes like the Independent Theatre its reason for existing. The committee plan, I may remind its critics, has been in operation in London for two hundred years in support of Italian opera.

Returning now to the actual state of things, it is clear that I have no grievance against our theatres. Knowing quite well what I was doing, I have heaped difficulties in the way of the performance of my plays by ignoring the majority of the manager's customers: nay, by positively making war on them. To the actor I have been more considerate, using all my cunning to enable him to make the most of his technical methods; but I have not hesitated on occasion to tax his intelligence very severely, making the stage effect depend not only on *nuances* of execution quite beyond the average skill produced by the routine of the English stage in its present condition, but on a perfectly sincere and straightforward conception of states of mind which still seem cynically perverse to most people, and on a good-humoredly contemptuous or profoundly pitiful attitude towards ethical conventions which seem to them validly heroic or venerable. It is inevitable that actors should suffer more than most of us from the sophistication of their consciousness by romance; and my view of romance as the great heresy to be swept off from art and life – as the food of modern pessimism and the bane of modern self-respect, is far more puzzling to the performers than it is to the pit. It is hard for an actor whose point of honor it is to be a perfect gentleman, to sympathize with an author who regards gentility as a dishonest folly, and gallantry and chivalry as treasonable to women and stultifying to men.

The misunderstanding is complicated by the fact that actors, in their demonstrations of emotion, have made a second nature of stage custom, which is often very much out of date as a representation of contemporary life. Sometimes the stage custom is not only obsolete, but fundamentally wrong: for instance, in the simple case of laughter and tears, in which it deals too liberally, it is certainly not based on the fact, easily enough discoverable in real life, that we only cry now in the effort to bear happiness, whilst we laugh and exult in destruction, confusion, and ruin. When a comedy is performed, it is nothing to me that the spectators laugh: any fool can make an audience laugh. I want to see how many of them, laughing or grave, are in the melting mood. And this result cannot be achieved, even by actors who thoroughly understand my purpose, except through an artistic beauty of execution unattainable without long and arduous practice, and an intellectual effort which my plays probably do not seem serious enough to call forth.

Beyond the difficulties thus raised by the nature and quality of my work, I have none to complain of. I have come upon no ill will, no inaccessibility, on the part of the very few managers with whom I have discussed it. As a rule I find that the actor-manager is over-sanguine, because he has the artist's habit of underrating the force of circumstances and exaggerating the power of the talented individual to prevail against them; whilst I have acquired the politician's habit of regarding the individual, however talented, as having no choice but to make the most of his circumstances. I half suspect that those managers who have had most to do with me, if asked to name the main obstacle to the performance of my plays, would unhesitatingly and unanimously reply 'The author'. And I confess that though as a matter of business I wish my plays to be performed, as a matter of instinct I fight against the inevitable misrepresentation of them with all the subtlety needed to conceal my ill will from myself as well as from the manager.

The main difficulty, of course, is the incapacity for serious drama of thousands of playgoers of all classes whose shillings and half guineas will buy as much in the market as if they delighted in the highest art. But with them I must frankly take the superior position. I know that many managers are wholly dependent on them, and that no manager is wholly independent of them; but I can no more write what they want than Joachim can put aside his fiddle and oblige a happy company of beanfeasters with a marching tune on the German concertina. They must keep away from my plays: that is all.

There is no reason, however, why I should take this haughty attitude towards those representative critics whose complaint is that my talent, though not unentertaining, lacks elevation of sentiment and seriousness of purpose. They can find, under the surface-brilliancy for which they give me credit, no coherent thought or sympathy, and accuse me, in various terms and degrees, of an inhuman and freakish wantonness; of preoccupation with 'the seamy side of life'; of paradox, cynicism, and eccentricity, reducible, as some contend, to a trite formula of treating bad as good and good as bad, important as trivial and trivial as important, serious as laughable and laughable as serious, and so forth. As to this formula I can only say that if any gentleman is simple enough to think that even a good comic opera can be produced by it, I invite him to try his hand, and see whether anything resembling one of my plays will reward him.

I could explain the matter easily enough if I chose; but the result would be that the people who misunderstand the plays would misunderstand the explanation ten times more. The particular exceptions taken are seldom more than symptoms of the underlying fundamental disagreement between the romantic morality of the critics and the natural morality of the plays. For example, I am quite aware that the much criticized Swiss officer in Arms and The Man is not a conventional stage soldier. He suffers from want of food and sleep; his nerves go to pieces after three days under fire, ending in the horrors of a rout and pursuit; he has found by experience that it is more important to have a few bits of chocolate to eat in the field than cartridges for his revolver. When many of my critics rejected these circumstances as fantastically improbable and cynically unnatural, it was not necessary to argue them into common sense: all I had to do was to brain them, so to speak, with the first half dozen military authorities at hand, beginning with the present Commander in Chief. But when it proved that such unromantic (but all the more dramatic) facts implied to them a denial of the existence of courage, patriotism, faith, hope, and charity, I saw that it was not really mere matter of fact that was at issue between us. One strongly Liberal critic, the late Moy Thomas, who had, in the teeth of a chorus of dissent, received my first play with the most generous encouragement, declared, when Arms and The Man was produced, that I had struck a wanton blow at the cause of liberty in the Balkan Peninsula by mentioning that it was not a matter of course for a Bulgarian in 1885 to wash his hands every day. He no doubt saw soon afterwards the squabble, reported all through Europe, between Stambouloff and an eminent lady of the Bulgarian court who took exception to his neglect of his fingernails. After that came the news of his ferocious assassination, with a description of the room prepared for the reception of visitors by his widow, who draped it with black, and decorated it with photographs of the mutilated body of her husband. Here was a sufficiently sensational confirmation of the accuracy of any sketch of the theatrical nature of the first apings of western civilization by spirited races just emerging from slavery. But it had no bearing on the real issue between my critic and myself, which was, whether the political and religious idealism which had inspired Gladstone to call for the rescue of these Balkan principalities from the despotism of the Turk, and converted miserably enslaved provinces into hopeful and gallant little States, will survive the general onslaught on idealism which is implicit, and indeed explicit, in Arms and The Man and the naturalist plays of the modern school. For my part I hope not; for idealism, which is only a flattering name for romance in politics and morals, is as obnoxious to me as romance in ethics or religion. In spite of a Liberal Revolution or two, I can no longer be satisfied with fictitious morals and fictitious good conduct, shedding fictitious glory on robbery, starvation, disease, crime, drink, war, cruelty, cupidity, and all the other commonplaces of civilization which drive men to the theatre to make foolish pretences that such things are progress, science, morals, religion, patriotism, imperial supremacy, national greatness and all the other names the newspapers call them. On the other hand, I see plenty of good in the world working itself out as fast as the idealists will allow it; and if they would only let it alone and learn to respect reality, which would include the beneficial exercise of respecting themselves, and incidentally respecting me, we should all get along much better and faster. At all events, I do not see moral chaos and anarchy as the alternative to romantic convention; and I am not going to pretend I do merely to please the people who are convinced that the world is held together only by the force of unanimous, strenuous, eloquent, trumpet-tongued lying. To me the tragedy and comedy of life lie in the consequences, sometimes terrible, sometimes ludicrous, of our persistent attempts to found our institutions on the ideals suggested to our imaginations by our half-satisfied passions, instead of on a genuinely scientific natural history. And with that hint as to what I am driving at, I withdraw and ring up the curtain.

ARMS AND THE MAN
1894

ARMS AND THE MAN

ACT I

Night: A lady's bedchamber in Bulgaria, in a small town near the Dragoman Pass, late in November in the year 1885. Through an open window with a little balcony a peak of the Balkans, wonderfully white and beautiful in the starlit snow, seems quite close at hand, though it is really miles away. The interior of the room is not like anything to be seen in the west of Europe. It is half rich Bulgarian, half cheap Viennese. Above the head of the bed, which stands against a little wall cutting off the left hand corner of the room, is a painted wooden shrine, blue and gold, with an ivory image of Christ, and a light hanging before it in a pierced metal ball suspended by three chains. The principal seat, placed towards the other side of the room and opposite the window, is a Turkish ottoman. The counterpane and hangings of the bed, the window curtains, the little carpet, and all the ornamental textile fabrics in the room are oriental and gorgeous; the paper on the walls is occidental and paltry. The washstand, against the wall on the side nearest the ottoman and window, consists of an enamelled iron basin with a pail beneath it in a painted metal frame, and a single towel on the rail at the side. The dressing table, between the bed and the window, is a common pine table, covered with a cloth of many colours, with an expensive toilet mirror on it. The door is on the side nearest the bed; and there is a chest of drawers between. This chest of drawers is also covered by a variegated native cloth; and on it there is a pile of paper backed novels, a box of chocolate creams, and a miniature easel with a large photograph of an extremely handsome officer, whose lofty bearing and magnetic glance can be felt even from the portrait. The room is lighted by a candle on the chest of drawers, and another on the dressing table with a box of matches beside it.

The window is hinged doorwise and stands wide open. Outside, a pair of wooden shutters, opening outwards, also stand open. On the balcony a young lady, intensely conscious of the romantic beauty of the night, and the fact that her own youth and beauty are part of it, is gazing at the snowy Balkans. She is in her nightgown, well covered by a long mantle of furs, worth, on a moderate estimate, about three times the furniture of the room.

Her reverie is interrupted by her mother, Catherine Petkoff, a woman over forty, imperiously energetic, with magnificent black hair and eyes, who might be a very splendid specimen of the wife of a mountain farmer, but is determined to be a Viennese lady, and to that end wears a fashionable tea gown on all occasions.

CATHERINE [*entering hastily, full of good news*] Raina! [*She pronounces it Rah-eena, with the stress on the ee*]. Raina! [*She goes to the bed, expecting to find Raina there*]. Why, where – ? [*Raina looks into the room*]. Heavens, child! are you out in the night air instead of in your bed? Youll catch your death. Louka told me you were asleep.

RAINA [*dreamily*] I sent her away. I wanted to be alone. The stars are so beautiful! What is the matter?

CATHERINE. Such news! There has been a battle.

RAINA [*her eyes dilating*] Ah! [*She comes eagerly to Catherine*].

CATHERINE. A great battle at Slivnitza! A victory! And it was won by Sergius.

RAINA [*with a cry of delight*] Ah! [*They embrace rapturously*] Oh, mother! [*Then, with sudden anxiety*] Is father safe?

CATHERINE. Of course! he sends me the news. Sergius is the hero of the hour, the idol of the regiment.

RAINA. Tell me, tell me. How was it? [*Ecstatically*] Oh, mother! mother! mother! [*She pulls her mother down on the ottoman; and they kiss one another frantically*].

CATHERINE [*with surging enthusiasm*] You cant guess how splendid it is. A cavalry charge! think of that! He defied our Russian commanders – acted without orders – led a charge on his own responsibility – headed it himself – was the first man to sweep through their guns. Cant you see it, Raina: our gallant splendid Bulgarians with their swords and eyes flashing, thundering down like an avalanche and scattering the wretched Serbs and their dandified Austrian officers like chaff. And you! you kept Sergius waiting a year before you would be betrothed to him. Oh, if you have a drop of Bulgarian blood in your veins, you will worship him when he comes back.

RAINA. What will he care for my poor little worship after the acclamations of a whole army of heroes? But no matter: I am so happy! so proud! [*She rises and walks about excitedly*]. It proves that all our ideas were real after all.

CATHERINE [*indignantly*] Our ideas real! What do you mean?

RAINA. Our ideas of what Sergius would do. Our patriotism. Our heroic ideals. I sometimes used to doubt whether they were anything but dreams. Oh, what faithless little creatures girls are! When I buckled on Sergius's sword he looked so noble: it was treason to think of disillusion or humiliation or failure. And yet – and yet – [*She sits down again suddenly*] Promise me youll never tell him.

CATHERINE. Dont ask me for promises until I know what I'm promising.

RAINA. Well, it came into my head just as he was holding me in his arms and looking into my eyes, that perhaps we only had our heroic ideas because we are so fond of reading Byron and Puskhin, and because we were so delighted with the opera that season at Bucharest. Real life is so seldom like that! indeed never, as far as I knew it then. [*Remorsefully*] Only think, mother: I doubted him: I wondered whether all his heroic qualities and his soldiership might not prove mere imagination when he went into a real battle. I had an uneasy fear that he might cut a poor figure there beside all those clever officers from the Tsar's court.

CATHERINE. A poor figure! Shame on you! The Serbs have Austrian officers who are just as clever as the Russians; but we have beaten them in every battle for all that.

RAINA [*laughing and snuggling against her mother*] Yes: I was only a prosaic little coward. Oh, to think that it was all true! that Sergius is just as splendid and noble as he looks! that the world is really a glorious world for women who can see its glory and men who can act its romance! What

21

happiness! what unspeakable fulfilment!

They are interrupted by the entry of Louka, a handsome proud girl in a pretty Bulgarian peasant's dress with double apron, so defiant that her servility to Raina is almost insolent. She is afraid of Catherine, but even with her goes as far as she dares.

LOUKA. If you please, madam, all the windows are to be closed and the shutters made fast. They say there may be shooting in the streets. [*Raina and Catherine rise together, alarmed*]. The Serbs are being chased right back through the pass; and they say they may run into the town. Our cavalry will be after them; and our people will be ready for them, you may be sure, now theyre running away. [*She goes out on the balcony, and pulls the outside shutters to; then steps back into the room*].

CATHERINE [*businesslike, housekeeping instincts aroused*] I must see that everything is made safe downstairs.

RAINA. I wish our people were not so cruel. What glory is there in killing wretched fugitives?

CATHERINE. Cruel! Do you suppose they would hesitate to kill you – or worse?

RAINA [*to Louka*] Leave the shutters so that I can just close them if I hear any noise.

CATHERINE [*authoritatively, turning on her way to the door*] Oh no, dear: you must keep them fastened. You would be sure to drop off to sleep and leave them open. Make them fast, Louka.

LOUKA. Yes, madam. [*She fastens them*].

RAINA. Dont be anxious about me. The moment I hear a shot, I shall blow out the candles and roll myself up in bed with my ears well covered.

CATHERINE. Quite the wisest thing you can do, my love. Goodnight.

RAINA. Goodnight. [*Her emotion comes back for a moment*]. Wish me joy [*They kiss*]. This is the happiest night of my life – if only there are no fugitives.

CATHERINE. Go to bed, dear; and dont think of them. [*She goes out*].

LOUKA [*secretly to Raina*] If you would like the shutters open, just give them a push like this [*she pushes them: they open: she pulls them to again*]. One of them ought to be bolted at the bottom; but the bolt's gone.

RAINA [*with dignity, reproving her*] Thanks, Louka; but we must do what we are told. [*Louka makes a grimace*]. Goodnight.

LOUKA [*carelessly*] Goodnight. [*She goes out, swaggering*].

Raina, left alone, takes off her fur cloak and throws it on the ottoman. Then she goes to the chest of drawers, and adores the portrait there with feelings that are beyond all expression. She does not kiss it or press it to her breast, or shew it any mark of bodily affection; but she takes it in her hands and elevates it, like a priestess.

RAINA [*looking up at the picture*] Oh, I shall never be unworthy of you any more, my soul's hero: never, never, never. [*She replaces it reverently. Then she selects a novel from the little pile of books. She turns over the leaves dreamily; finds her page; turns the book inside out at it; and, with a happy sigh, gets into bed and prepares to read herself to sleep. But before abandoning herself to fiction, she raises her eyes once more, thinking of the blessed reality, and murmurs*] My hero! my hero!

A distant shot breaks the quiet of the night. She starts, listening; and two more shots, much nearer, follow, startling her so that she scrambles out of bed, and hastily blows out the candle on the chest of drawers. Then, putting her fingers in her ears, she runs to the dressing table, blows out the light there, and hurries back to bed in the dark, nothing being visible but the glimmer of the light in the pierced ball before the image, and the starlight seen through the slits at the top of the shutters. The firing breaks out again: there is a startling fusillade quite close at hand. Whilst it is still echoing, the shutters disappear, pulled open from without; and for an instant the rectangle of snowy starlight flashes out with the figure of a man silhouetted in black upon it. The shutters close immediately; and the room is dark again. But the silence is now broken by the sound of panting. Then there is a scratch; and the flame of a match is seen in the middle of the room.

RAINA [*crouching on the bed*] Who's there? [*The match is out instantly*]. Who's there? Who is that?

A MAN'S VOICE [*in the darkness, subduedly, but threateningly*] Sh – sh! Dont call out; or youll be shot. Be good; and no harm will happen to you. [*She is heard leaving her bed, and making for the door*]. Take care: it's no use trying to run away.

RAINA. But who –

THE VOICE [*warning*] Remember: if you raise your voice my revolver will go off. [*Commandingly*]. Strike a light and let me see you. Do you hear. [*Another moment of silence and darkness as she retreats to the chest of drawers. Then she lights a candle; and the mystery is at an end. He is a man of about 35, in a deplorable plight, bespattered with mud and blood and snow, his belt and the strap of his revolver-case keeping together the torn ruins of the blue tunic of a Serbian artillery officer. All that the candlelight and his unwashed unkempt condition make it possible to discern is that he is of middling stature and undistinguished appearance, with strong neck and shoulders, roundish obstinate looking head covered with short crisp bronze curls, clear quick eyes and good brows and mouth, hopelessly prosaic nose like that of a strong minded baby, trim soldierlike carriage and energetic manner, and with all his wits about him in spite of his desperate predicament: even with a sense of the humor of it, without, however, the least intention of trifling with it or throwing away a chance. Reckoning up what he can guess about Raina: her age, her social position, her character, and the extent to which she is frightened, he continues, more politely but still determinedly*] Excuse my disturbing you; but you recognize my uniform? Serb! If I'm caught I shall be killed. [*Menacingly*] Do you understand that?

RAINA. Yes.

THE MAN. Well, I dont intend to get killed if I can help it. [*Still more formidably*] Do you understand that? [*He locks the door quickly but quietly*].

RAINA [*disdainfully*] I suppose not. [*She draws herself up superbly, and looks him straight in the face, adding, with cutting emphasis*] Some soldiers, I know, are afraid to die.

THE MAN [*with grim goodhumor*] All of them, dear lady, all of them, believe me. It is our duty to live as long as we can. Now, if you raise an alarm –

RAINA [*cutting him short*] You will shoot me. How do you know that *I* am afraid to die?

THE MAN [*cunningly*] Ah; but suppose I dont shoot you, what will happen then? A lot of your cavalry will burst into this pretty room of yours and slaughter me here like a pig; for I'll fight like a demon: they shant get me into the street to amuse themselves with: I know what they are. Are you prepared to receive that sort of company in your present undress? [*Raina, suddenly conscious of her nightgown, instinctively shrinks and gathers it more closely about her neck. He watches her and adds pitilessly*] Hardly presentable, eh? [*She turns to the ottoman. He raises his pistol instantly, and cries*] Stop! [*She stops*]. Where are you going?

RAINA [*with dignified patience*] Only to get my cloak.

THE MAN [*passing swiftly to the ottoman and snatching the cloak*] A good idea! I'll keep the cloak; and youll take care that nobody comes in and sees you without it. This is a better weapon than the revolver: eh? [*He throws the pistol down on the ottoman*].

RAINA [*revolted*] It is not the weapon of a gentleman!

THE MAN. It's good enough for a man with only you to stand between him and death. [*As they look at one another for a moment, Raina hardly able to believe that even a Serbian officer can be so cynically and selfishly unchivalrous, they are startled by a sharp fusillade in the street. The chill of imminent death hushes the man's voice as he adds*] Do you hear? If you are going to bring those blackguards in on me you shall receive them as you are.

Clamor and disturbance. The pursuers in the street batter at the house door, shouting Open the door! Open the door! Wake up, will you! *A man servant's voice calls to them angrily from within* This is Major Petkoff's house: you cant come in here; *but a renewal of the clamor, and a torrent of blows on the door, end with his letting a chain down with a clank, followed by a rush of heavy footsteps and a din of triumphant yells, dominated at last by the voice of Catherine, indignantly addressing an officer with* What does this mean, sir? Do you know where you are? *The noise subsides suddenly.*

LOUKA [*outside, knocking at the bedroom door*] My lady! my lady! get up quick and open the door. If you dont they will break it down.

The fugitive throws up his head with the gesture of a man who sees that it is all over with him, and drops the manner he has been assuming to intimidate Raina.

THE MAN [*sincerely and kindly*] No use, dear: I'm done for. [*Flinging the cloak to her*] Quick! wrap yourself up: theyre coming.

RAINA. Oh, thank you. [*She wraps herself up with intense relief*].

THE MAN [*between his teeth*] Dont mention it.

RAINA [*anxiously*] What will you do?

THE MAN [*grimly*] The first man in will find out. Keep out of the way; and dont look. It wont last long; but it will not be nice. [*He draws his sabre and faces the door, waiting.*]

RAINA [*impulsively*] I'll help you. I'll save you.

THE MAN. You cant.

RAINA. I can. I'll hide you. [*She drags him towards the window*]. Here! behind the curtains.

THE MAN [*yielding to her*] Theres just half a chance, if you keep your head.

RAINA [*drawing the curtain before him*] S-sh! [*She makes for the ottoman*].

THE MAN [*putting out his head*] Remember –

RAINA [*running back to him*] Yes?

THE MAN. – nine soldiers out of ten are born fools.

RAINA. Oh! [*She draws the curtain angrily before him*].

THE MAN [*looking out at the other side*] If they find me, I promise you a fight: a devil of a fight.

She stamps at him. He disappears hastily. She takes off her cloak, and throws it across the foot of the bed. Then, with a sleepy, disturbed air, she opens the door. Louka enters excitedly.

LOUKA. One of those beasts of Serbs has been seen climbing up the waterpipe to your balcony. Our men want to search for him; and they are so wild and drunk and furious. [*She makes for the other side of the room to get as far from the door as possible*]. My lady says you are to dress at once, and to — [*She sees the revolver lying on the ottoman, and stops, petrified*].

RAINA [*as if annoyed at being disturbed*] They shall not search here. Why have they been let in?

CATHERINE [*coming in hastily*] Raina, darling, are you safe? Have you seen anyone or heard anything?

RAINA. I heard the shooting. Surely the soldiers will not dare come in here?

CATHERINE. I have found a Russian officer, thank Heaven: he knows Sergius. [*Speaking through the door to someone outside*] Sir: will you come in now. My daughter will receive you.

A young Russian officer, in Bulgarian uniform, enters, sword in hand.

OFFICER [*with soft feline politeness and stiff military carriage*] Good evening, gracious lady. I am sorry to intrude; but there is a Serb hiding on the balcony. Will you and the gracious lady your mother please to withdraw whilst we search?

RAINA [*petulantly*] Nonsense, sir: you can see that there is no one on the balcony. [*She throws the shutters wide open and stands with her back to the curtain where the man is hidden, pointing to the moonlit balcony. A couple of shots are fired right under the window; and a bullet shatters the glass opposite Raina, who winks and gasps, but stands her ground; whilst Catherine screams, and the officer, with a cry of* Take care! *rushes to the balcony*].

THE OFFICER [*on the balcony, shouting savagely down to the street*] Cease firing there, you fools: do you hear? Cease firing, damn you! [*He glares down for a moment; then turns to Raina, trying to resume his polite manner*]. Could anyone have got in without your knowledge? Were you asleep?

RAINA. No: I have not been to bed.

THE OFFICER [*impatiently, coming back into the room*] Your

neighbors have their heads so full of runaway Serbs that they see them everywhere. [*Politely*] Gracious lady: a thousand pardons. Goodnight. [*Military bow, which Raina returns coldly. Another to Catherine, who follows him out*].

Raina closes the shutters. She turns and sees Louka, who has been watching the scene curiously.

RAINA. Dont leave my mother, Louka, until the soldiers go away.

Louka glances at Raina, at the ottoman, at the curtain; then purses her lips secretively, laughs insolently, and goes out. Raina, highly offended by this demonstration, follows her to the door, and shuts it behind her with a slam, locking it violently. The man immediately steps out from behind the curtain, sheathing his sabre. Then, dismissing the danger from his mind in a businesslike way, he comes affably to Raina.

THE MAN. A narrow shave; but a miss is as good as a mile. Dear young lady: your servant to the death. I wish for your sake I had joined the Bulgarian army instead of the other one. I am not a native Serb.

RAINA [*haughtily*] No: you are one of the Austrians who set the Serbs on to rob us of our national liberty, and who officer their army for them. We hate them!

THE MAN. Austrian! not I. Dont hate me, dear young lady. I am a Swiss, fighting merely as a professional soldier. I joined the Serbs because they came first on the road from Switzerland. Be generous: youve beaten us hollow.

RAINA. Have I not been generous?

THE MAN. Noble! Heroic! But I'm not saved yet. This particular rush will soon pass through; but the pursuit will go on all night by fits and starts. I must take my chance to get off in a quiet interval. [*Pleasantly*] You dont mind my waiting just a minute or two, do you?

RAINA [*putting on her most genteel society manner*] Oh, not at all. Wont you sit down?

THE MAN. Thanks [*He sits on the foot of the bed*].

Raina walks with studied elegance to the ottoman and sits down. Unfortunately she sits on the pistol, and jumps up with a shriek. The man, all nerves, shies like a frightened horse to the other side of the room.

THE MAN [*irritably*] Dont frighten me like that. What is it?

RAINA. Your revolver! It was staring that officer in the face all the time. What an escape!

THE MAN [*vexed at being unnecessarily terrified*] Oh, is that all?

RAINA [*staring at him rather superciliously as she conceives a poorer and poorer opinion of him, and feels proportionately more and more at her ease*] I am sorry I frightened you. [*She takes up the pistol and hands it to him*]. Pray take it to protect yourself against me.

THE MAN [*grinning wearily at the sarcasm as he takes the pistol*] No use, dear young lady: theres nothing in it. It's not loaded. [*He makes a grimace at it, and drops it disparagingly into his revolver case.*]

RAINA. Load it by all means.

THE MAN. Ive no ammunition. What use are cartridges in battle? I always carry chocolate instead; and I finished the last cake of that hours ago.

RAINA [*outraged in her most cherished ideals of manhood*] Chocolate! Do you stuff your pockets with sweets – like a schoolboy – even in the field?

THE MAN [*grinning*] Yes: isnt it contemptible? [*Hungrily*] I wish I had some now.

RAINA. Allow me. [*She sails away scornfully to the chest of drawers, and returns with the box of confectionery in her hand*]. I am sorry I have eaten them all except these. [*She offers him the box*].

THE MAN [*ravenously*] Youre an angel! [*He gobbles the contents*]. Creams! Delicious! [*He looks anxiously to see whether there are any more. There are none: he can only scrape the box with his fingers and suck them. When that nourishment is exhausted he accepts the inevitable with pathetic goodhumor, and says, with grateful emotion*] Bless you, dear lady! You can always tell an old soldier by the inside of his holsters and cartridge boxes. The young ones carry pistols and cartridges: the old ones, grub. Thank you. [*He hands back the box. She snatches it contemptuously from him and throws it away. He shies again, as if she had meant to strike him*]. Ugh! Dont do things so suddenly, gracious lady. It's mean to revenge yourself because I frightened you just now.

RAINA [*loftily*] Frighten me! Do you know, sir, that though I am only a woman, I think I am at heart as brave as you.

THE MAN. I should think so. You havnt been under fire for three days as I have. I can stand two days without shewing it much: but no man can stand three days; I'm as nervous as a mouse. [*He sits down on the ottoman, and takes his head in his hands*]. Would you like to see me cry?

RAINA [*alarmed*] No.

THE MAN. If you would, all you have to do is to scold me just as if I were a little boy and you my nurse. If I were in camp now, theyd play all sorts of tricks on me.

RAINA [*a little moved*] I'm sorry. I wont scold you. [*Touched by the sympathy in her tone, he raises his head and looks gratefully at her: she immediately draws back and says stiffly*] You must excuse me: our soldiers are not like that. [*She moves away from the ottoman*].

THE MAN. Oh yes they are. There are only two sorts of soldiers: old ones and young ones. Ive served fourteen years: half of your fellows never smelt powder before. Why, how is it that youve just beaten us? Sheer ignorance of the art of war, nothing else. [*Indignantly*] I never saw anything so unprofessional.

RAINA [*ironically*] Oh! was it unprofessional to beat you?

THE MAN. Well, come! is it professional to throw a regiment of cavalry on a battery of machine guns, with the dead certainty that if the guns go off not a horse or man will ever get within fifty yards of the fire? I couldnt believe my eyes when I saw it.

RAINA [*eagerly turning to him, as all her enthusiasm and her dreams of glory rush back to her*] Did you see the great cavalry charge? Oh, tell me about it. Describe it to me.

THE MAN. You never saw a cavalry charge, did you?

RAINA. How could I?

THE MAN. Ah, perhaps not. No: of course not! Well, it's a funny sight. It's like slinging a handful of peas against a window pane: first one comes; then two or three close behind him; and then all the rest in a lump.

RAINA [*her eyes dilating as she raises her clasped hands ecstatically*] Yes, first One! the bravest of the brave!

THE MAN [*prosaically*] Hm! you should see the poor devil pulling at his horse.

RAINA. Why should he pull at his horse?

THE MAN [*impatient of so stupid a question*] It's running away with him, of course: do you suppose the fellow wants to get there before the others and be killed? Then they all come. You can tell the young ones by their wildness and their slashing. The old ones come bunched up under the number one guard: they know that theyre mere projectiles, and that its no use trying to fight. The wounds are mostly broken knees, from the horses cannoning together.

RAINA. Ugh! But I dont believe the first man is a coward. I know he is a hero!

THE MAN [*goodhumoredly*] Thats what youd have said if youd seen the first man in the charge today.

RAINA [*breathless, forgiving him everything*] Ah, I knew it! Tell me. Tell me about him.

THE MAN. He did it like an operatic tenor. A regular handsome fellow, with flashing eyes and lovely moustache, shouting his war-cry and charging like Don Quixote at the windmills. We did laugh.

RAINA. You dared to laugh!

THE MAN. Yes; but when the sergeant ran up as white as a sheet, and told us theyd sent us the wrong ammunition, and that we couldnt fire a round for the next ten minutes, we laughed at the other side of our mouths. I never felt so sick in my life; though Ive been in one or two very tight places. And I hadnt even a revolver cartridge: only chocolate. We'd no bayonets: nothing. Of course, they just cut us to bits. And there was Don Quixote flourishing like a drum major, thinking he'd done the cleverest thing ever known, whereas he ought to be courtmartialled for it. Of all the fools ever let loose on a field of battle, that man must be the very maddest. He and his regiment simply committed suicide; only the pistol missed fire: thats all.

RAINA [*deeply wounded, but steadfastly loyal to her ideals*] Indeed! Would you know him again if you saw him?

THE MAN. Shall I ever forget him!

She again goes to the chest of drawers. He watches her with a vague hope that she may have something more for him to eat. She takes the portrait from its stand and brings it to him.

RAINA. That is a photograph of the gentleman – the patriot and hero – to whom I am betrothed.

THE MAN [*recognizing it with a shock*] I'm really very sorry. [*Looking at her*] Was it fair to lead me on? [*He looks at the portrait again*] Yes: thats Don Quixote: not a doubt of it. [*He stifles a laugh.*]

RAINA [*quickly*] Why do you laugh?

THE MAN [*apologetic, but still greatly tickled*] I didnt laugh, I assure you. At least I didnt mean to. But when I think of him charging the windmills and imagining he was doing the finest thing – [*He chokes with suppressed laughter*].

RAINA [*sternly*] Give me back the portrait, sir.

THE MAN [*with sincere remorse*] Of course. Certainly. I'm really very sorry. [*He hands her the picture. She deliberately kisses it and looks him straight in the face before returning to the chest of drawers to replace it. He follows her, apologizing*]. Perhaps I'm quite wrong, you know: no doubt I am. Most likely he had got wind of the cartridge business somehow, and knew it was a safe job.

RAINA. That is to say, he was a pretender and a coward! You did not dare say that before.

THE MAN [*with a comic gesture of despair*] It's no use, dear lady: I cant make you see it from the professional point of view. [*As he turns away to get back to the ottoman, a couple of distant shots threaten renewed trouble*].

RAINA [*sternly, as she sees him listening to the shots*] So much the better for you!

THE MAN [*turning*] How?

RAINA. You are my enemy; and you are at my mercy. What would I do if I were a professional soldier?

THE MAN. Ah, true, dear young lady: youre always right. I know how good youve been to me: to my last hour I shall remember those three chocolate creams. It was unsoldierly; but it was angelic.

RAINA [*coldly*] Thank you. And now I will do a soldierly thing. You cannot stay here after what you have just said about my future husband; but I will go out on the balcony and see whether it is safe for you to climb down into the street. [*She turns to the window*].

THE MAN [*changing countenance*] Down that waterpipe! Stop! Wait! I cant! I darent! The very thought of it makes me giddy. I came up it fast enough with death behind me. But to face it now in cold blood — ! [*He sinks on the ottoman*]. It's no use: I give up: I'm beaten. Give the alarm. [*He drops his head on his hands in the deepest dejection*].

RAINA [*disarmed by pity*] Come: dont be disheartened. [*She stoops over him almost maternally: he shakes his head*]. Oh, you are a very poor soldier: a chocolate cream soldier! Come, cheer up! it takes less courage to climb down than to face capture: remember that.

THE MAN [*dreamily, lulled by her voice*] No: capture only means death; and death is sleep: oh, sleep, sleep, sleep, undisturbed sleep! Climbing down the pipe means doing something — exerting myself — thinking! Death ten times over first.

RAINA [*softly and wonderingly, catching the rhythm of his weariness*] Are you as sleepy as that?

THE MAN. Ive not had two hours undisturbed sleep since I joined. I havnt closed my eyes for forty-eight hours.

RAINA [*at her wit's end*] But what am I to do with you?

THE MAN [*staggering up, roused by her desperation*] Of course. I must do something. [*He shakes himself; pulls himself together; and speaks with rallied vigor and courage*]. You see, sleep or no sleep, hunger or no hunger, tired or not tired, you can always do a thing when you know it must be done. Well, that pipe must be got down: [*he hits himself on the chest*] do you hear that, you chocolate cream soldier? [*He turns to the window*].

RAINA [*anxiously*] But if you fall?

THE MAN. I shall sleep as if the stones were a feather bed. Goodbye. [*He makes boldly for the window; and his hand is on the shutter when there is a terrible burst of firing in the street beneath*].

RAINA [*rushing to him*] Stop! [*She seizes him recklessly, and pulls him quite round*]. Theyll kill you.

THE MAN [*coolly, but attentively*] Never mind: this sort of thing is all in my day's work. I'm bound to take my chance. [*Decisively*] Now do what I tell you. Put out the candle; so that they shant see the light when I open the shutters. And keep away from the window, whatever you do. If they see me theyre sure to have a shot at me.

RAINA [*clinging to him*] Theyre sure to see you: it's bright moonlight. I'll save you. Oh, how can you be so indifferent! You want me to save you, dont you?

THE MAN. I really dont want to be troublesome. [*She shakes him in her impatience*]. I am not indifferent, dear young lady, I assure you. But how is it to be done?

RAINA. Come away from the window. [*She takes him firmly back to the middle of the room. The moment she releases him he turns mechanically towards the window again. She seizes him and turns him back, exclaiming*] Please! [*He becomes motionless, like a hypnotized rabbit, his fatigue gaining fast on him. She releases him, and addresses him patronizingly*]. Now listen. You must trust to our hospitality. You do not yet know in whose house you are. I am a Petkoff.

THE MAN. A pet what?

RAINA [*rather indignantly*] I mean that I belong to the family of the Petkoffs, the richest and best known in our country.

THE MAN. Oh yes, of course. I beg your pardon. The Petkoffs, to be sure. How stupid of me!

RAINA. You know you never heard of them until this

moment. How can you stoop to pretend!

THE MAN. Forgive me: I'm too tired to think; and the change of subject was too much for me. Dont scold me.

RAINA. I forgot. It might make you cry. [*He nods, quite seriously. She pouts and then resumes her patronizing tone*]. I must tell you that my father holds the highest command of any Bulgarian in our army. He is [*proudly*] a Major.

THE MAN [*prentending to be deeply impressed*] A Major! Bless me! Think of that!

RAINA. You shewed great ignorance in thinking that it was necessary to climb up to the balcony because ours is the only private house that has two rows of windows. There is a flight of stairs inside to get up and down by.

THE MAN. Stairs! How grand! You live in great luxury indeed, dear young lady.

RAINA. Do you know what a library is?

THE MAN. A library? A roomful of books?

RAINA. Yes. We have one, the only one in Bulgaria.

THE MAN. Actually a real library! I should like to see that.

RAINA [*affectedly*] I tell you these things to shew you that you are not in the house of ignorant country folk who would kill you the moment they saw your Serbian uniform, but among civilized people. We go to Bucharest every year for the opera season; and I have spent a whole month in Vienna.

THE MAN. I saw that, dear young lady. I saw at once that you knew the world.

RAINA. Have you ever seen the opera of Ernani?

THE MAN. Is that the one with the devil in it in red velvet, and a soldiers' chorus?

RAINA [*contemptuously*] No!

THE MAN [*stifling a heavy sigh of weariness*] Then I dont know it.

RAINA. I thought you might have remembered the great scene where Ernani, flying from his foes just as you are tonight, takes refuge in the castle of his bitterest enemy, an old Castilian noble. The noble refuses to give him up. His guest is sacred to him.

THE MAN [*quickly, waking up a little*] Have your people got that notion?

RAINA [*with dignity*] My mother and I can understand that notion, as you call it. And if instead of threatening me with your pistol as you did you had simply thrown yourself as a fugitive on our hospitality, you would have been as safe as in your father's house.

THE MAN. Quite sure?

RAINA [*turning her back on him in disgust*] Oh, it is useless to try to make you understand.

THE MAN. Dont be angry: you see how awkward it would be for me if there was any mistake. My father is a very hospitable man: he keeps six hotels; but I couldnt trust him as far as that. What about your father?

RAINA. He is away at Slivnitza fighting for his country. I answer for your safety. There is my hand in pledge of it. Will that reassure you? [*She offers him her hand*].

THE MAN [*looking dubiously at his own hand*] Better not touch my hand, dear young lady. I must have a wash first.

RAINA [*touched*] That is very nice of you. I see that you are a gentleman.

THE MAN [*puzzled*] Eh?

RAINA. You must not think I am surprised. Bulgarians of really good standing – people in our position – wash their hands nearly every day. So you see I can appreciate your delicacy. You may take my hand. [*She offers it again*].

THE MAN [*kissing it with his hands behind his back*] Thanks, gracious young lady: I feel safe at last. And now would you mind breaking the news to your mother? I had better not stay here secretly longer than is necessary.

RAINA. If you will be so good as to keep perfectly still whilst I am away.

THE MAN. Certainly. [*He sits down on the ottoman*].

    Raina goes to the bed and wraps herself in the fur cloak. His eyes close. She goes to the door. Turning for a last look at him, she sees that he is dropping off to sleep.

RAINA [*at the door*] You are not going asleep, are you? [*He murmurs inarticulately: she runs to him and shakes him*]. Do you hear? Wake up: you are falling asleep.

THE MAN. Eh? Falling aslee–? Oh no: not the least in the world: I was only thinking. It's all right: I'm wide awake.

RAINA [*severely*] Will you please stand up while I am away. [*He rises reluctantly*]. All the time, mind.

THE MAN [*standing unsteadily*] Certainly. Certainly: you may depend on me.

Raina looks doubtfully at him. He smiles weakly. She goes reluctantly, turning again at the door, and almost catching him in the act of yawning. She goes out.

THE MAN [*drowsily*] Sleep, sleep, sleep, sleep, slee– [*The words trail off into a murmur. He wakes again with a shock on the point of falling*]. Where am I? That's what I want to know: where am I? Must keep awake. Nothing keeps me awake except danger: remember that: [*intently*] danger, danger, danger, dan – [*trailing off again; another shock*] Wheres danger? Mus' find it. [*He starts off vaguely round the room in search of it*]. What am I looking for? Sleep – danger – dont know. [*He stumbles against the bed*]. Ah yes: now I know. All right now. I'm to go to bed, but not to sleep. Be sure not to sleep, because of danger. Not to lie down either, only sit down. [*He sits on the bed. A blissful expression comes into his face*]. Ah! [*With a happy sigh he sinks back at full length; lifts his boots into the bed with a final effort; and falls fast asleep instantly*].

Catherine comes in, followed by Raina.

RAINA [*looking at the ottoman*] He's gone! I left him here.

CATHERINE. Here! Then he must have climbed down from the –

RAINA [*seeing him*] Oh! [*She points*].

CATHERINE [*scandalized*] Well! [*She strides to the bed, Raina following until she is opposite her on the other side*]. He's fast asleep. The brute!

RAINA [*anxiously*] Sh!

CATHERINE [*shaking him*] Sir! [*Shaking him again, harder*] Sir!! [*Vehemently, shaking very hard*] Sir!!!

RAINA [*catching her arm*] Dont, mamma: the poor darling is worn out. Let him sleep.

CATHERINE [*letting him go, and turning amazed to Raina*] The poor darling! Raina!!! [*She looks sternly at her daughter*]. *The man sleeps profoundly.*

*The sixth of March, 1886. In the garden of Major Petkoff's house.
It is a fine spring morning: the garden looks fresh and pretty. Beyond
the paling the tops of a couple of minarets can be seen, shewing that
there is a valley there, with the little town in it. A few miles further the
Balkan mountains rise and shut in the landscape. Looking towards
them from within the garden, the side of the house is seen on the left,
with a garden door reached by a little flight of steps. On the right the
stable yard, with its gateway, encroaches on the garden. There are
fruit bushes along the paling and house, covered with washing spread
out to dry. A path runs by the house, and rises by two steps at the
corner, where it turns out of sight. In the middle, a small table, with
two bent wood chairs at it, is laid for breakfast with Turkish coffee
pot, cups, rolls, etc.; but the cups have been used and the bread
broken. There is a wooden garden seat against the wall on the right.*

*Louka, smoking a cigaret, is standing between the table and the
house, turning her back with angry disdain on a man servant who is
lecturing her. He is a middle-aged man of cool temperament and low
but clear and keen intelligence, with the complacency of the servant
who values himself on his rank in servitude, and the imperturbability
of the accurate calculator who has no illusions. He wears a white
Bulgarian costume: jacket with embroidered border, sash, wide
knickerbockers, and decorated gaiters. His head is shaved up to the
crown, giving him a high Japanese forehead. His name is Nicola.*

NICOLA. Be warned in time, Louka: mend your manners. I
know the mistress. She is so grand that she never dreams
that any servant could dare be disrespectful to her; but if
she once suspects that you are defying her, out you go.

LOUKA. I do defy her. I will defy her. What do I care for
her?

NICOLA. If you quarrel with the family, I never can marry
you. It's the same as if you quarrelled with me!

LOUKA. You take her part against me, do you?

NICOLA [*sedately*] I shall always be dependent on the good
will of the family. When I leave their service and start a

shop in Sofia, their custom will be half my capital: their bad word would ruin me.

LOUKA. You have no spirit. I should like to catch them saying a word against me!

NICOLA [*pityingly*] I should have expected more sense from you, Louka. But youre young: youre young!

LOUKA. Yes; and you like me the better for it, dont you? But I know some family secrets they wouldnt care to have told, young as I am. Let them quarrel with me if they dare!

NICOLA [*with compassionate superiority*] Do you know what they would do if they heard you talk like that?

LOUKA. What could they do?

NICOLA. Discharge you for untruthfulness. Who would believe any stories you told after that? Who would give you another situation? Who in this house would dare be seen speaking to you ever again? How long would your father be left on his little farm? [*She impatiently throws away the end of her cigaret, and stamps on it*]. Child: you dont know the power such high people have over the like of you and me when we try to rise out of our poverty against them. [*He goes close to her and lowers his voice*]. Look at me, ten years in their service. Do you think I know no secrets? I know things about the mistress that she wouldnt have the master know for a thousand levas. I know things about him that she wouldnt let him hear the last of for six months if I blabbed them to her. I know things about Raina that would break off her match with Sergius if —

LOUKA [*turning on him quickly*] How do you know? I never told you!

NICOLA [*opening his eyes cunningly*] So thats your little secret, is it? Thought it might be something like that. Well, you take my advice and be respectful; and make the mistress feel that no matter what you know or dont know, she can depend on you to hold your tongue and serve the family faithfully. Thats what they like; and thats how youll make most out of them.

LOUKA [*with searching scorn*] You have the soul of a servant, Nicola.

NICOLA [*complacently*] Yes: thats the secret of success in service.

> *A loud knocking with a whip handle on a wooden door is heard from the stable yard.*

MALE VOICE OUTSIDE. Hollo! Hollo there! Nicola!

LOUKA. Master! back from the war!

NICOLA [*quickly*] My word for it, Louka, the war's over. Off with you and get some fresh coffee. [*He runs out into the stable yard*].

LOUKA [*as she collects the coffee pot and cups on the tray, and carries it into the house*] Youll never put the soul of a servant into me.

> *Major Petkoff comes from the stable yard, followed by Nicola. He is a cheerful, excitable, insignificant, unpolished man of about 50, naturally unambitious except as to his income and his importance in local society, but just now greatly pleased with the military rank which the war has thrust on him as a man of consequence in his town. The fever of plucky patriotism which the Serbian attack roused in all the Bulgarians has pulled him through the war; but he is obviously glad to be home again.*

PETKOFF [*pointing to the table with his whip*] Breakfast out here, eh?

NICOLA. Yes, sir. The mistress and Miss Raina have just gone in.

PETKOFF [*sitting down and taking a roll*] Go in and say Ive come; and get me some fresh coffee.

NICOLA. It's coming, sir. [*He goes to the house door. Louka, with fresh coffee, a clean cup, and a brandy bottle on her tray, meets him*]. Have you told the mistress?

LOUKA. Yes: she's coming.

> *Nicola goes into the house. Louka brings the coffee to the table.*

PETKOFF. Well: the Serbs havnt run away with you, have they?

LOUKA. No, sir.

PETKOFF. Thats right. Have you brought me some cognac?

LOUKA [*putting the bottle on the table*] Here, sir.

PETKOFF. Thats right. [*He pours some into his coffee*].

Catherine, who, having at this early hour made only a very perfunctory toilet, wears a Bulgarian apron over a once brilliant but now half worn-out dressing gown, and a colored handkerchief tied over her thick black hair, comes from the house with Turkish slippers on her bare feet, looking astonishingly handsome and stately under all the circumstances. Louka goes into the house.

CATHERINE. My dear Paul: what a surprise for us! [*She stoops over the back of his chair to kiss him*]. Have they brought you fresh coffee?

PETKOFF. Yes: Louka's been looking after me. The war's over. The treaty was signed three days ago at Bucharest; and the decree for our army to demobilize was issued yesterday.

CATHERINE [*springing erect, with flashing eyes*] Paul: have you let the Austrians force you to make peace?

PETKOFF [*submissively*] My dear: they didnt consult me. What could *I* do? [*She sits down and turns away from him*]. But of course we saw to it that the treaty was an honorable one. It declares peace –

CATHERINE [*outraged*] Peace!

PETKOFF [*appeasing her*] – but not friendly relations: remember that. They wanted to put that in; but I insisted on its being struck out. What more could I do?

CATHERINE. You could have annexed Serbia and made Prince Alexander Emperor of the Balkans. Thats what I would have done.

PETKOFF. I dont doubt it in the least, my dear. But I should have had to subdue the whole Austrian Empire first; and that would have kept me too long away from you. I missed you greatly.

CATHERINE [*relenting*] Ah! [*She stretches her hand affectionately across the table to squeeze his*].

PETKOFF. And how have you been, my dear?

CATHERINE. Oh, my usual sore throats: thats all.

PETKOFF [*with conviction*] That comes from washing your neck every day. Ive often told you so.

CATHERINE. Nonsense, Paul!

PETKOFF [*over his coffee and cigaret*] I dont believe in going too far with these modern customs. All this washing cant be good for the health: it's not natural. There was an Englishman at Philippopolis who used to wet himself all over with cold water every morning when he got up. Disgusting! It all comes from the English: their climate makes them so dirty that they have to be perpetually washing themselves. Look at my father! he never had a bath in his life; and he lived to be ninety-eight, the healthiest man in Bulgaria. I dont mind a good wash once a week to keep up my position; but once a day is carrying the thing to a ridiculous extreme.

CATHERINE. You are a barbarian at heart still, Paul. I hope you behaved yourself before all those Russian officers.

PETKOFF. I did my best. I took care to let them know that we have a library.

CATHERINE. Ah; but you didnt tell them that we have an electric bell in it? I have had one put up.

PETKOFF. Whats an electric bell?

CATHERINE. You touch a button; something tinkles in the kitchen; and then Nicola comes up.

PETKOFF. Why not shout for him?

CATHERINE. Civilized people never shout for their servants. Ive learnt that while you were away.

PETKOFF. Well, I'll tell you something Ive learnt too. Civilized people dont hang out their washing to dry where visitors can see it; so youd better have all that [*indicating the clothes on the bushes*] put somewhere else.

CATHERINE. Oh, thats absurd, Paul: I dont believe really refined people notice such things.

SERGIUS [*knocking at the stable gates*] Gate, Nicola!

PETKOFF. Theres Sergius. [*Shouting*] Hollo, Nicola!

CATHERINE. Oh, dont shout, Paul: it really isnt nice.

PETKOFF. Bosh! [*He shouts louder than before*] Nicola!

NICOLA [*appearing at the house door*] Yes, sir.

PETKOFF. Are you deaf? Dont you hear Major Saranoff knocking? Bring him round this way. [*He pronounces the name with the stress on the second syllable: Sarahnoff*].

NICOLA. Yes, Major. [*He goes into the stable yard*].

PETKOFF. You must talk to him, my dear, until Raina takes him off our hands. He bores my life out about our not promoting him. Over my head, if you please.

CATHERINE. He certainly ought to be promoted when he marries Raina. Besides, the country should insist on having at least one native general.

PETKOFF. Yes; so that he could throw away whole brigades instead of regiments. It's no use, my dear: he hasnt the slightest chance of promotion until we're quite sure that the peace will be a lasting one.

NICOLA [*at the gate, announcing*] Major Sergius Saranoff! [*He goes into the house and returns presently with a third chair, which he places at the table. He then withdraws*].

Major Sergius Saranoff, the original of the portrait in Raina's room, is a tall romantically handsome man, with the physical hardihood, the high spirit, and the susceptible imagination of an untamed mountaineer chieftain. But his remarkable personal distinction is of a characteristically civilized type. The ridges of his eyebrows, curving with an interrogative twist round the projections at the outer corners; his jealously observant eye; his nose, thin, keen, and apprehensive in spite of the pugnacious high bridge and large nostril; his assertive chin, would not be out of place in a Parisian salon, shewing that the clever imaginative barbarian has an acute critical faculty which has been thrown into intense activity by the arrival of western civilization in the Balkans. The result is precisely what the advent of nineteenth century thought first produced in England: to wit, Byronism. By his brooding on the perpetual failure, not only of others, but of himself, to live up to his ideals; by his consequent cynical scorn for humanity; by his jejune credulity as to the absolute validity of his concepts and the unworthiness of the world in disregarding them; by his wincings and mockeries under the sting of the petty disillusions which every

*hour spent among men brings to his sensitive observations, he has
acquired the half tragic, half ironic air, the mysterious moodiness,
the suggestion of a strange and terrible history that has left nothing
but undying remorse, by which Childe Harold fascinated the grand-
mothers of his English contemporaries. It is clear that here or no-
where is Raina's ideal hero. Catherine is hardly less enthusiastic
about him than her daughter, and much less reserved in shewing her
enthusiasm. As he enters from the stable gate, she rises effusively to
greet him. Petkoff is distinctly less disposed to make a fuss about him.*

PETKOFF. Here already, Sergius! Glad to see you.

CATHERINE. My dear Sergius! [*She holds out both her
hands*].

SERGIUS [*kissing them with scrupulous gallantry*] My dear
mother, if I may call you so.

PETKOFF [*drily*] Mother-in-law, Sergius: mother-in-law!
Sit down; and have some coffee.

SERGIUS. Thank you: none for me. [*He gets away from the
table with a certain distaste for Petkoff's enjoyment of it, and posts
himself with conscious dignity against the rail of the steps leading
to the house*].

CATHERINE. You look superb. The campaign has improved
you, Sergius. Everybody here is mad about you. We were
all wild with enthusiasm about this magnificent cavalry
charge.

SERGIUS [*with grave irony*] Madam: it was the cradle and the
grave of my military reputation.

CATHERINE. How so?

SERGIUS. I won the battle the wrong way when our worthy
Russian generals were losing it the right way. In short, I
upset their plans, and wounded their self-esteem. Two
Cossack colonels had their regiments routed on the most
correct principles of scientific warfare. Two major-
generals got killed strictly according to military etiquette.
The two colonels are now major-generals; and I am still
a simple major.

CATHERINE. You shall not remain so, Sergius. The women
are on your side; and they will see that justice is done you.

SERGIUS. It is too late. I have only waited for the peace to send in my resignation.

PETKOFF [*dropping his cup in his amazement*] Your resignation!

CATHERINE. Oh, you must withdraw it!

SERGIUS [*with resolute measured emphasis, folding his arms*] I never withdraw.

PETKOFF [*vexed*] Now who could have supposed you were going to do such a thing?

SERGIUS [*with fire*] Everyone that knew me. But enough of myself and my affairs. How is Raina; and where is Raina?

RAINA [*suddenly coming round the corner of the house and standing at the top of the steps in the path*] Raina is here.

> *She makes a charming picture as they turn to look at her. She wears an underdress of pale green silk, draped with an overdress of thin ecru canvas embroidered with gold. She is crowned with a dainty eastern cap of gold tinsel. Sergius goes impulsively to meet her. Posing regally, she presents her hand; he drops chivalrously on one knee and kisses it.*

PETKOFF [*aside to Catherine, beaming with parental pride*] Pretty, isnt it? She always appears at the right moment.

CATHERINE [*impatiently*] Yes: she listens for it. It is an abominable habit.

> *Sergius leads Raina forward with splendid gallantry. When they arrive at the table, she turns to him with a bend of the head: he bows; and thus they separate, he coming to his place and she going behind her father's chair.*

RAINA [*stooping and kissing her father*] Dear father! Welcome home!

PETKOFF [*patting her cheek*] My little pet girl. [*He kisses her. She goes to the chair left by Nicola for Sergius, and sits down*].

CATHERINE. And so youre no longer a soldier, Sergius.

SERGIUS. I am no longer a soldier. Soldiering, my dear madam, is the coward's art of attacking mercilessly when you are strong, and keeping out of harm's way when you are weak. That is the whole secret of successful fighting. Get your enemy at a disadvantage; and never, on any account, fight him on equal terms.

PETKOFF. They wouldnt let us make a fair stand-up fight of it. However, I suppose soldiering has to be a trade like any other trade.

SERGIUS. Precisely. But I have no ambition to shine as a tradesman; so I have taken the advice of that bagman of a captain that settled the exchange of prisoners with us at Pirot, and given it up.

PETKOFF. What! that Swiss fellow? Sergius: Ive often thought of that exchange since. He over-reached us about those horses.

SERGIUS. Of course he over-reached us. His father was a hotel and livery stable keeper; and he owed his first step to his knowledge of horse-dealing. [*With mock enthusiasm*] Ah, he was a soldier: every inch a soldier! If only I had bought the horses for my regiment instead of foolishly leading it into danger, I should have been a field-marshal now!

CATHERINE. A Swiss? What was he doing in the Serbian army?

PETKOFF. A volunteer, of course: keen on picking up his profession. [*Chuckling*] We shouldnt have been able to begin fighting if these foreigners hadnt shewn us how to do it: we knew nothing about it; and neither did the Serbs. Egad, there'd have been no war without them!

RAINA. Are there many Swiss officers in the Serbian Army?

PETKOFF. No. All Austrians, just as our officers were all Russians. This was the only Swiss I came across. I'll never trust a Swiss again. He humbugged us into giving him fifty ablebodied men for two hundred worn out chargers. They werent even eatable!

SERGIUS. We were two children in the hands of that consummate soldier, Major: simply two innocent little children.

RAINA. What was he like?

CATHERINE. Oh, Raina, what a silly question!

SERGIUS. He was like a commercial traveller in uniform. Bourgeois to his boots!

PETKOFF [*grinning*] Sergius: tell Catherine that queer story

his friend told us about how he escaped after Slivnitza.
You remember. About his being hid by two women.

SERGIUS [*with bitter irony*] Oh yes: quite a romance! He was
serving in the very battery I so unprofessionally charged.
Being a thorough soldier, he ran away like the rest of
them, with our cavalry at his heels. To escape their sabres
he climbed a waterpipe and made his way into the
bedroom of a young Bulgarian lady. The young lady
was enchanted by his persuasive commercial traveller's
manners. She very modestly entertained him for an hour
or so, and then called in her mother lest her conduct
should appear unmaidenly. The old lady was equally
fascinated; and the fugitive was sent on his way in the
morning, disguised in an old coat belonging to the master
of the house, who was away at the war.

RAINA [*rising with marked stateliness*] Your life in the camp
has made you coarse, Sergius. I did not think you would
have repeated such a story before me. [*She turns away
coldly*].

CATHERINE [*also rising*] She is right, Sergius. If such women
exist, we should be spared the knowledge of them.

PETKOFF. Pooh! nonsense! what does it matter?

SERGIUS [*ashamed*] No, Petkoff: I was wrong. [*To Raina,
with earnest humility*] I beg your pardon. I have behaved
abominably. Forgive me, Raina. [*She bows reservedly*]. And
you too, madam. [*Catherine bows graciously and sits down.
He proceeds solemnly, again addressing Raina*] The glimpses I
have had of the seamy side of life during the last few
months have made me cynical; but I should not have
brought my cynicism here: least of all into your presence,
Raina. I — [*Here, turning to the others, he is evidently going to
begin a long speech when the Major interrupts him*].

PETKOFF. Stuff and nonsense, Sergius! Thats quite enough
fuss about nothing: a soldier's daughter should be able to
stand up without flinching to a little strong conversation.
[*He rises*]. Come: it's time for us to get to business. We have
to make up our minds how those three regiments are to get

back to Philippopolis: theres no forage for them on the Sofia route. [*He goes towards the house*]. Come along. [*Sergius is about to follow him when Catherine rises and intervenes*].

CATHERINE. Oh, Paul, cant you spare Sergius for a few moments? Raina has hardly seen him yet. Perhaps I can help you to settle about the regiments.

SERGIUS [*protesting*] My dear madam, impossible: you –

CATHERINE [*stopping him playfully*] You stay here, my dear Sergius: theres no hurry. I have a word or two to say to Paul. [*Sergius instantly bows and steps back*]. Now, dear [*taking Petroff's arm*]: come and see the electric bell.

PETKOFF. Oh, very well, very well.

They go into the house together affectionately. Sergius, left alone with Raina, looks anxiously at her, fearing that she is still offended. She smiles, and stretches out her arms to him.

SERGIUS [*hastening to her*] Am I forgiven?

RAINA [*placing her hands on his shoulders as she looks up at him with admiration and worship*] My hero! My king!

SERGIUS. My queen! [*He kisses her on the forehead*].

RAINA. How I have envied you, Sergius! You have been out in the world, on the field of battle, able to prove yourself there worthy of any woman in the world; whilst I have had to sit at home inactive – dreaming – useless – doing nothing that could give me the right to call myself worthy of any man.

SERGIUS. Dearest: all my deeds have been yours. You inspired me. I have gone through the war like a knight in a tournament with his lady looking down at him!

RAINA. And you have never been absent from my thoughts for a moment. [*Very solemnly*] Sergius: I think we two have found the higher love. When I think of you, I feel that I could never do a base deed, or think an ignoble thought.

SERGIUS. My lady and my saint! [*He clasps her reverently*].

RAINA [*returning his embrace*] My lord and my –

SERGIUS. Sh – sh! Let me be the worshipper, dear. You little know how unworthy even the best man is of a girl's pure passion!

RAINA. I trust you. I love you. You will never disappoint me, Sergius. [*Louka is heard singing within the house. They quickly release each other*]. I cant pretend to talk indifferently before her: my heart is too full. [*Louka comes from the house with her tray. She goes to the table, and begins to clear it, with her back turned to them*]. I will get my hat; and then we can go out until lunch time. Wouldnt you like that?

SERGIUS. Be quick. If you are away five minutes, it will seem five hours. [*Raina runs to the top of the steps, and turns there to exchange looks with him and wave him a kiss with both hands. He looks after her with emotion for a moment; then turns slowly away, his face radiant with the loftiest exaltation. The movement shifts his field of vision, into the corner of which there now comes the tail of Louka's double apron. His attention is arrested at once. He takes a stealthy look at her, and begins to twirl his moustache mischievously, with his left hand akimbo on his hip. Finally, striking the ground with his heels in something of a cavalry swagger, he strolls over to the other side of the table, opposite her, and says*] Louka: do you know what the higher love is?

LOUKA [*astonished*] No, sir.

SERGIUS. Very fatiguing thing to keep up for any length of time, Louka. One feels the need of some relief after it.

LOUKA [*innocently*] Perhaps you would like some coffee, sir? [*She stretches her hand across the table for the coffee pot*].

SERGIUS [*taking her hand*] Thank you, Louka.

LOUKA [*pretending to pull*] Oh, sir, you know I didnt mean that. I'm surprised at you!

SERGIUS [*coming clear of the table and drawing her with him*] I am surprised at myself, Louka. What would Sergius, the hero of Slivnitza, say if he saw me now? What would Sergius, the apostle of the higher love, say if he saw me now? What would the half dozen Sergiuses who keep popping in and out of this handsome figure of mine say if they caught us here? [*Letting go her hand and slipping his arm dexterously round her waist*] Do you consider my figure handsome, Louka?

LOUKA. Let me go, sir. I shall be disgraced. [*She struggles: he holds her inexorably*]. Oh, will you let go?

SERGIUS [*looking straight into her eyes*] No.

LOUKA. Then stand back where we cant be seen. Have you no common sense?

SERGIUS. Ah! thats reasonable. [*He takes her into the stable yard gateway, where they are hidden from the house*].

LOUKA [*plaintively*] I may have been seen from the windows: Miss Raina is sure to be spying about after you.

SERGIUS [*stung: letting her go*] Take care, Louka. I may be worthless enough to betray the higher love; but do not you insult it.

LOUKA [*demurely*] Not for the world, sir, I'm sure. May I go on with my work, please, now?

SERGIUS [*again putting his arm round her*] You are a provoking little witch, Louka. If you were in love with me, would you spy out of windows on me?

LOUKA. Well, you see, sir, since you say you are half a dozen different gentlemen all at once, I should have a great deal to look after.

SERGIUS [*charmed*] Witty as well as pretty. [*He tries to kiss her*].

LOUKA [*avoiding him*] No: I dont want your kisses. Gentlefolk are all alike: you making love to me behind Miss Raina's back; and she doing the same behind yours.

SERGIUS [*recoiling a step*] Louka!

LOUKA. It shews how little you really care.

SERGIUS [*dropping his familiarity, and speaking with freezing politeness*] If our conversation is to continue, Louka, you will please remember that a gentleman does not discuss the conduct of the lady he is engaged to with her maid.

LOUKA. It's so hard to know what a gentleman considers right. I thought from your trying to kiss me that you had given up being so particular.

SERGIUS [*turning from her and striking his forehead as he comes back into the garden from the gateway*] Devil! devil!

LOUKA. Ha! ha! I expect one of the six of you is very like me, sir; though I am only Miss Raina's maid. [*She goes back to her work at the table, taking no further notice of him*].

SERGIUS [*speaking to himself*] Which of the six is the real man?

Thats the question that torments me. One of them is a hero, another a buffoon, another a humbug, another perhaps a bit of a blackguard. [*He pauses, and looks furtively at Louka as he adds, with deep bitterness*] And one, at least, is a coward: jealous, like all cowards. [*He goes to the table*]. Louka.

LOUKA. Yes?

SERGIUS. Who is my rival?

LOUKA. You shall never get that out of me, for love or money.

SERGIUS. Why?

LOUKA. Never mind why. Besides, you would tell that I told you; and I should lose my place.

SERGIUS [*holding out his right hand in affirmation*] No! on the honor of a – [*He checks himself; and his hand drops, nerveless, as he concludes sardonically*] – of a man capable of behaving as I have been behaving for the last five minutes. Who is he?

LOUKA. I dont know. I never saw him. I only heard his voice through the door of her room.

SERGIUS. Damnation! How dare you?

LOUKA [*retreating*] Oh, I mean no harm; youve no right to take up my words like that. The mistress knows all about it. And I tell you that if that gentleman ever comes here again, Miss Raina will marry him, whether he likes it or not. I know the difference between the sort of manner you and she put on before one another and the real manner.

Sergius shivers as if she had stabbed him. Then, setting his face like iron, he strides grimly to her, and grips her above the elbows with both hands.

SERGIUS. Now listen you to me.

LOUKA [*wincing*] Not so tight: youre hurting me.

SERGIUS. That doesnt matter. You have stained my honor by making me a party to your eavesdropping. And you have betrayed your mistress.

LOUKA [*writhing*] Please –

SERGIUS. That shews that you are an abominable little clod of common clay, with the soul of a servant. [*He lets her go as if she were an unclean thing, and turns away, dusting his hands of her, to the bench by the wall, where he sits down with averted head, meditating gloomily].*

LOUKA [*whimpering angrily with her hands up her sleeves, feeling her bruised arms*] You know how to hurt with your tongue as well as with your hands. But I dont care, now Ive found out that whatever clay I'm made of, youre made of the same. As for her, she's a liar; and her fine airs are a cheat; and I'm worth six of her. [*She shakes the pain off hardily; tosses her head; and sets to work to put the things on the tray].*

He looks doubtfully at her. She finishes packing the tray, and laps the cloth over the edges, so as to carry all out together. As she stoops to lift it, he rises.

SERGIUS. Louka! [*She stops and looks defiantly at him].* A gentleman has no right to hurt a woman under any circumstances. [*With profound humility, uncovering his head*] I beg your pardon.

LOUKA. That sort of apology may satisfy a lady. Of what use is it to a servant?

SERGIUS [*rudely crossed in his chivalry, throws it off with a bitter laugh, and says slightingly*] Oh! you wish to be paid for the hurt! [*He puts on his shako, and takes some money from his pocket].*

LOUKA [*her eyes filling with tears in spite of herself*] No: I want my hurt made well.

SERGIUS [*sobered by her tone*] How?

She rolls up her left sleeve; clasps her arm with the thumb and fingers of her right hand; and looks down at the bruise. Then she raises her head and looks straight at him. Finally, with a superb gesture, she presents her arm to be kissed. Amazed, he looks at her; at the arm; at her again; hesitates; and then, with shuddering intensity, exclaims Never! *and gets away as far as possible from her.*

Her arm drops. Without a word, and with unaffected dignity, she takes her tray, and is approaching the house when Raina returns, wearing a hat and jacket in the height of the Vienna fashion of the previous year, 1885. Louka makes way proudly for her, and then goes into the house.

RAINA. I'm ready. Whats the matter? [*Gaily*] Have you been flirting with Louka?

SERGIUS [*hastily*] No, no. How can you think such a thing?

RAINA [*ashamed of herself*] Forgive me, dear: it was only a jest. I am so happy today.

He goes quickly to her, and kisses her hand remorsefully. Catherine comes out and calls to them from the top of the steps.

CATHERINE [*coming down to them*] I am sorry to disturb you, children; but Paul is distracted over those three regiments. He doesnt know how to send them to Philippopolis; and he objects to every suggestion of mine. You must go and help him, Sergius. He is in the library.

RAINA [*disappointed*] But we are just going out for a walk.

SERGIUS. I shall not be long. Wait for me just five minutes. [*He runs up the steps to the door*].

RAINA [*following him to the foot of the steps and looking up at him with timid coquetry*] I shall go round and wait in full view of the library windows. Be sure you draw father's attention to me. If you are a moment longer than five minutes, I shall go in and fetch you, regiments or no regiments.

SERGIUS [*laughing*] Very well. [*He goes in*].

Raina watched him until he is out of her sight. Then, with a perceptible relaxation of manner, she begins to pace up and down the garden in a brown study.

CATHERINE. Imagine their meeting that Swiss and hearing the whole story! The very first thing your father asked for was the old coat we sent him off in. A nice mess you have got us into!

RAINA [*gazing thoughtfully at the gravel as she walks*] The little beast!

CATHERINE. Little beast! What little beast?

RAINA. To go and tell! Oh, if I had him here, I'd cram him with chocolate creams til he couldnt ever speak again!

CATHERINE. Dont talk such stuff. Tell me the truth, Raina. How long was he in your room before you came to me?

RAINA [*whisking round and recommencing her march in the opposite direction*] Oh, I forget.

CATHERINE. You cannot forget! Did he really climb up after the soldiers were gone; or was he there when that officer searched the room?

RAINA. No. Yes: I think he must have been there then.

CATHERINE. You think! Oh, Raina! Raina! Will anything ever make you straightforward? If Sergius finds out, it will be all over between you.

RAINA [*with cool impertinence*] Oh, I know Sergius is your pet. I sometimes wish you could marry him instead of me. You would just suit him. You would pet him, and spoil him, and mother him to perfection.

CATHERINE [*opening her eyes very widely indeed*] Well, upon my word!

RAINA [*capriciously: half to herself*] I always feel a longing to do or say something dreadful to him – to shock his propriety – to scandalize the five senses out of him. [*To Catherine, perversely*] I dont care whether he finds out about the chocolate cream soldier or not. I half hope he may. [*She again turns and strolls flippantly away up the path to the corner of the house*].

CATHERINE. And what should I be able to say to your father, pray?

RAINA [*over her shoulder, from the top of the two steps*] Oh, poor father! As if he could help himself! [*She turns the corner and passes out of sight*].

CATHERINE [*looking after her, her fingers itching*] Oh, if you were only ten years younger! [*Louka comes from the house with a salver, which she carries hanging down by her side*]. Well?

LOUKA. Theres a gentleman just called, madam. A Serbian officer.

CATHERINE [*flaming*] A Serb! And how dare he – [*checking herself bitterly*] Oh, I forgot. We are at peace now. I suppose we shall have them calling every day to pay their compliments. Well: if he is an officer why dont you tell your master? He is in the library with Major Saranoff. Why do you come to me?

LOUKA. But he asks for you, madam. And I dont think he

knows who you are: he said the lady of the house. He gave me this little ticket for you. [*She takes a card out of her bosom; puts in on the salver; and offers it to Catherine*].

CATHERINE [*reading*] 'Captain Bluntschli'? Thats a German name.

LOUKA. Swiss, madam, I think.

CATHERINE [*with a bound that makes Louka jump back*] Swiss! What is he like?

LOUKA [*timidly*] He has a big carpet bag, madam.

CATHERINE. Oh Heavens! he's come to return the coat. Send him away: say we're not at home: ask him to leave his address and I'll write to him. Oh stop: that will never do. Wait! [*She throws herself into a chair to think it out. Louka waits*]. The master and Major Saranoff are busy in the library, arnt they?

LOUKA. Yes, madam.

CATHERINE [*decisively*] Bring the gentleman out here at once. [*Peremptorily*] And be very polite to him. Dont delay. Here [*impatiently snatching the salver from her*]: leave that here; and go straight back to him.

LOUKA. Yes, madam [*going*].

CATHERINE. Louka!

LOUKA [*stopping*] Yes, madam.

CATHERINE. Is the library door shut?

LOUKA. I think so, madam.

CATHERINE. If not, shut it as you pass through.

LOUKA. Yes, madam [*going*].

CATHERINE. Stop! [*Louka stops*]. He will have to go that way [*indicating the gate of the stable yard*]. Tell Nicola to bring his bag here after him. Dont forget.

LOUKA [*surprised*] His bag?

CATHERINE. Yes: here: as soon as possible. [*Vehemently*] Be quick! [*Louka runs into the house. Catherine snatches her apron off and throws it behind a bush. She then takes up the salver and uses it as a mirror, with the result that the handkerchief tied round her head follows the apron. A touch to her hair and a shake to her dressing gown make her presentable*]. Oh, how? how? how can a man be such a fool! Such a moment to select! [*Louka appears at the door of the house, announcing* Captain Bluntschli. *She stands aside at the top of the steps to let him pass before she goes in again. He is the man of the midnight adventure in Raina's room, clean, well brushed, smartly uniformed, and out of trouble, but still unmistakably the same man. The moment Louka's back is turned, Catherine swoops on him with impetuous, urgent, coaxing appeal*]. Captain Bluntschli: I am very glad to see you; but you must leave this house at once. [*He raises his eyebrows*]. My husband has just returned with my future son-in-law; and they know nothing. If they did, the consequences would be terrible. You are a foreigner: you do not feel our national animosities as we do. We still hate the Serbs: the effect of the peace on my husband has been to make him feel like a lion baulked on his prey. If he discovers our secret, he will never forgive me; and my daughter's life will hardly be safe. Will you, like the chivalrous gentleman and soldier you are, leave at once before he finds you here?

BLUNTSCHLI [*disappointed, but philosophical*] At once, gracious lady. I only came to thank you and return the coat you lent me. If you will allow me to take it out of my bag and leave it with your servant as I pass out, I need detain you no further. [*He turns to go into the house*].

CATHERINE [*catching him by the sleeve*] Oh, you must not think of going back that way. [*Coaxing him across to the stable gates*] This is the shortest way out. Many thanks. So glad to have been of service to you. Good-bye.

BLUNTSCHLI. But my bag?

CATHERINE. It shall be sent on. You will leave me your address.

BLUNTSCHLI. True. Allow me. [*He takes out his card-case, and stops to write his address, keeping Catherine in an agony of impatience. As he hands her the card, Petkoff, hatless, rushes from the house in a fluster of hospitality, followed by Sergius*].

PETKOFF [*as he hurries down the steps*] My dear Captain Bluntschli –

CATHERINE. Oh Heavens! [*She sinks on the seat against the wall*].

57

PETKOFF [*too preoccupied to notice her as he shakes Bluntschli's hand heartily*] Those stupid people of mine thought I was out here, instead of in the – haw! – library [*he cannot mention the library without betraying how proud he is of it*]. I saw you through the window. I was wondering why you didnt come in. Saranoff is with me: you remember him, dont you?

SERGIUS [*saluting humorously, and then offering his hand with great charm of manner*] Welcome, our friend the enemy!

PETKOFF. No longer the enemy, happily. [*Rather anxiously*] I hope youve called as a friend, and not about horses or prisoners.

CATHERINE. Oh, quite as a friend, Paul. I was just asking Captain Bluntschli to stay to lunch; but he declares he must go at once.

SERGIUS [*sardonically*] Impossible, Bluntschli. We want you here badly. We have to send on three cavalry regiments to Philippopolis; and we dont in the least know how to do it.

BLUNTSCHLI [*suddenly attentive and businesslike*] Philippopolis? The forage is the trouble, I suppose.

PETKOFF [*eagerly*] Yes: thats it. [*To Sergius*] He sees the whole thing at once.

BLUNTSCHLI. I think I can shew you how to manage that.

SERGIUS. Invaluable man! Come along! [*Towering over Bluntschli, he puts his hand on his shoulder and takes him to the steps, Petkoff following*].

Raina comes from the house as Bluntschli puts his foot on the first step.

RAINA. Oh! The chocolate cream soldier!

Bluntschli stands rigid. Sergius, amazed, looks at Raina, then at Petkoff, who looks back at him and then at his wife.

CATHERINE [*with commanding presence of mind*] My dear Raina, dont you see that we have a guest here? Captain Bluntschli: one of our new Serbian friends.

Raina bows: Bluntschli bows.

RAINA. How silly of me! [*She comes down into the centre of the group, between Bluntschli and Petkoff*]. I made a beautiful ornament this morning for the ice pudding; and that stupid

Nicola has just put down a pile of plates on it and spoilt it. [*To Bluntschli, winningly*] I hope you didnt think that you were the chocolate cream soldier, Captain Bluntschli.

BLUNTSCHLI [*laughing*] I assure you I did. [*Stealing a whimsical glance at her*] Your explanation was a relief.

PETKOFF [*suspiciously, to Raina*] And since when, pray, have you taken to cooking?

CATHERINE. Oh, whilst you were away. It is her latest fancy.

PETKOFF [*testily*] And has Nicola taken to drinking? He used to be careful enough. First he shews Captain Bluntschli out here when he knew quite well I was in the library; and then he goes downstairs and breaks Raina's chocolate soldier. He must – [*Nicola appears at the top of the steps with the bag. He descends; places it respectfully before Bluntschli; and waits for further orders. General amazement. Nicola, unconscious of the effect he is producing, looks perfectly satisfied with himself. When Petkoff recovers his power of speech, he breaks out at him with*] Are you mad, Nicola?

NICOLA [*taken aback*] Sir?

PETKOFF. What have you brought that for?

NICOLA. My lady's orders, major. Louka told me that –

CATHERINE [*interrupting him*] My orders! Why should I order you to bring Captain Bluntschli's luggage out here? What are you thinking of, Nicola?

NICOLA [*after a moment's bewilderment, picking up the bag as he addresses Bluntschli with the very perfection of servile discretion*] I beg your pardon, captain, I am sure. [*To Catherine*] My fault, madam: I hope youll overlook it. [*He bows, and is going to the steps with the bag, when Petkoff addresses him angrily*].

PETKOFF. Youd better go and slam that bag, too, down on Miss Raina's ice pudding! [*This is too much for Nicola. The bag drops from his hand almost on his master's toes, eliciting a roar of*] Begone, you butter-fingered donkey.

NICOLA [*snatching up the bag, and escaping into the house*] Yes, major.

CATHERINE. Oh, never mind. Paul: dont be angry.

PETKOFF [*blustering*] Scoundrel! He's got out of hand while I was away. I'll teach him. Infernal blackguard! The sack next Saturday! I'll clear out the whole establishment – [*He is stifled by the caresses of his wife and daughter, who hang round his neck, petting him*].

CATHERINE
RAINA } [*together*] {
Now, now, now, it mustnt be angry. He meant no harm. Be good to please me, dear. Sh-sh-sh-sh!

Wow, wow, wow: not on your first day at home. I'll make another ice pudding. Tch-ch-ch!

PETKOFF [*yielding*] Oh well, never mind. Come, Bluntschli: lets have no more nonsense about going away. You know very well youre not going back to Switzerland yet. Until you do go back youll stay with us.

RAINA. Oh, do, Captain Bluntschli.

PETKOFF [*to Catherine*] Now, Catherine: it's of you he's afraid. Press him: and he'll stay.

CATHERINE. Of course I shall be only too delighted if [*appealingly*] Captain Bluntschli really wishes to stay. He knows my wishes.

BLUNTSCHLI [*in his driest military manner*] I am at madam's orders.

SERGIUS [*cordially*] That settles it!

PETKOFF [*heartily*] Of course!

RAINA. You see you must stay.

BLUNTSCHLI [*smiling*] Well, if I must, I must.

   Gesture of despair from Catherine.

ACT III

In the library after lunch. It is not much of a library. Its literary equipment consists of a single fixed shelf stocked with old paper covered novels, broken backed, coffee stained, torn and thumbed; and a couple of little hanging shelves with a few gift books on them: the rest of the wall space being occupied by trophies of war and the chase. But it is a most comfortable sitting room. A row of three large windows shews a mountain panorama, just now seen in one of its friendliest aspects in the mellowing afternoon light. In the corner next the right hand window a square earthenware stove, a perfect tower of glistening pottery, rises nearly to the ceiling and guarantees plenty of warmth. The ottoman is like that in Raina's room, and similarly placed; and the window seats are luxurious with decorated cushions. There is one object, however, hopelessly out of keeping with its surroundings. This is a small kitchen table, much the worse for wear, fitted as a writing table with an old canister full of pens, an eggcup filled with ink, and a deplorable scrap of heavily used pink blotting paper.

At the side of this table, which stands to the left of anyone facing the window, Bluntschli is hard at work with a couple of maps before him, writing orders. At the head of it sits Sergius, who is supposed to be also at work, but is actually gnawing the feather of a pen, and contemplating Bluntschli's quick, sure, businesslike progress with a mixture of envious irritation at his own incapacity and awestruck wonder at an ability which seems to him almost miraculous, though its prosaic character forbids him to esteem it. The Major is comfortably established on the ottoman, with a newspaper in his hand and the tube of his hookah within easy reach. Catherine sits at the stove, with her back to them, embroidering. Raina, reclining on the divan, is gazing in a daydream out at the Balkan landscape, with a neglected novel in her lap.

The door is on the same side as the stove, farther from the window. The button of the electric bell is at the opposite side, behind Bluntschli.

PETKOFF [*looking up from his paper to watch how they are getting on at the table*] Are you sure I cant help in any way, Bluntschli?

BLUNTSCHLI [*without interrupting his writing or looking up*] Quite sure, thank you. Saranoff and I will manage it.

SERGIUS [*grimly*] Yes: we'll manage it. He finds out what to do; draws up the orders; and I sign em. Division of labor! [*Bluntschli passes him a paper*]. Another one? Thank you. [*He plants the paper squarely before him; sets his chair carefully parallel to it; and signs with his cheek on his elbow and his protruded tongue following the movements of his pen*]. This hand is more accustomed to the sword than to the pen.

PETKOFF. It's very good of you, Bluntschli: it is indeed, to let yourself be put upon in this way. Now are you quite sure I can do nothing?

CATHERINE [*in a low warning tone*] You can stop interrupting, Paul.

PETKOFF [*starting and looking round at her*] Eh? Oh! Quite right, my love: quite right. [*He takes his newspaper up again, but presently lets it drop*]. Ah, you havnt been campaigning, Catherine: you dont know how pleasant it is for us to sit here, after a good lunch, with nothing to do but enjoy ourselves. Theres only one thing I want to make me thoroughly comfortable.

CATHERINE. What is that?

PETKOFF. My old coat. I'm not at home in this one: I feel as if I were on parade.

CATHERINE. My dear Paul, how absurd you are about that old coat! It must be hanging in the blue closet where you left it.

PETKOFF. My dear Catherine, I tell you Ive looked there. Am I to believe my own eyes or not? [*Catherine rises and crosses the room to press the button of the electric bell*]. What are you shewing off that bell for? [*She looks at him majestically, and silently resumes her chair and her needlework*]. My dear: if you think the obstinacy of your sex can make a coat out of two old dressing gowns of Raina's, your waterproof, and my mackintosh, youre mistaken. Thats exactly what the blue closet contains at present.

Nicola presents himself.

CATHERINE. Nicola: go to the blue closet and bring your master's old coat here: the braided one he wears in the house.

NICOLA. Yes, madam. [*He goes out*].

PETKOFF. Catherine.

CATHERINE. Yes, Paul.

PETKOFF. I bet you any piece of jewellery you like to order from Sofia against a week's housekeeping money that the coat isnt there.

CATHERINE. Done, Paul!

PETKOFF [*excited by the prospect of a gamble*] Come: heres an opportunity for some sport. Wholl bet on it? Bluntschli: I'll give you six to one.

BLUNTSCHLI [*imperturbably*] It would be robbing you, major. Madame is sure to be right. [*Without looking up, he passes another bunch of papers to Sergius*].

SERGIUS [*also excited*] Bravo, Switzerland! Major: I bet my best charger against an Arab mare for Raina that Nicola finds the coat in the blue closet.

PETKOFF [*eagerly*] Your best char –

CATHERINE [*hastily interrupting him*] Dont be foolish, Paul. An Arabian mare will cost you 50,000 levas.

RAINA [*suddenly coming out of her picturesque revery*] Really, mother, if you are going to take the jewellery, I dont see why you should grudge me my Arab.

Nicola comes back with the coat, and brings it to Petkoff, who can hardly believe his eyes.

CATHERINE. Where was it, Nicola?

NICOLA. Hanging in the blue closet, madame.

PETKOFF. Well, I am d –

CATHERINE [*stopping him*] Paul!

PETKOFF. I could have sworn it wasnt there. Age is beginning to tell on me. I'm getting hallucinations. [*To Nicola*] Here: help me to change. Excuse me, Bluntschli. [*He begins changing coats, Nicola acting as valet*]. Remember: I didnt take that bet of yours, Sergius. Youd better give Raina that Arab steed yourself, since youve roused her expectations.

Eh, Raina? [*He looks round at her; but she is again rapt in the landscape. With a little gush of parental affection and pride, he points her out to them, and says*] She's dreaming, as usual.

SERGIUS. Assuredly she shall not be the loser.

PETKOFF. So much the better for her. *I* shant come off so cheaply, I expect. [*The change is now complete. Nicola goes out with the discarded coat*]. Ah, now I feel at home at last. [*He sits down and takes his newspaper with a grunt of relief*].

BLUNTSCHLI [*to Sergius, handing a paper*] Thats the last order.

PETKOFF [*jumping up*] What! Finished?

BLUNTSCHLI. Finished.

PETKOFF [*with childlike envy*] Havnt you anything for me to sign?

BLUNTSCHLI. Not necessary. His signature will do.

PETKOFF [*inflating his chest and thumping it*] Ah well, I think weve done a thundering good day's work. Can I do anything more?

BLUNTSCHLI. You had better both see the fellows that are to take these. [*Sergius rises*] Pack them off at once; and shew them that Ive marked on the orders the time they should hand them in by. Tell them that if they stop to drink or tell stories – if theyre five minutes late, theyll have the skin taken off their backs.

SERGIUS [*stiffening indignantly*] I'll say so. [*He strides to the door*]. And if one of them is man enough to spit in my face for insulting him, I'll buy his discharge and give him a pension. [*He goes out*].

BLUNTSCHLI [*confidentially*] Just see that he talks to them properly, major, will you?

PETKOFF [*officiously*] Quite right, Bluntschi, quite right. I'll see to it. [*He goes to the door importantly, but hesitates on the threshold*]. By the bye, Catherine, you may as well come too. Theyll be far more frightened of you than of me.

CATHERINE [*putting down her embroidery*] I daresay I had better. You would only splutter at them. [*She goes out, Petkoff holding the door for her and following her*].

BLUNTSCHLI. What an army! They make cannons out of

cherry trees; and the officers send for their wives to keep discipline! [*He begins to fold and docket the papers*].

Raina, who has risen from the divan, marches slowly down the room with her hands clasped behind her, and looks mischievously at him.

RAINA. You look ever so much nicer than when we last met. [*He looks up, surprised*]. What have you done to yourself?

BLUNTSCHLI. Washed; brushed; good night's sleep and breakfast. That's all.

RAINA. Did you get back safely that morning?

BLUNTSCHLI. Quite, thanks.

RAINA. Were they angry with you for running away from Sergius's charge?

BLUNTSCHLI [*grinning*] No: they were glad; because theyd all just run away themselves.

RAINA [*going to the table, and leaning over it towards him*] It must have made a lovely story for them: all that about me and my room.

BLUNTSCHLI. Capital story. But I only told it to one of them: a particular friend.

RAINA. On whose discretion you could absolutely rely?

BLUNTSCHLI. Absolutely.

RAINA. Hm! He told it all to my father and Sergius the day you exchanged the prisoners. [*She turns away and strolls carelessly across to the other side of the room*].

BLUNTSCHLI [*deeply concerned, and half incredulous*] No! You dont mean that, do you?

RAINA [*turning, with sudden earnestness*] I do indeed. But they dont know that it was in this house you took refuge. If Sergius knew, he would challenge you and kill you in a duel.

BLUNTSCHLI. Bless me! then dont tell him.

RAINA. Please be serious, Captain Bluntschli. Can you not realize what it is to me to deceive him? I want to be quite perfect with Sergius: no meanness, no smallness, no deceit. My relation to him is the one really beautiful and noble part of my life. I hope you can understand that.

BLUNTSCHLI [*sceptically*] You mean that you wouldnt like him to find out that the story about the ice pudding was a –a – a – You know.

RAINA [*wincing*] Ah, dont talk of it in that flippant way. I lied: I know it. But I did it to save your life. He would have killed you. That was the second time I ever uttered a falsehood. [*Bluntschli rises quickly and looks doubtfully and somewhat severely at her*]. Do you remember the first time?

BLUNTSCHLI. I! No. Was I present?

RAINA. Yes; and I told the officer who was searching for you that you were not present.

BLUNTSCHLI. True. I should have remembered it.

RAINA [*greatly encouraged*] Ah, it is natural that you should forget it first. It cost you nothing: it cost me a lie! A lie!
She sits down on the ottoman, looking straight before her with her hands clasped round her knee. Bluntschli, quite touched, goes to the ottoman with a particularly reassuring and considerate air, and sits down beside her.

BLUNTSCHLI. My dear young lady, dont let this worry you. Remember: I'm a soldier. Now what are the two things that happen to a soldier so often that he comes to think nothing of them? One is hearing people tell lies [*Raina recoils*]: the other is getting his life saved in all sorts of ways by all sorts of people.

RAINA [*rising in indignant protest*] And so he becomes a creature incapable of faith and of gratitude.

BLUNTSCHLI [*making a wry face*] Do you like gratitude? I dont. If pity is akin to love, gratitude is akin to the other thing.

RAINA. Gratitude! [*Turning on him*] If you are incapable of gratitude you are incapable of any noble sentiment. Even animals are grateful. Oh, I see now exactly what you think of me! You were not surprised to hear me lie. To you it was something I probably did every day! every hour? That is how men think of women. [*She paces the room tragically*].

BLUNTSCHLI [*dubiously*] Theres reason in everything. You said youd told only two lies in your whole life. Dear young lady: isnt that rather a short allowance? I'm quite a straightforward man myself; but it wouldnt last me a whole morning.

RAINA [*staring haughtily at him*] Do you know, sir, that you are insulting me?

BLUNTSCHLI. I cant help it. When you strike that noble attitude and speak in that thrilling voice, I admire you; but I find it impossible to believe a single word you say.

RAINA [*superbly*] Captain Bluntschli!

BLUNTSCHLI [*unmoved*] Yes?

RAINA [*standing over him, as if she could not believe her senses*] Do you mean what you said just now? Do you know what you said just now?

BLUNTSCHLI. I do.

RAINA [*gasping*] I! I!!! [*She points to herself incredulously, meaning 'I, Raina Petkoff tell lies!' He meets her gaze unflinchingly. She suddenly sits down beside him, and adds, with a complete change of manner from the heroic to a babyish familiarity*] How did you find me out?

BLUNTSCHLI [*promptly*] Instinct, dear young lady. Instinct, and experience of the world.

RAINA [*wonderingly*] Do you know, you are the first man I ever met who did not take me seriously?

BLUNTSCHLI. You mean, dont you, that I am the first man that has ever taken you quite seriously?

RAINA. Yes: I suppose I do mean that. [*Cosily, quite at her ease with him*] How strange it is to be talked to in such a way! You know, I've always gone on like that.

BLUNTSCHLI. You mean the – ?

RAINA. I mean the noble attitude and the thrilling voice. [*They laugh together*]. I did it when I was a tiny child to my nurse. She believed in it. I do it before my parents. They believe in it. I do it before Sergius. He believes in it.

BLUNTSCHLI. Yes: he's a little in that line himself, isnt he?

RAINA [*startled*] Oh! Do you think so?

BLUNTSCHLI. You know him better than I do.

RAINA. I wonder – I wonder is he? If I thought that – !

[*Discouraged*] Ah, well: what does it matter? I suppose, now youve found me out, you despise me.

BLUNTSCHLI [*warmly, rising*] No, my dear young lady, no, no, no a thousand times. It's part of your youth: part of your charm. I'm like all the rest of them: the nurse, your parents, Sergius: I'm your infatuated admirer.

RAINA [*pleased*] Really?

BLUNTSCHLI [*slapping his breast smartly with his hand, German fashion*] Hand aufs Herz! Really and truly.

RAINA [*very happy*] But what did you think of me for giving you my portrait?

BLUNTSCHLI [*astonished*] Your portrait! You never gave me your portrait.

RAINA [*quickly*] Do you mean to say you never got it?

BLUNTSCHLI. No. [*He sits down beside her, with renewed interest, and says with some complacency*] When did you send it to me?

RAINA [*indignantly*] I did not send it to you. [*She turns her head away, and adds, reluctantly*] It was in the pocket of that coat.

BLUNTSCHLI [*pursing his lips and rounding his eyes*] Oh-o-oh! I never found it. It must be there still.

RAINA [*springing up*] There still! for my father to find the first time he puts his hand in his pocket! Oh, how could you be so stupid?

BLUNTSCHLI [*rising also*] It doesnt matter: I suppose it's only a photograph: how can he tell who it was intended for? Tell him he put it there himself.

RAINA [*bitterly*] Yes: that is so clever! isnt it? [*Distractedly*] Oh! what shall I do?

BLUNTSCHLI. Ah, I see. You wrote something on it. That was rash.

RAINA [*vexed almost to tears*] Oh, to have done such a thing for you, who care no more – except to laugh at me – oh! Are you sure nobody has touched it?

BLUNTSCHLI. Well, I cant be quite sure. You see, I couldnt carry it about with me all the time: one cant take much luggage on active service.

RAINA. What did you do with it?

BLUNTSCHLI. When I got through to Pirot I had to put it in safe keeping somehow. I thought of the railway cloak room; but thats the surest place to get looted in modern warfare. So I pawned it.

RAINA. Pawned it!!!

BLUNTSCHLI. I know it doesnt sound nice: but it was much the safest plan. I redeemed it the day before yesterday. Heaven only knows whether the pawnbroker cleared out the pockets or not.

RAINA [*furious: throwing the words right into his face*] You have a low shopkeeping mind. You think of things that would never come into a gentleman's head.

BLUNTSCHLI [*phlegmatically*] Thats the Swiss national character, dear lady. [*He returns to the table*].

RAINA. Oh, I wish I had never met you. [*She flounces away, and sits at the window fuming*].

    Louka comes in with a heap of letters and telegrams on her salver, and crosses, with her bold free gait, to the table. Her left sleeve is looped up to the shoulder with a brooch, shewing her naked arm, with a broad gilt bracelet covering the bruise.

LOUKA [*to Bluntschli*] For you. [*She empties the salver with a fling on to the table*]. The messenger is waiting. [*She is determined not to be civil to an enemy, even if she must bring him his letters*].

BLUNTSCHLI [*to Raina*] Will you excuse me: the last postal delivery that reached me was three weeks ago. These are the subsequent accumulations. Four telegrams: a week old. [*He opens one*]. Oho! Bad news!

RAINA [*rising and advancing a little remorsefully*] Bad news?

BLUNTSCHLI. My father's dead. [*He looks at the telegram with his lips pursed, musing on the unexpected change in his arrangements. Louka crosses herself hastily*].

RAINA. Oh, how very sad!

BLUNTSCHLI. Yes: I shall have to start for home in an hour. He has left a lot of big hotels behind him to be looked after. [*He takes up a fat letter in a long blue envelope*]. Here's a whacking letter from the family solicitor. [*He puts out the enclosures and glances over them*]. Great Heavens! Seventy! Two hundred! [*In a crescendo of dismay*] Four hundred! Four thousand!! Nine thousand six hundred!!! What on earth am I to do with them all?

RAINA [*timidly*] Nine thousand hotels?

BLUNTSCHLI. Hotels! nonsense. If you only knew! Oh, it's too ridiculous! Excuse me: I must give my fellow orders about starting. [*He leaves the room hastily, with the documents in his hand*].

LOUKA [*knowing instinctively that she can annoy Raina by disparaging Bluntschli*] He has not much heart, that Swiss. He has not a word of grief for his poor father.

RAINA [*bitterly*] Grief! A man who has been doing nothing but killing people for years! What does he care? What does any soldier care? [*She goes to the door, restraining her tears with difficulty*].

LOUKA. Major Saranoff has been fighting too; and he has plenty of heart left. [*Raina, at the door, draws herself up haughtily and goes out*]. Aha! I thought you wouldnt get much feeling out of your soldier. [*She is following Raina when Nicola enters with an armful of logs for the stove*].

NICOLA [*grinning amorously at her*] Ive been trying all the afternoon to get a minute alone with you, my girl. [*His countenance changes as he notices her arm*]. Why, what fashion is that of wearing your sleeve, child?

LOUKA [*proudly*] My own fashion.

NICOLA. Indeed! If the mistress catches you, she'll talk to you. [*He puts the logs down, and seats himself comfortably on the ottoman*].

LOUKA. Is that any reason why you should take it on yourself to talk to me?

NICOLA. Come! dont be so contrary with me. Ive some good news for you. [*She sits down beside him. He takes out some paper money. Louka, with an eager gleam in her eyes, tries to snatch it; but he shifts it quickly to his left hand, out of her reach*]. See! a twenty leva bill! Sergius gave me that, out of pure swagger. A fool and his money are soon parted. Theres ten levas more. The Swiss gave me that for backing up the mistress's and Raina's lies about him. He's no fool, he isnt. You should have heard old Catherine downstairs as polite as you please to me, telling me not to mind the Major being a little impatient; for they knew what a good servant I was — after making a fool and a liar of me before them all! The twenty will go to our savings; and you shall have the ten to spend if youll only talk to me so as to remind me I'm a human being. I get tired of being a servant occasionally.

LOUKA. Yes: sell your manhood for 30 levas, and buy me for 10! [*Rising scornfully*] Keep your money. You were born to be a servant. I was not. When you set up your shop you will only be everybody's servant instead of somebody's servant. [*She goes moodily to the table and seats herself regally in Sergius's chair*].

NICOLA [*picking up his logs, and going to the stove*] Ah, wait til you see. We shall have our evenings to ourselves; and I shall be master in my own house, I promise you. [*He throws the logs down and kneels at the stove*].

LOUKA. You shall never be master in mine.

NICOLA [*turning, still on his knees, and squatting down rather forlornly on his calves, daunted by her implacable disdain*] You have a great ambition in you, Louka. Remember: if any luck comes to you, it was I that made a woman of you.

LOUKA. You!

NICOLA [*scrambling up and going to her*] Yes, me. Who was it made you give up wearing a couple of pounds of false black hair on your head and reddening your lips and cheeks like any other Bulgarian girl! I did. Who taught you to trim your nails, and keep your hands clean, and be dainty about yourself, like a fine Russian lady! Me: do you hear that? Me! [*She tosses her head defiantly; and he turns away, adding more coolly*] Ive often thought that if Raina were out of the way, and you just a little less of a fool and Sergius just a little more of one, you might come to be one of my grandest customers, instead of only being my wife and costing me money.

LOUKA. I believe you would rather be my servant than my

husband. You would make more out of me. Oh, I know that soul of yours.

NICOLA [*going closer to her for greater emphasis*] Never you mind my soul; but just listen to my advice. If you want to be a lady, your present behaviour to me wont do at all, unless when we're alone. It's too sharp and impudent; and impudence is a sort of familiarity: it shews affection for me. And dont you try being high and mighty with me, either. Youre like all country girls: you think it's genteel to treat a servant the way I treat a stableboy. Thats only your ignorance; and dont you forget it. And dont be so ready to defy everybody. Act as if you expected to have your own way, not as if you expected to be ordered about. The way to get on as a lady is the same as the way to get on as a servant: youve got to know your place: thats the secret of it. And you may depend on me to know my place if you get promoted. Think over it, my girl. I'll stand by you: one servant should always stand by another.

LOUKA [*rising impatiently*] Oh, I must behave in my own way. You take all the courage out of me with your cold-blooded wisdom. Go and put those logs on the fire: thats the sort of thing you understand.

Before Nicola can retort, Sergius comes in. He checks himself a moment on seeing Louka; then goes to the stove.

SERGIUS [*to Nicola*] I am not in the way of your work, I hope.

NICOLA [*in a smooth, elderly manner*] Oh no, sir: thank you kindly. I was only speaking to this foolish girl about her habit of running up here to the library whenever she gets a chance, to look at the books. Thats the worst of her education, sir: it gives her habits above her station. [*To Louka*] Make that table tidy, Louka, for the Major. [*He goes out sedately*].

Louka, without looking at Sergius, pretends to arrange the papers on the table. He crosses slowly to her, and studies the arrangement of her sleeve reflectively.

SERGIUS. Let me see: is there a mark there? [*He turns up the bracelet and sees the bruise made by his grasp. She stands motion-*

less, not looking at him: fascinated, but on her guard] Ffff! Does
it hurt?

LOUKA. Yes.

SERGIUS. Shall I cure it?

LOUKA [*instantly withdrawing herself proudly, but still not looking
at him*] No. You cannot cure it now.

SERGIUS [*masterfully*] Quite sure? [*He makes a movement as if
to take her in his arms*].

LOUKA. Dont trifle with me, please. An officer should not
trifle with a servant.

SERGIUS [*indicating the bruise with a merciless stroke of his forefinger*] That was no trifle, Louka.

LOUKA [*flinching; then looking at him for the first time*] Are you
sorry?

SERGIUS [*with measured emphasis, folding his arms*] I am never
sorry.

LOUKA [*wistfully*] I wish I could believe a man could be as
unlike a woman as that. I wonder are you really a brave
man?

SERGIUS [*unaffectedly, relaxing his attitude*] Yes: I am a brave
man. My heart jumped like a woman's at the first shot;
but in the charge I found that I was brave. Yes: that at
least is real about me.

LOUKA. Did you find in the charge that the men whose
fathers are poor like mine were any less brave than the
men who are rich like you?

SERGIUS [*with bitter levity*] Not a bit. They all slashed and
cursed and yelled like heroes. Psha! the courage to rage and
kill is cheap. I have an English bull terrier who has as much
of that sort of courage as the whole Bulgarian nation, and
the whole Russian nation at its back. But he lets my groom
thrash him, all the same. Thats your soldier all over! No,
Louka: your poor men can cut throats; but they are afraid
of their officers; they put up with insults and blows; they
stand by and see one another punished like children: aye,
and help to do it when they are ordered. And the officers! ! !
Well [*with a short harsh laugh*] I am an officer. Oh, [*fervently*]

73

give me the man who will defy to the death any power on earth or in heaven that sets itself up against his own will and conscience: he alone is the brave man.

LOUKA. How easy it is to talk! Men never seem to me to grow up: they all have schoolboy's ideas. You dont know what true courage is.

SERGIUS [*ironically*] Indeed! I am willing to be instructed. [*He sits on the ottoman, sprawling magnificently*].

LOUKA. Look at me! how much am I allowed to have my own will? I have to get your room ready for you: to sweep and dust, to fetch and carry. How could that degrade me if it did not degrade you to have it done for you? But [*with subdued passion*] if I were Empress of Russia, above everyone in the world, then!! Ah then, though according to you I could shew no courage at all, you should see, you should see.

SERGIUS. What would you do, most noble Empress?

LOUKA. I would marry the man I loved, which no other queen in Europe has the courage to do. If I loved you, though you would be as far beneath me as I am beneath you, I would dare to be the equal of my inferior. Would you dare as much if you loved me? No: if you felt the beginnings of love for me you would not let it grow. You would not dare: you would marry a rich man's daughter because you would be afraid of what other people would say to you.

SERGIUS [*bounding up*] You lie: it is not so, by all the stars! If I loved you, and I were the Czar himself, I would set you on the throne by my side. You know that I love another woman, a woman as high above you as heaven is above earth. And you are jealous of her.

LOUKA. I have no reason to be. She will never marry you now. The man I told you of has come back. She will marry the Swiss.

SERGIUS [*recoiling*] The Swiss!

LOUKA. A man worth ten of you. Then you can come to me; and I will refuse you. You are not good enough for me. [*She turns to the door*].

SERGIUS [*springing after her and catching her fiercely in his arms*] I will kill the Swiss; and afterwards I will do as I please with you.

LOUKA [*in his arms, passive and steadfast*] The Swiss will kill you, perhaps. He has beaten you in love. He may beat you in war.

SERGIUS [*tormentedly*] Do you think I believe that she – she! whose worst thoughts are higher than your best ones, is capable of trifling with another man behind my back?

LOUKA. Do you think she would believe the Swiss if he told her now that I am in your arms?

SERGIUS [*releasing her in despair*] Damnation! Oh, damnation! Mockery! mockery everywhere! everything I think is mocked by everything I do. [*He strikes himself frantically on the breast*]. Coward! liar! fool? Shall I kill myself like a man, or live and pretend to laugh at myself? [*She again turns to go*]. Louka! [*She stops near the door*]. Remember: you belong to me.

LOUKA [*turning*] What does that mean? An insult?

SERGIUS [*commandingly*] It means that you love me, and that I have had you here in my arms, and will perhaps have you there again. Whether that is an insult I neither know nor care: take it as you please. But [*vehemently*] I will not be a coward and a trifler. If I choose to love you, I dare marry you, in spite of all Bulgaria. If these hands ever touch you again, they shall touch my affianced bride.

LOUKA. We shall see whether you dare keep your word. And take care. I will not wait long.

SERGIUS [*again folding his arms and standing motionless in the middle of the room*] Yes: we shall see. And you shall wait my pleasure.

    Bluntschli, much preoccupied, with his papers still in his hand, enters, leaving the door open for Louka to go out. He goes across to the table, glancing at her as he passes. Sergius, without altering his resolute attitude, watches him steadily. Louka goes out, leaving the door open.

BLUNTSCHLI [*absently, sitting at the table as before, and putting down his papers*] Thats a remarkable looking young woman.

SERGIUS [*gravely, without moving*] Captain Bluntschli.

BLUNTSCHLI. Eh?

SERGIUS. You have deceived me. You are my rival. I brook no rivals. At six o'clock I shall be in the drilling-ground on the Klissoura road, alone, on horseback, with my sabre. Do you understand?

BLUNTSCHLI [*staring, but sitting quite at his ease*] Oh, thank you: thats a cavalry man's proposal. I'm in the artillery; and I have the choice of weapons. If I go, I shall take a machine gun. And there shall be no mistake about the cartridges this time.

SERGIUS [*flushing, but with deadly coldness*] Take care, sir. It is not our custom in Bulgaria to allow invitations of that kind to be trifled with.

BLUNTSCHLI [*warmly*] Pooh! dont talk to me about Bulgaria. You dont know what fighting is. But have it your own way. Bring your sabre along. I'll meet you.

SERGIUS [*fiercely delighted to find his opponent a man of spirit*] Well said, Switzer. Shall I lend you my best horse?

BLUNTSCHLI. No: damn your horse! thank you all the same, my dear fellow. [*Raina comes in, and hears the next sentence*]. I shall fight you on foot. Horseback's too dangerous; I dont want to kill you if I can help it.

RAINA [*hurrying forward anxiously*] I have heard what Captain Bluntschli said, Sergius. You are going to fight. Why? [*Sergius turns away in silence, and goes to the stove, where he stands watching her as she continues, to Bluntschli*] What about?

BLUNTSCHLI. I dont know: he hasnt told me. Better not interfere, dear young lady. No harm will be done: I've often acted as sword instructor. He wont be able to touch me; and I'll not hurt him. It will save explanations. In the morning I shall be off home; and youll never see me or hear of me again. You and he will then make it up and live happily ever after.

RAINA [*turning away deeply hurt, almost with a sob in her voice*] I never said I wanted to see you again.

SERGIUS [*striding forward*] Ha! That is a confession.

RAINA [*haughtily*] What do you mean?

SERGIUS. You love that man!

RAINA [*scandalized*] Sergius!

SERGIUS. You allow him to make love to you behind my back, just as you treat me as your affianced husband behind his. Bluntschli: you knew our relations; and you deceived me. It is for that I call you to account, not for having received favors *I* never enjoyed.

BLUNTSCHLI [*jumping up indignantly*] Stuff! Rubbish! I have received no favors. Why, the young lady doesnt even know whether I'm married or not.

RAINA [*forgetting herself*] Oh! [*Collapsing on the ottoman*] Are you?

SERGIUS. You see the young lady's concern, Captain Bluntschli. Denial is useless. You have enjoyed the privilege of being received in her own room, late at night –

BLUNTSCHLI [*interrupting him pepperily*] Yes, you blockhead! she received me with a pistol at her head. Your cavalry were at my heels. I'd have blown out her brains if she'd uttered a cry.

SERGIUS [*taken aback*] Bluntschli! Raina: is this true?

RAINA [*rising in wrathful majesty*] Oh, how dare you, how dare you?

BLUNTSCHLI. Apologize, man: apologize. [*He resumes his seat at the table*].

SERGIUS [*with the old measured emphasis, folding his arms*] I never apologize!

RAINA [*passionately*] This is the doing of that friend of yours, Captain Bluntschli. It is he who is spreading this horrible story about me. [*She walks about excitedly*].

BLUNTSCHLI. No: he's dead. Burnt alive.

RAINA [*stopping, shocked*] Burnt alive!

BLUNTSCHLI. Shot in the hip in a woodyard. Couldnt drag himself out. Your fellows' shells set the timber on fire and burnt him, with half a dozen other poor devils in the same predicament.

RAINA. How horrible!

SERGIUS. And how ridiculous! Oh, war! war! the dream of patriots and heroes! A fraud, Bluntschli. A hollow sham, like love.

RAINA [*outraged*] Like love! You say that before me!

BLUNTSCHLI. Come, Saranoff: that matter is explained.

SERGIUS. A hollow sham, I say. Would you have come back here if nothing had passed between you except at the muzzle of your pistol? Raina is mistaken about your friend who was burnt. He was not my informant.

RAINA. Who then? [*Suddenly guessing the truth*] Ah, Louka! my maid! my servant! You were with her this morning all that time after – after – Oh, what sort of god is this I have been worshipping! [*He meets her gaze with sardonic enjoyment of her disenchantment. Angered all the more, she goes closer to him, and says, in a lower, intenser tone*] Do you know that I looked out of the window as I went upstairs, to have another sight of my hero; and I saw something I did not understand then. I know now that you were making love to her.

SERGIUS [*with grim humor*] You saw that?

RAINA. Only too well. [*She turns away, and throws herself on the divan under the centre window, quite overcome*].

SERGIUS [*cynically*] Raina: our romance is shattered. Life's a farce.

BLUNTSCHLI [*to Raina, whimsically*] You see: he's found himself out now.

SERGIUS [*going to him*] Bluntschli: I have allowed you to call me a blockhead. You may now call me a coward as well. I refuse to fight you. Do you know why?

BLUNTSCHLI. No; but it doesnt matter. I didnt ask the reason when you cried on; and I dont ask the reason now that you cry off. I'm a professional soldier: I fight when I have to, and am very glad to get out of it when I havnt to. Youre only an amateur: you think fighting's an amusement.

SERGIUS [*sitting at the table, nose to nose with him*] You shall hear the reason all the same, my professional. The reason is that it takes two men – real men – men of heart, blood and honor – to make a genuine combat. I could no more fight with you than I could make love to an ugly woman. Youve no magnetism: youre not a man: youre a machine.

BLUNTSCHLI [*apologetically*] Quite true, quite true. I always was that sort of chap. I'm very sorry.

SERGIUS. Psha!

BLUNTSCHLI. But now that youve found that life isnt a farce, but something quite sensible and serious, what further obstacle is there to your happiness?

RAINA [*rising*] You are very solicitous about my happiness and his. Do you forget his new love – Louka? It is not you that he must fight now, but his rival, Nicola.

SERGIUS. Rival!! [*bounding half across the room*].

RAINA. Dont you know that theyre engaged?

SERGIUS. Nicola! Are fresh abysses opening? Nicola!

RAINA [*sarcastically*] A shocking sacrifice, isnt it? Such beauty! such intellect! such modesty! wasted on a middle-aged servant man. Really, Sergius, you cannot stand by and allow such a thing. It would be unworthy of your chivalry.

SERGIUS [*losing all self-control*] Viper! Viper! [*He rushes to and fro, raging*].

BLUNTSCHLI. Look here, Saranoff: youre getting the worst of this.

RAINA [*getting angrier*] Do you realize what he has done, Captain Bluntschli? He has set this girl as a spy on us; and her reward is that he makes love to her.

SERGIUS. False! Monstrous!

RAINA. Monstrous! [*Confronting him*] Do you deny that she told you about Captain Bluntschli being in my room?

SERGIUS. No; but –

RAINA [*interrupting*] Do you deny that you were making love to her when she told you?

SERGIUS. No; but I tell you –

RAINA [*cutting him short contemptuously*] It is unnecessary to tell us anything more. That is quite enough for us. [*She turns away from him and sweeps majestically back to the window*].

BLUNTSCHLI [*quietly, as Sergius, in an agony of mortification, sinks on the ottoman, clutching his averted head between his fists*] I told you you were getting the worst of it, Saranoff.

SERGIUS. Tiger cat!

RAINA [*running excitedly to Bluntschli*] You hear this man calling me names, Captain Bluntschli?

BLUNTSCHLI. What else can he do, dear lady? He must defend himself somehow. Come [*very persuasively*]: dont quarrel. What good does it do?

Raina, with a gasp, sits down on the ottoman, and after a vain effort to look vexedly at Bluntschli, falls a victim to her sense of humor, and actually leans back babyishly against the writhing shoulder of Sergius.

SERGIUS. Engaged to Nicola! Ha! ha! Ah well, Bluntschli, you are right to take this huge imposture of a world coolly.

RAINA [*quaintly to Bluntschli, with an intuitive guess at his state of mind*] I daresay you think us a couple of grown-up babies, dont you?

SERGIUS [*grinning savagely*] He does: he does. Swiss civilization nursetending Bulgarian barbarism, eh?

BLUNTSCHLI [*blushing*] Not at all, I assure you. I'm only very glad to get you two quieted. There! there! let's be pleasant and talk it over in a friendly way. Where is this other young lady?

RAINA. Listening at the door, probably.

SERGIUS [*shivering as if a bullet had struck him, and speaking with quiet but deep indignation*] I will prove that that, at least, is a calumny. [*He goes with dignity to the door and opens it. A yell of fury bursts from him as he looks out. He darts into the passage, and returns dragging in Louka, whom he flings violently against the table, exclaiming*] Judge her, Bluntschli. You, the cool impartial man: judge the eavesdropper.

Louka stands her ground, proud and silent.

BLUNTSCHLI [*shaking his head*] I mustnt judge her. I once listened myself outside a tent when there was a mutiny brewing. It's all a question of the degree of provocation. My life was at stake.

80

LOUKA. My love was at stake. I am not ashamed.

RAINA [*contemptuously*] Your love! Your curiosity, you mean.

LOUKA [*facing her and returning her contempt with interest*] My love, stronger than anything you can feel, even for your chocolate cream soldier.

SERGIUS [*with quick suspicion, to Louka*] What does that mean?

LOUKA [*fiercely*] It means –

SERGIUS [*interrupting her slightingly*] Oh, I remember: the ice pudding. A paltry taunt, girl!

Major Petkoff enters, in his shirtsleeves.

PETKOFF. Excuse my shirtsleeves, gentlemen. Raina: somebody has been wearing that coat of mine: I'll swear it. Somebody with a differently shaped back. It's all burst open at the sleeve. Your mother is mending it. I wish she'd make haste: I shall catch cold. [*He looks more attentively at them*]. Is anything the matter?

RAINA. No. [*She sits down at the stove, with a tranquil air*].

SERGIUS. Oh no. [*He sits down at the end of the table, as at first*].

BLUNTSCHLI [*who is already seated*] Nothing. Nothing.

PETKOFF [*sitting down on the ottoman in his old place*] Thats all right. [*He notices Louka*]. Anything the matter, Louka?

LOUKA. No, sir.

PETKOFF [*genially*] Thats all right. [*He sneezes*] Go and ask your mistress for my coat, like a good girl, will you?

Nicola enters with the coat. Louka makes a pretence of having business in the room by taking the little table with the hookah away to the wall near the windows.

RAINA [*rising quickly as she sees the coat on Nicola's arm*] Here it is, papa. Give it to me, Nicola; and do you put some more wood on the fire. [*She takes the coat, and brings it to the Major, who stands up to put it on. Nicola attends to the fire*].

PETKOFF [*to Raina, teasing her affectionately*] Aha! Going to be very good to poor old papa just for one day after his return from the wars, eh?

RAINA [*with solemn reproach*] Ah, how can you say that to me, father?

PETKOFF. Well, well, only a joke, little one. Come: give me a kiss. [*She kisses him*]. Now give me the coat.

RAINA. No: I am going to put it on for you. Turn your back. [*He turns his back and feels behind him with his arms for the sleeves. She dexterously takes the photograph from the pocket and throws it on the table before Bluntschli, who covers it with a sheet of paper under the very nose of Sergius, who looks on amazed, with his suspicions roused in the highest degree. She then helps Petkoff on with his coat*]. There, dear! Now are you comfortable?

PETKOFF. Quite, little love. Thanks. [*He sits down, and Raina returns to her seat near the stove*]. Oh, by the bye, Ive found something funny. Whats the meaning of this? [*He puts his hand into the picked pocket*]. Eh? Hallo! [*He tries the other pocket*]. Well, I could have sworn – ! [*Much puzzled, he tries the breast pocket*]. I wonder – [*trying the original pocket*]. Where can it – ? [*He rises, exclaiming*] Your mother's taken it!

RAINA [*very red*] Taken what?

PETKOFF. Your photograph, with the inscription: 'Raina, to her Chocolate Cream Soldier: a Souvenir.' Now you know theres something more in this than meets the eye; and I'm going to find it out. [*Shouting*] Nicola!

NICOLA [*coming to him*] Sir!

PETKOFF. Did you spoil any pastry of Miss Raina's th morning?

NICOLA. You heard Miss Raina say that I did, sir.

PETKOFF. I know that, you idiot. Was it true?

NICOLA. I am sure Miss Raina is incapable of saying anything that is not true, sir.

PETKOFF. Are you? Then I'm not. [*Turning to the others*] Come: do you think I dont see it all? [*He goes to Sergius, and slaps him on the shoulder*]. Sergius: youre the chocolate cream soldier, arnt you?

SERGIUS [*starting up*] I! A chocolate cream soldier! Certainly not.

PETKOFF. Not! [*He looks at them. They are all very serious and very conscious*]. Do you mean to tell me that Raina sends things like that to other men?

SERGIUS [*enigmatically*] The world is not such an innocent place as we used to think, Petkoff.

BLUNTSCHLI [*rising*] It's all right, Major. I'm the chocolate cream soldier. [*Petkoff and Sergius are equally astonished*]. The gracious young lady saved my life by giving me chocolate creams when I was starving: shall I ever forget their flavour! My late friend Stolz told you the story at Pirot. I was the fugitive.

PETKOFF. You! [*He gasps*]. Sergius: do you remember how those two women went on this morning when we mentioned it? [*Sergius smiles cynically. Petkoff confronts Raina severely*]. Youre a nice young woman, arnt you?

RAINA [*bitterly*] Major Saranoff has changed his mind. And when I wrote that on the photograph, I did not know that Captain Bluntschli was married.

BLUNTSCHLI [*startled into vehement protest*] I'm not married.

RAINA [*with deep reproach*] You said you were.

BLUNTSCHLI. I did not. I positively did not. I never was married in my life.

PETKOFF [*exasperated*] Raina: will you kindly inform me, if I am not asking too much, which of these gentlemen you are engaged to?

RAINA. To neither of them. This young lady [*introducing Louka, who faces them all proudly*] is the object of Major Saranoff's affections at present.

PETKOFF. Louka! Are you mad, Sergius? Why, this girl's engaged to Nicola.

NICOLA. I beg your pardon, sir. There is a mistake. Louka is not engaged to me.

PETKOFF. Not engaged to you, you scoundrel! Why, you had twenty-five levas from me on the day of your betrothal; and she had that gilt bracelet from Miss Raina.

NICOLA [*with cool unction*] We gave it out so, sir. But it was only to give Louka protection. She had a soul above her station; and I have been no more than her confidential servant. I intend, as you know, sir, to set up a shop later on in Sofia; and I look forward to her custom and recommendation should she marry into the nobility. [*He goes out with impressive discretion, leaving them all staring after him*].

PETKOFF [*breaking the silence*] Well, I am – hm!

SERGIUS. This is either the finest heroism or the most crawling baseness. Which is it, Bluntschli?

BLUNTSCHLI. Never mind whether it's heroism or baseness. Nicola's the ablest man Ive met in Bulgaria. I'll make him manager of a hotel if he can speak French and German.

LOUKA [*suddenly breaking out at Sergius*] I have been insulted by everyone here. You set them the example. You owe me an apology.

Sergius, like a repeating clock of which the spring has been touched, immediately begins to fold his arms.

BLUNTSCHLI [*before he can speak*] It's no use. He never apologizes.

LOUKA. Not to you, his equal and his enemy. To me, his poor servant, he will not refuse to apologize.

SERGIUS [*approvingly*] You are right. [*He bends his knee in his grandest manner*] Forgive me.

LOUKA. I forgive you. [*She timidly gives him her hand, which he kisses*]. That touch makes me your affianced wife.

SERGIUS [*springing up*] Ah! I forgot that.

LOUKA [*coldly*] You can withdraw if you like.

SERGIUS. Withdraw! Never! You belong to me. [*He puts his arm about her*].

Catherine comes in and finds Louka in Sergius's arms, with all the rest gazing at them in bewildered astonishment.

CATHERINE. What does this mean?

Sergius releases Louka.

PETKOFF. Well, my dear, it appears that Sergius is going to marry Louka instead of Raina. [*She is about to break out indignantly at him: he stops her by exclaiming testily*] Dont blame me: Ive nothing to do with it. [*He retreats to the stove*].

CATHERINE. Marry Louka! Sergius: you are bound by your word to us!

SERGIUS [*folding his arms*] Nothing binds me.

BLUNTSCHLI [*much pleased by this piece of common sense*] Saranoff: your hand. My congratulations. These heroics of yours have their practical side after all. [*To Louka*] Gracious young lady: the best wishes of a good Republican! [*He kisses her hand, to Raina's great disgust, and returns to his seat*].

CATHERINE. Louka: you have been telling stories.

LOUKA. I have done Raina no harm.

CATHERINE [*haughtily*] Raina!

Raina, equally indignant, almost snorts at the liberty.

LOUKA. I have a right to call her Raina: she calls me Louka. I told Major Saranoff she would never marry him if the Swiss gentleman came back.

BLUNTSCHLI [*rising, much surprised*] Hallo!

LOUKA [*turning to Raina*] I thought you were fonder of him than of Sergius. You know best whether I was right.

BLUNTSCHLI. What nonsense! I assure you, my dear Major, my dear Madame, the gracious young lady simply saved my life, nothing else. She never cared two straws for me. Why, bless my heart and soul, look at the young lady and look at me. She, rich, young, beautiful, with her imagination full of fairy princes and noble natures and cavalry charges and goodness knows what! And I, a commonplace Swiss soldier who hardly knows what a decent life is after fifteen years of barracks and battles: a vagabond, a man who has spoiled all his chances in life through an incurably romantic disposition, a man –

SERGIUS [*starting as if a needle had pricked him and interrupting Bluntschli in incredulous amazement*] Excuse me, Bluntschli: what did you say had spoiled your chances in life?

BLUNTSCHLI [*promptly*] An incurably romantic disposition. I ran away from home twice when I was a boy. I went into the army instead of into my father's business. I climbed the balcony of this house when a man of sense would have dived into the nearest cellar. I came sneaking back here to have another look at the young lady when any other man of my age would have sent the coat back –

PETKOFF. My coat!

BLUNTSCHLI. – yes: thats the coat I mean – would have sent

it back and gone quietly home. Do you suppose I am the sort of fellow a young girl falls in love with? Why, look at our ages! I'm thirty-four: I dont suppose the young lady is much over seventeen. [*This estimate produces a marked sensation, all the rest turning and staring at one another. He proceeds innocently*] All that adventure which was life or death to me, was only a schoolgirl's game to her – chocolate creams and hide and seek. Heres the proof! [*He takes the photograph from the table*]. Now, I ask you, would a woman who took the affair seriously have sent me this and written on it 'Raina, to her Chocolate Cream Soldier: a Souvenir'? [*He exhibits the photograph triumphantly, as if it settled the matter beyond all possibility of refutation*].

PETKOFF. Thats what I was looking for. How the deuce did it get there? [*He comes from the stove to look at it, and sits down on the ottoman*].

BLUNTSCHLI [*to Raina, complacently*] I have put everything right, I hope, gracious young lady.

RAINA [*going to the table to face him*] I quite agree with your account of yourself. You are a romantic idiot. [*Bluntschli is unspeakably taken aback*]. Next time, I hope you will know the difference between a schoolgirl of seventeen and a woman of twenty-three.

BLUNTSCHLI [*stupefied*] Twenty-three!

Raina snaps the photograph contemptuously from his hand; tears it up; throws the pieces in his face; and sweeps back to her former place.

SERGIUS [*with grim enjoyment of his rival's discomfiture*] Bluntschli: my one last belief is gone. Your sagacity is a fraud, like everything else. You have less sense than even I!

BLUNTSCHLI [*overwhelmed*] Twenty-three! Twenty-three!! [*He considers*]. Hm! [*Swiftly making up his mind and coming to his host*] In that case, Major Petkoff, I beg to propose formally to become a suitor for your daughter's hand, in place of Major Saranoff retired.

RAINA. You dare!

BLUNTSCHLI. If you were twenty-three when you said

86

those things to me this afternoon, I shall take them
seriously.

CATHERINE [*loftily polite*] I doubt, sir, whether you quite
realize either my daughter's position or that of Major
Sergius Saranoff, whose place you propose to take. The
Petkoffs and the Saranoffs are known as the richest and
most important families in the country. Our position is
almost historical: we can go back for twenty years.

PETKOFF. Oh, never mind that, Catherine. [*To Bluntschli*]
We should be most happy, Bluntschli, if it were only a
question of your position; but hang it, you know, Raina
is accustomed to a very comfortable establishment.
Sergius keeps twenty horses.

BLUNTSCHLI. But who wants twenty horses? We're not
going to keep a circus.

CATHERINE [*severely*] My daughter, sir, is accustomed to a
first-rate stable.

RAINA. Hush, mother: youre making me ridiculous.

BLUNTSCHLI. Oh well, if it comes to a question of an
establishment, here goes! [*He darts impetuously to the table;
seizes the papers in the blue envelope; and turns to Sergius*]. How
many horses did you say?

SERGIUS. Twenty, noble Switzer.

BLUNTSCHLI. I have two hundred horses. [*They are
amazed*]. How many carriages?

SERGIUS. Three.

BLUNTSCHLI. I have seventy. Twenty-four of them will
hold twelve inside, besides two on the box, without counting the driver and conductor. How many tablecloths have
you?

SERGIUS. How the deuce do I know?

BLUNTSCHLI. Have you four thousand?

SERGIUS. No.

BLUNTSCHLI. I have. I have nine thousand six hundred
pairs of sheets and blankets, with two thousand four hundred eider-down quilts. I have ten thousand knives and
forks, and the same quantity of dessert spoons. I have three

hundred servants. I have six palatial establishments, besides two livery stables, a tea gardens, and a private house. I have four medals for distinguished services; I have the rank of an officer and the standing of a gentleman; and I have three native languages. Shew me any man in Bulgaria that can offer as much!

PETKOFF [*with childish awe*] Are you Emperor of Switzerland?

BLUNTSCHLI. My rank is the highest known in Switzerland: I am a free citizen.

CATHERINE. Then, Captain Bluntschli, since you are my daughter's choice –

RAINA [*mutinously*] He's not.

CATHERINE [*ignoring her*] – I shall not stand in the way of her happiness. [*Petkoff is about to speak*] That is Major Petkoff's feeling also.

PETKOFF. Oh, I shall be only too glad. Two hundred horses! Whew!

SERGIUS. What says the lady?

RAINA [*pretending to sulk*] The lady says that he can keep his tablecloths and his omnibuses. I am not here to be sold to the highest bidder. [*She turns her back on him*].

BLUNTSCHLI. I wont take that answer. I appealed to you as a fugitive, a beggar, and a starving man. You accepted me. You gave me your hand to kiss, your bed to sleep in, and your roof to shelter me.

RAINA. I did not give them to the Emperor of Switzerland.

BLUNTSCHLI. Thats just what I say. [*He catches her by the shoulders and turns her face-to-face with him*]. Now tell us whom you did give them to.

RAINA [*succumbing with a shy smile*] To my chocolate cream soldier.

BLUNTSCHLI [*with a boyish laugh of delight*] Thatll do. Thank you. [*He looks at his watch and suddenly becomes businesslike*]. Time's up, Major. Youve managed those regiments so well that youre sure to be asked to get rid of some of the infantry of the Timok division. Send them home by way of Lom Palanka. Saranoff: dont get married until I come back: I shall be here punctually at five in the evening on Tuesday fortnight. Gracious ladies [*his heels click*] good evening. [*He makes them a military bow, and goes*].

SERGIUS. What a man! Is he a man!

CANDIDA
1895

CANDIDA

ACT I

A fine morning in October 1894 in the north east quarter of London, a vast district miles away from the London of Mayfair and St James's, and much less narrow, squalid, fetid and airless in its slums. It is strong in unfashionable middle class life: wide-streeted; myriad-populated; well served with ugly iron urinals, Radical clubs, and tram lines carrying a perpetual stream of yellow cars; enjoying in its main thoroughfares the luxury of grass-grown 'front gardens' untrodden by the foot of man save as to the path from the gate to the hall door; blighted by a callously endured monotony of miles and miles of unlovely brick houses, black iron railings, stony pavements, slated roofs, and respectably ill dressed or disreputably worse dressed people, quite accustomed to the place, and mostly plodding uninterestedly about somebody else's work. The little energy and eagerness that crop up shew themselves in cockney cupidity and business 'push'. Even the policemen and the chapels are not infrequent enough to break the monotony. The sun is shining cheerfully: there is no fog; and though the smoke effectually prevents anything, whether faces and hands or bricks and mortar, from looking fresh and clean, it is not hanging heavily enough to trouble a Londoner.

This desert of unattractiveness has its oasis. Near the outer end of the Hackney Road is a park of 217 acres, fenced in, not by railings, but by a wooden paling, and containing plenty of greensward, trees, a lake for bathers, flower beds which are triumphs of the admired cockney art of carpet gardening, and a sandpit, originally imported from the seaside for the delight of children, but speedily deserted on its becoming a natural vermin preserve for all the petty fauna of Kingsland, Hackney, and Hoxton. A bandstand, an unfurnished forum for religious, anti-religious, and political orators, cricket pitches, a gymnasium, and an old fashioned stone kiosk are among its attractions. Wherever the prospect is bounded by trees or rising green grounds, it is a pleasant place. Where the ground stretches flat to the grey palings, with bricks and mortar, sky signs, crowded chimneys and smoke beyond, the prospect makes it desolate and sordid.

The best view of Victoria Park is commanded by the front window of St Dominic's Parsonage, from which not a brick is visible. The parsonage is semi-detached, with a front garden and a porch. Visitors go up the flight of steps to the porch: tradespeople and members of the family go down by a door under the steps to the basement, with a breakfast room, used for all meals, in front, and the kitchen at the back. Upstairs, on the level of the hall door, is the drawing room, with its large plate glass window looking out on the park. In this, the only sitting room that can be spared from the children and the family meals, the parson, the Reverend James Mavor Morell, does his work. He is sitting in a strong round backed revolving chair at the end of a long table, which stands across the window, so that he can cheer himself with a view of the park over his left shoulder. At the opposite end of the table, adjoining it, is a little table only half as wide as the other, with a typewriter on it. His typist is sitting at this machine, with her back to the window. The large table is littered with pamphlets, journals, letters, nests of drawers, an office diary, postage scales and the like. A spare chair for visitors having business with the parson is in the middle, turned to his end. Within reach of his hand is a stationery case, and a photograph in a frame. The wall behind him is fitted with bookshelves, on which an adept eye can measure the parson's casuistry and divinity by Maurice's Theological Essays and a complete set of Browning's poems, and the reformer's politics by a yellow backed Progress and Poverty, Fabian Essays, A Dream of John Ball, Marx's Capital, and half a dozen other literary landmarks in Socialism. Facing him on the other side of the room, near the typewriter, is the door. Further down opposite the fireplace, a bookcase stands on a cellaret, with a sofa near it. There is a generous fire burning; and the hearth, with a comfortable armchair and a black japanned flower-painted coal scuttle at one side, a miniature chair for children on the other, a varnished wooden mantelpiece, with neatly moulded shelves, tiny bits of mirror let into the panels, a travelling clock in a leather case (the inevitable wedding present), and on the wall above a large autotype of the chief figure in Titian's Assumption of the Virgin, is very inviting. Altogether the room is the room of a good housekeeper, vanquished, as far as the table is concerned, by an untidy man, but elsewhere mistress of the situation. The furniture, in its ornamental aspect, betrays the style of the advertized 'drawing-room suite' of the pushing suburban furniture dealer; but there is nothing useless or pretentious in the room, money being too scarce in the house of an east end parson to be wasted on snobbish trimmings.

The Reverend James Mavor Morell is a Christian Socialist clergyman of the Church of England, and an active member of the Guild of St Matthew and the Christian Social Union. A vigorous, genial, popular man of forty, robust and goodlooking, full of energy, with pleasant, hearty, considerate manners, and a sound unaffected voice, which he used with the clean athletic articulation of a practised orator, and with a wide range and perfect command of expression. He is a first rate clergyman, able to say what he likes to whom he likes, to lecture people without setting himself up against them, to impose his authority on them without humiliating them, and, on occasion, to interfere in their business without impertinence. His well-spring of enthusiasm and sympathetic emotion has never run dry for a moment: he still eats and sleeps heartily enough to win the daily battle between exhaustion and recuperation triumphantly. Withal, a great baby, pardonably vain of his powers and unconsciously pleased with himself. He has a healthy complexion: good forehead, with the brows somewhat blunt, and the eyes bright and eager, mouth resolute but not particularly well cut, and a substantial nose, with the mobile spreading nostrils of the dramatic orator, void, like all his features, of subtlety.

The typist, Miss Proserpine Garnett, is a brisk little woman of about 30, of the lower middle class, neatly but cheaply dressed in a black merino skirt and a blouse, notably pert and quick of speech, and not very civil in her manner, but sensitive and affectionate. She is clattering away busily at her machine whilst Morell opens the last of his morning's letters. He realizes its contents with a comic groan of despair.

PROSERPINE. Another lecture?

MORELL. Yes. The Hoxton Freedom Group want me to address them on Sunday morning [*he lays great emphasis on Sunday, this being the unreasonable part of the business*]. What are they?

PROSERPINE. Communist Anarchists, I think.

MORELL. Just like Anarchists not to know that they cant have a parson on Sunday! Tell them to come to church if they want to hear me: it will do them good. Say I can come on Mondays and Thursdays only. Have you the diary there?

PROSERPINE [*taking up the diary*] Yes.

MORELL. Have I any lecture on for next Monday?

PROSERPINE [*referring to the diary*] Tower Hamlets Radical Club.

MORELL. Well, Thursday then?

PROSERPINE. English Land Restoration League.

MORELL. What next?

PROSERPINE. Guild of St Matthew on Monday. Independent Labor Party, Greenwich Branch, on Thursday. Monday, Social-Democratic Federation, Mile End Branch. Thursday, first Confirmation class. [*Impatiently*] Oh, I'd better tell them you cant come. Theyre only half a dozen ignorant conceited costermongers without five shillings between them.

MORELL [*amused*] Ah; but you see theyre near relatives of mine.

PROSERPINE [*staring at him*] Relatives of yours!

MORELL. Yes: we have the same father – in Heaven.

PROSERPINE [*relieved*] Oh, is that all?

MORELL [*with a sadness which is a luxury to a man whose voice expresses it so finely*] Ah, you dont believe it. Everybody says it: nobody believes it: nobody. [*Briskly, getting back to business*] Well, well! Come, Miss Proserpine: cant you find a date for the costers? what about the 25th? That was vacant the day before yesterday.

PROSERPINE [*referring to diary*] Engaged. The Fabian Society.

MORELL. Bother the Fabian Society! Is the 28th gone too?

PROSERPINE. City dinner. Youre invited to dine with the Founders' Company.

MORELL. Thatll do: I'll go to the Hoxton Group of Freedom instead. [*She enters the engagement in silence, with implacable disparagement of the Hoxton Anarchists in every line of her face.*

Morell bursts open the cover of a copy of The Church Reformer, *which has come by post, and glances through Mr Stewart Headlam's leader and the Guild of St Matthew news. These proceedings are presently enlivened by the appearance of Morell's curate, the Reverend Alexander Mill, a young gentleman gathered by Morell from the nearest University settlement, whither he had come from Oxford to give the east end of London the benefit of his university training. He is a conceitedly well intentioned, enthusiastic, immature novice, with nothing positively unbearable about him except a habit of speaking with his lips carefully closed a full half inch from each corner for the sake of a finicking articulation and a set of university vowels, this being his chief means so far of bringing his Oxford refinement (as he calls his habits) to bear on Hackney vulgarity. Morell, whom he has won over by a doglike devotion, looks up indulgently from* The Church Reformer, *and remarks]* Well, Lexy? Late again, as usual?

LEXY. I'm afraid so. I wish I could get up in the morning.

MORELL [*exulting in his own energy*] Ha! ha! [*Whimsically*] Watch and pray. Lexy: watch and pray.

LEXY. I know. [*Rising wittily to the occasion*] But how can I watch and pray when I am asleep? Isnt that so, Miss Prossy? [*He makes for the warmth of the fire*].

PROSERPINE [*sharply*] Miss Garnett, if you please.

LEXY. I beg your pardon. Miss Garnett.

PROSERPINE. Youve got to do all the work today.

LEXY [*on the hearth*] Why?

PROSERPINE. Never mind why. It will do you good to earn your supper before you eat it, for once in a way, as I do. Come! dont dawdle. You should have been off on your rounds half an hour ago.

LEXY [*perplexed*] Is she in earnest, Morell?

MORELL [*in the highest spirits; his eyes dancing*] Yes. *I* am going to dawdle today.

LEXY. You! You dont know how.

MORELL [*rising*] Ha! ha! dont I? I'm going to have this morning all to myself. My wife's coming back; she's due here at 11.45.

97

LEXY [*surprised*] Coming back already! with the children? I thought they were to stay to the end of the month.

MORELL. So they are: she's only coming up for two days, to get some flannel things for Jimmy, and to see how we're getting on without her.

LEXY [*anxiously*] But, my dear Morell, if what Jimmy and Fluffy had was scarlatina, do you think it wise –

MORELL. Scarlatina! Rubbish! it was German measles. I brought it into the house myself from the Pycroft Street school. A parson is like a doctor, my boy: he must face infection as a soldier must face bullets. [*He claps Lexy manfully on the shoulders*]. Catch the measles if you can, Lexy: she'll nurse you; and what a piece of luck that will be for you! Eh?

LEXY [*smiling uneasily*] It's so hard to understand you about Mrs Morell –

MORELL [*tenderly*] Ah, my boy, get married; get married to a good woman; and then youll understand. Thats a foretaste of what will be best in the Kingdom of Heaven we are trying to establish on earth. That will cure you of dawdling. An honest man feels that he must pay Heaven for every hour of happiness with a good spell of hard unselfish work to make others happy. We have no more right to consume happiness without producing it than to consume wealth without producing it. Get a wife like my Candida; and youll always be in arrear with your repayment. [*He pats Lexy affectionately and moves to leave the room*].

LEXY. Oh, wait a bit: I forgot. [*Morell halts and turns with the door knob in his hand*]. Your father-in-law is coming round to see you.

Morell, surprised and not pleased, shuts the door again, with a complete change of manner.

MORELL. Mr Burgess?

LEXY. Yes. I passed him in the park, arguing with somebody. He asked me to let you know that he was coming.

MORELL [*half incredulous*] But he hasnt called here for three years. Are you sure, Lexy? Youre not joking, are you?

LEXY [*earnestly*] No sir, really.

MORELL [*thoughtfully*] Hm! Time for him to take another look at Candida before she grows out of his knowledge. [*He resigns himself to the inevitable, and goes out*].

> *Lexy looks after him with beaming worship. Miss Garnett, not being able to shake Lexy, relieves her feelings by worrying the typewriter.*

LEXY. What a good man! What a thorough loving soul he is! [*He takes Morell's place at the table, making himself very comfortable as he takes out a cigaret*].

PROSERPINE [*impatiently, pulling the letter she has been working at off the typewriter and folding it*] Oh, a man ought to be able to be fond of his wife without making a fool of himself about her.

LEXY [*shocked*] Oh, Miss Prossy!

PROSERPINE [*snatching at the stationery case for an envelope, in which she encloses the letter as she speaks*] Candida here, and Candida there, and Candida everywhere! [*She licks the envelope*]. It's enough to drive anyone out of their senses [*thumping the envelope to make it stick*] to hear a woman raved about in that absurd manner merely because she's got good hair and a tolerable figure.

LEXY [*with reproachful gravity*] I think her extremely beautiful, Miss Garnett. [*He takes the photograph up; looks at it; and adds, with even greater impressiveness*] extremely beautiful. How fine her eyes are!

PROSERPINE. Her eyes are not a bit better than mine: now! [*He puts down the photograph and stares austerely at her*]. And you know very well you think me dowdy and second rate enough.

LEXY [*rising majestically*] Heaven forbid that I should think of any of God's creatures in such a way! [*He moves stiffly away from her across the room to the neighbourhood of the bookcase*].

PROSERPINE [*sarcastically*] Thank you. Thats very nice and comforting.

LEXY [*saddening by her depravity*] I had no idea you had any feeling against Mrs Morell.

PROSERPINE [*indignantly*] I have no feeling against her. She's very nice, very good-hearted: I'm very fond of her, and can appreciate her real qualities far better than any man can. [*He shakes his head sadly. She rises and comes at him with intense pepperiness*]. You dont believe me? You think I'm jealous? Oh, what a knowledge of the human heart you have, Mr Lexy Mill! How well you know the weaknesses of Woman, dont you? It must be so nice to be a man and have a fine penetrating intellect instead of mere emotions like us, and to know that the reason we dont share your amorous delusions is that we're all jealous of one another! [*She abandons him with a toss of her shoulders, and crosses to the fire to warm her hands*].

LEXY. Ah, if you women only had the same clue to Man's strength that you have to his weakness, Miss Prossy, there would be no Woman Question.

PROSERPINE [*over her shoulder, as she stoops, holding her hands to the blaze*] Where did you hear Morell say that? You didnt invent it yourself: youre not clever enough.

LEXY. That's quite true, I am not ashamed of owing him that, as I owe him so many other spiritual truths. He said it at the annual conference of the Women's Liberal Federation. Allow me to add that though they didnt appreciate it, I, a mere man, did. [*He turns to the bookcase again, hoping that this may leave her crushed*].

PROSERPINE [*putting her hair straight at a panel of mirror in the mantelpiece*] Well, when you talk to me, give me your own ideas, such as they are, and not his. You never cut a poorer figure than when you are trying to imitate him.

LEXY [*stung*] I try to follow his example, not to imitate him.

PROSERPINE [*coming at him again on her way back to her work*] Yes, you do: you imitate him. Why do you tuck your umbrella under your left arm instead of carrying it in your hand like anyone else? Why do you walk with your chin stuck out before you, hurrying along with that eager look in your eyes? you! who never get up before half past nine in the morning. Why do you say 'knoaledge' in church, though you always say 'knolledge' in private conversation! Bah! do you think I dont know? [*She goes back to the typewriter*]. Here! come and set about your work: weve wasted enough time for one morning. Here's a copy of the diary for today. [*She hands him a memorandum*].

LEXY [*deeply offended*] Thank you. [*He takes it and stands at the table with his back to her, reading it. She begins to transcribe her shorthand notes on the typewriter without troubling herself about his feelings*].

The door opens; and Mr Burgess enters unannounced. He is a man of sixty, made coarse and sordid by the compulsory selfishness of petty commerce, and later on softened into sluggish bumptiousness by overfeeding and commercial success. A vulgar ignorant guzzling man, offensive and contemptuous to people whose labor is cheap, respectful to wealth and rank, and quite sincere and without rancor or envy in both attitudes. The world has offered him no decently paid work except that of a sweater; and he has become, in consequence, somewhat hoggish. But he has no suspicion of this himself, and honestly regards his commercial prosperity as the inevitable and socially wholesome triumph of the ability, industry, shrewdness, and experience in business of a man who in private is easygoing, affectionate, and humorously convivial to a fault. Corporeally he is podgy, with a snoutish nose in the centre of a flat square face, a dust colored beard with a patch of grey in the centre under his chin, and small watery blue eyes with a plaintively sentimental expression, which he transfers easily to his voice by his habit of pompously intoning his sentences.

BURGESS [*stopping on the threshold, and looking round*] They told me Mr Morell was here.

PROSERPINE [*rising*] I'll fetch him for you.

BURGESS [*staring disappointedly at her*] Youre not the same young lady as hused to typewrite for him?

PROSERPINE. No.

BURGESS [*grumbling on his way to the hearth-rug*] No: she was young-er. [*Miss Garnett stares at him; then goes out, slamming the door*]. Startin on your rounds, Mr Mill?

LEXY [*folding his memorandum and pocketing it*] Yes: I must be off presently.

BURGESS [*momentously*] Dont let me detain you, Mr Mill. What I come about is p r i v a t e between me and Mr Morell.

LEXY [*huffily*] I have no intention of intruding, I am sure, Mr Burgess. Good morning.

BURGESS [*patronizingly*] Oh, good morning to you.

Morell returns as Lexy is making for the door.

MORELL [*to Lexy*] Off to work?

LEXY. Yes, sir.

MORELL. Take my silk handkerchief and wrap your throat up. Theres a cold wind. Away with you.

Lexy, more than consoled for Burgess's rudeness, brightens up and goes out.

BURGESS. Spoilin your korates as usu'l, James. Good mornin. When I pay a man, an' 'is livin depens on me, I keep him in 'is place.

MORELL [*rather shortly*] I always keep my curates in their places as my helpers and comrades. If you get as much work out of your clerks and warehousemen as I do out of my curates, you must be getting rich pretty fast. Will you take your old chair.

He points with curt authority to the armchair beside the fireplace; then takes the spare chair from the table and sits down at an unfamiliar distance from his visitor.

BURGESS [*without moving*] Just the same as hever, James!

MORELL. When you last called – it was about three years ago, I think – you said the same thing a little more frankly. Your exact words then were 'Just as big a fool as ever, James!'

BURGESS [*soothingly*] Well, praps I did; but [*with conciliatory cheerfulness*] I meant no hoffence by it. A clorgyman is privileged to be a bit of a fool, you know: it's ony becomin in 'is profession that he should. Anyhow, I come here, not to rake up hold differences, but to let bygones be bygones. [*Suddenly becoming very solemn, and approaching Morell*] James: three years ago, you done me a hil turn. You done me hout of a contrac: as when I gev you arsh words in my natral disappointment, you turned my daughrter again me. Well, Ive come to hact the part of a Kerischin [*Offering his hand*] I forgive you, James.

MORELL [*starting up*] Confound your impudence!

BURGESS [*retreating, with almost lachrymose deprecation of this treatment*] Is that becomin language for a clorgyman, James? And you so particlar, too!

MORELL [*hotly*] No, sir: it is not becoming language for a clergyman. I used the wrong word. I should have said damn your impudence: thats what St Paul or any honest priest would have said to you. Do you think I have forgotten that tender of yours for the contract to supply clothing to the workhouse?

BURGESS [*in a paroxysm of public spirit*] I hacted in the hinterest of the ratepayers, James. It was the lowest tender: you carnt deny that.

MORELL. Yes, the lowest, because you paid worse wages than any other employer – starvation wages – aye, worse than starvation wages – to the women who made the clothing. Your wages would have driven them to the streets to keep body and soul together. [*Getting angrier and angrier*] Those women were my parishioners. I shamed the Guardians out of accepting your tender: I shamed the ratepayers out of letting them do it: I shamed everybody but you. [*Boiling over*]. How dare you, sir, come here and offer to forgive me, and talk about your daughter, and –

BURGESS. Heasy, James! heasy! heasy! Dont git hinto a fluster about nothink. Ive howned I was wrong.

MORELL. Have you? I didn't hear you.

BURGESS. Of course I did. I hown it now. Come: I harsk your pardon for the letter I wrote you. Is that enough?

MORELL [*snapping his fingers*] Thats nothing. Have you raised the wages?

BURGESS [*triumphantly*] Yes.

MORELL. What!

BURGESS [*unctuously*] Ive turned a moddle hemployer. I

dont hemploy no women now: theyre all sacked; and the work is done by machinery. Not a man 'as less than sixpence a *hour*; and the skilled ands gits the Trade Union rate. [*Proudly*] What ave you to say to me now?

MORELL [*overwhelmed*] Is it possible! Well, theres more joy in heaven over one sinner that repenteth! – [*Going to Burgess with an explosion of apologetic cordiality*] My dear Burgess: how splendid of you! I most heartily beg your pardon for my hard thoughts. [*Grasping his hand*] And now, dont you feel the better for the change? Come! confess! youre happier. You look happier.

BURGESS [*ruefully*] Well, praps I do. I spose I must, since you notice it. At all events, I git my contrax assepted by the County Council. [*Savagely*] They dussent ave nothink to do with me unless I paid fair wages: curse em for a parcel o meddlin fools!

MORELL [*dropping his hand, utterly discouraged*] So that was why you raised the wages! [*He sits down moodily*].

BURGESS [*severely, in spreading, mounting tones*] Woy helse should I do it? What does it lead to but drink and huppishness in workin men? [*He seats himself magisterially in the easy chair*]. It's hall very well for you, James: it gits you hinto the papers and makes a great man of you; but you never think of the arm you do, puttin money into the pockets of workin men that they dunno ow to spend, and takin it from people that might be makin a good huse on it.

MORELL [*with a heavy sigh, speaking with cold politeness*] What is your business with me this morning? I shall not pretend to believe that you are here merely out of family sentiment.

BURGESS [*obstinately*] Yes I ham: just family sentiment and nothink helse.

MORELL [*with weary calm*] I dont believe you.

BURGESS [*rising threateningly*] Dont say that to me again, James Mavor Morell.

MORELL [*unmoved*] I'll say it just as often as may be necessary to convince you that it's true. I dont believe you.

BURGESS [*collapsing into an abyss of wounded feeling*] Oh, well, if youre determined to be hunfriendly, I spose I'd better go. [*He moves reluctantly towards the door. Morell makes no sign. He lingers*]. I didnt hexpect to find a hunforgivin spirit in you, James. [*Morell still not responding, he takes a few more reluctant steps doorwards. Then he comes back, whining*]. We huseter git on well enough, spite of our different hopinions. Woy are you so changed to me? I give you my word I come here in peeorr [pure] frenliness, not wishin to be hon bad terms with my hown daughrter's usban. Come, James: be a Kerischin, and shake ands. [*He puts his hand sentimentally on Morell's shoulder*].

MORELL [*looking up at him thoughtfully*] Look here, Burgess. Do you want to be as welcome here as you were before you lost that contract?

BURGESS. I do, James. I do – *h*onest.

MORELL. Then why dont you behave as you did then?

BURGESS [*cautiously removing his hand*] Ow d'y'mean?

MORELL. I'll tell you. You thought me a young fool then.

BURGESS [*coaxingly*] No I didnt, James. I –

MORELL [*cutting him short*] Yes, you did. And I thought you an old scoundrel.

BURGESS [*most vehemently deprecating this gross self-accusation on Morell's part*] No you didnt, James. Now you do yourself a hinjustice.

MORELL. Yes I did. Well, that did not prevent our getting on very well together. God made you what I call a scoundrel as He made me what you call a fool. [*The effect of this observation on Burgess is to remove the keystone of his moral arch. He becomes bodily weak, and, with his eyes fixed on Morell in a helpless stare, puts out his hand apprehensively to balance himself, as if the floor had suddenly sloped under him. Morell proceeds, in the same tone of quiet conviction*] It was not for me to quarrel with His handiwork in the one case more than in the other. So long as you come here honestly as a self-respecting, thorough, convinced, scoundrel, justifying your scoundrelism and proud of it, you are welcome. But [*and now Morell's tone becomes formidable; and he rises and strikes the back of the chair for greater emphasis*] I wont have you here snivelling about being a model employer and a converted man when youre only an apostate with your coat turned for the sake of a County Council contract. [*He nods at him to enforce the point; then goes to the hearth-rug, where he takes up a comfortably commanding position with his back to the fire, and continues*] No: I like a man to be true to himself, even in wickedness. Come now: either take your hat and go; or else sit down and give me a good scoundrelly reason for wanting to be friends with me. [*Burgess, whose emotions have subsided sufficiently to be expressed by a dazed grin, is relieved by this concrete proposition. He ponders it for a moment, and then, slowly and very modestly sits down in the chair Morell has just left*]. Thats right. Now out with it.

BURGESS [*chuckling in spite of himself*] Well, you orr a queer bird, James, and no mistake. But [*almost enthusiastically*] one carnt elp likin you: besides, as I said afore, of course one dont take hall a clorgyman says seriously, or the world couldnt go on. Could it now? [*He composes himself for graver discourse, and, turning his eyes on Morell, proceeds with dull seriousness*] Well, I dont mind tellin you, since it's your wish we should be free with one another, that I did think you a bit of a fool once; but I'm beginnin to think that praps I was be'ind the times a bit.

MORELL [*exultant*] Aha! Youre finding that out at last, are you?

BURGESS [*portentously*] Yes: times 'as changed mor'n I could a believed. Five yorr [year] ago, no sensible man would a thought o takin hup with your hidears. I hused to wonder you was let preach at all. Why, I know a clorgyman what 'as bin kep hout of his job for yorrs by the Bishop o London, although the pore feller's not a bit more religious than you are. But today, if hennyone was to horffer to bet me a thousan poun that youll hend by being a bishop yourself, I dussent take the bet. [*Very impressively*] You and your crew are gittin hinfluential: I can see that. Theyll ave to give you somethink someday, if it's honly to stop your mouth.

You ad the right instinc arter all, James: the line you took is the payin line in the long run for a man o your sort.

MORELL [*offering his hand with thorough decision*] Shake hands, Burgess. Now youre talking honestly. I dont think theyll make me a bishop; but if they do, I'll introduce you to the biggest jobbers I can get to come to my dinner parties.

BURGESS [*who has risen with a sheepish grin and accepted the hand of friendship*] You will ave your joke, James. Our quarrel made up now, ain it?

A WOMAN'S VOICE. Say yes, James.

Startled, they turn quickly and find that Candida has just come in, and is looking at them with an amused maternal indulgence which is her characteristic expression. She is a woman of 33, well built, well nourished, likely, one guesses, to become matronly later on, but now quite at her best, with the double charm of youth and motherhood. Her ways are those of a woman who has found that she can always manage people by engaging their affection, and who does so frankly and instinctively without the smallest scruple. So far, she is like any other pretty woman who is just clever enough to make the most of her sexual attractions for trivially selfish ends; but Candida's serene brow, courageous eyes, and well set mouth and chin signify largeness of mind and dignity of character to ennoble her cunning in the affections. A wise-hearted observer, looking at her, would at once guess that whoever had placed the Virgin of the Assumption over her hearth did so because he fancied some spiritual resemblance between them, and yet would not suspect either her husband or herself of any such idea, or indeed of any concern with the art of Titian.

Just now she is in bonnet and mantle, carrying a strapped rug with her umbrella stuck through it, a hand-bag, and a supply of illustrated papers.

MORELL [*shocked at his remissness*] Candida! Why – [*he looks at his watch, and is horrified to find it so late*]. My darling! [*Hurrying to her and seizing the rug strap, pouring forth his remorseful regrets all the time*] I intended to meet you at the train. I let the time slip. [*Flinging the rug on the sofa*] I was so engrossed by – [*returning to her*] – I forgot – oh! [*He embraces her with penitent emotion*].

BURGESS [*a little shamefaced and doubtful of his reception*] How orr you, Candy? [*She, still in Morell's arms, offers him her cheek, which he kisses*]. James and me is come to a nunner-stannin. A honorable unnerstannin. Ain we, James?

MORELL [*impetuously*] Oh bother your understanding! youve kept me late for Candida. [*With compassionate fervor*] My poor love: how did you manage about the luggage? How –

CANDIDA [*stopping him and disengaging herself*] There! there! there! I wasnt alone. Eugene has been down with us; and we travelled together.

MORELL [*pleased*] Eugene!

CANDIDA. Yes: he's struggling with my luggage, poor boy. Go out, dear, at once; or he'll pay for the cab; and I dont want that. [*Morell hurries out. Candida puts down her hand-bag; then takes off her mantle and bonnet and puts them on the sofa with the rug, chatting meanwhile*]. Well, papa: how are you getting on at home?

BURGESS. The ouse aint worth livin in since you left it, Candy. I wish youd come round and give the gurl a talkin to. Who's this Eugene thats come with you?

CANDIDA. Oh, Eugene's one of James's discoveries. He found him sleeping on the Embankment last June. Havnt you noticed our new picture [*pointing to the Virgin*]? He gave us that.

BURGESS [*incredulously*] Garn! D'you mean to tell me – your hown father! – that cab touts or such like, orf the Embankment, buys pictures like that? [*Severely*] Dont deceive me, Candy: it's a 'Igh Church picture; and James chose it hisself.

CANDIDA. Guess again. Eugene isnt a cab tout.

BURGESS. Then what is he? [*Sarcastically*] A nobleman, I spose.

CANDIDA [*nodding delightedly*] Yes. His uncle's a peer! A real live earl.

BURGESS [*not daring to believe such good news*] No!

CANDIDA. Yes. He had a seven day bill for £55 in his pocket when James found him on the Embankment. He thought he couldnt get any money for it until the seven days were up; and he was too shy to ask for credit. Oh, he's a dear boy! We are very fond of him.

BURGESS [*pretending to belittle the aristocracy, but with his eyes gleaming*] Hm! I thort you wouldnt git a hearl's nevvy visitin in Victawriar Pawrk unless he were a bit of a flat. [*Looking again at the picture*] Of course I dont old with that picture, Candy; but still it's a 'igh class fust rate work of ort: I can see that. Be sure you hintrodooce me to im, Candy. [*He looks at his watch anxiously*]. I can ony stay about two minutes.

Morell comes back with Eugene, whom Burgess contemplates moist-eyed with enthusiasm. He is a strange, shy youth of eighteen, slight, effeminate, with a delicate childish voice, and a hunted tormented expression and shrinking manner that shew the painful sensitiveness of very swift and acute apprehensiveness in youth, before the character has grown to its full strength. Miserably irresolute, he does not know where to stand or what to do. He is afraid of Burgess, and would run away into solitude if he dared; but the very intensity with which he feels a perfectly commonplace position comes from excessive nervous force; and his nostrils, mouth, and eyes betray a fiercely petulant wilfulness, as to the bent of which his brow, already lined with pity, is reassuring. He is so uncommon as to be almost unearthly; and to prosaic people there is something noxious in this unearthliness, just as to poetic people there is something angelic in it. His dress is anarchic. He wears an old blue serge jacket, unbuttoned, over a woollen lawn tennis shirt, with a silk handkerchief for a cravat, trousers matching the jacket, and brown canvas shoes. In these garments he has apparently lain in the heather and waded through the waters; and there is no evidence of his having ever brushed them.

As he catches sight of a stranger on entering, he stops, and edges along the wall on the opposite side of the room.

MORELL [*as he enters*] Come along: you can spare us quarter of an hour at all events. This is my father-in-law. Mr Burgess – Mr Marchbanks.

MARCHBANKS [*nervously backing against the bookcase*] Glad to meet you, sir.

BURGESS [*crossing to him with great heartiness, whilst Morell joins Candida at the fire*] Glad to meet you, I'm shore, Mr Morchbanks. [*Forcing him to shake hands*] Ow do you find yoreself this weather? Ope you aint lettin James put no foolish ideas into your ed?

MARCHBANKS. Foolish ideas? Oh, you mean Socialism? No.

BURGESS. Thats right. [*Again looking at his watch*] Well, I must go now: theres no elp for it. Yore not comin my way, orr you, Mr Morchbanks?

MARCHBANKS. Which way is that?

BURGESS. Victawriar Pawrk Station. Theres a city train at 12.25.

MORELL. Nonsense. Eugene will stay to lunch with us, I expect.

MARCHBANKS [*anxiously excusing himself*] No – I – I –

BURGESS. Well, well, I shornt press you: I bet youd rather lunch with Candy. Some night, I ope, youll come and dine with me at my club, the Freeman Founders in Nortn Folgit. Come: say you will!

MARCHBANKS. Thank you, Mr Burgess. Where is Norton Folgate. Down in Surrey, isnt it?

Burgess, inexpressibly tickled, begins to splutter with laughter.

CANDIDA [*coming to the rescue*] Youll lose your train, papa, if you dont go at once. Come back in the afternoon and tell Mr Marchbanks where to find the club.

BURGESS [*roaring with glee*] Down in Surrey! Har, har! thats not a bad one. Well, I never met a man as didnt know Nortn Folgit afore. [*Abashed at his own noisiness*] Goodbye, Mr Morchbanks: I know yore too ighbred to take my pleasantry in bad part. [*He again offers his hand*].

MARCHBANKS [*taking it with a nervous jerk*] Not at all.

BURGESS. Bye, bye, Candy. I'll look in again later on. So long, James.

MORELL. Must you go?

BURGESS. Dont stir. [*He goes out with unabated heartiness*].

MORELL. Oh, I'll see you off. [*He follows him*].

Eugene stares after them apprehensively, holding his breath until Burgess disappears.

CANDIDA [*laughing*] Well, Eugene? [*He turns with a start, and comes eagerly towards her, but stops irresolutely as he meets her amused look*]. What do you think of my father?

MARCHBANKS. I – I hardly know him yet. He seems to be a very nice old gentleman.

CANDIDA [*with gentle irony*] And youll go to the Freeman Founders to dine with him, wont you?

MARCHBANKS [*miserably, taking it quite seriously*] Yes, if it will please you.

CANDIDA [*touched*] Do you know, you are a very nice boy, Eugene, with all your queerness. If you had laughed at my father I shouldnt have minded; but I like you ever so much better for being nice to him.

MARCHBANKS. Ought I to have laughed? I noticed that he said something funny; but I am so ill at ease with strangers; and I never can see a joke. I'm very sorry. [*He sits down on the sofa, his elbows on his knees and his temples between his fists with an expression of hopeless suffering*].

CANDIDA [*bustling him goodnaturedly*] Oh come! You great baby, you! You are worse than usual this morning. Why were you so melancholy as we came along in the cab?

MARCHBANKS. Oh, that was nothing. I was wondering how much I ought to give the cabman. I know it's utterly silly; but you dont know how dreadful such things are to me – how I shrink from having to deal with strange people. [*Quickly and reassuringly*] But it's all right. He beamed all over and touched his hat when Morell gave him two shillings. I was on the point of offering him ten.

Morell comes back with a few letters and newspapers which have come by the midday post.

CANDIDA. Oh, James dear, he was going to give the cabman

ten shillings! ten shillings for a three minutes drive! Oh dear!

MORELL [*at the table, glancing through the letters*] Never mind her, Marchbanks. The overpaying instinct is a generous one: better than the underpaying instinct, and not so common.

MARCHBANKS [*relapsing into dejection*] No: cowardice, incompetence. Mrs Morell's quite right.

CANDIDA. Of course she is. [*She takes up her hand-bag*]. And now I must leave you to James for the present. I suppose you are too much of a poet to know the state a woman finds her house in when she's been away for three weeks. Give me my rug. [*Eugene takes the strapped rug from the couch, and gives it to her. She takes it in her left hand, having the bag in her right*]. Now hang my cloak across my arm. [*He obeys*]. Now my hat. [*He puts it into the hand which has the bag*]. Now open the door for me. [*He hurries before her and opens the door*]. Thanks. [*She goes out; and Marchbanks shuts the door*].

MORELL [*still busy at the table*] Youll stay to lunch, Marchbanks, of course.

MARCHBANKS [*scared*] I mustnt. [*He glances quickly at Morell, but at once avoids his frank look, and adds, with obvious disingenuousness*] I mean I cant.

MORELL. You mean you wont.

MARCHBANKS [*earnestly*] No: I should like to, indeed. Thank you very much. But – but –

MORELL. But – but – but – but – Bosh! If youd like to stay, stay. If youre shy, go and take a turn in the park and write poetry until half past one; and then come in and have a good feed.

MARCHBANKS. Thank you, I should like that very much. But I really musnt. The truth is, Mrs Morell told me not to. She said she didnt think youd ask me to stay to lunch, but that I was to remember, if you did, that you didnt really want me to. [*Plaintively*] She said I'd understand; but I dont. Please dont tell her I told you.

MORELL [*drolly*] Oh, is that all? Wont my suggestion that

you should take a turn in the park meet the difficulty?

MARCHBANKS. How?

MORELL [*exploding good-humoredly*] Why, you duffer – [*But this boisterousness jars himself as well as Eugene. He checks himself*]. No: I wont put it in that way. [*He comes to Eugene with affectionate seriousness*]. My dear lad: in a happy marriage like ours, there is something very sacred in the return of the wife to her home. [*Marchbanks looks quickly at him, half anticipating his meaning*]. An old friend or a truly noble and sympathetic soul is not in the way on such occasions; but a chance visitor is. [*The hunted horror-stricken expression comes out with sudden vividness in Eugene's face as he understands. Morell, occupied with his own thoughts, goes on without noticing this*]. Candida thought I would rather not have you here; but she was wrong. I'm very fond of you, my boy; and I should like you to see for yourself what a happy thing it is to be married as I am.

MARCHBANKS. Happy! Your marriage! You think that! You believe that!

MORELL [*buoyantly*] I know it, my lad. Larochefoucauld said that there are convenient marriages but no delightful ones. You dont know the comfort of seeing through and through a thundering liar and rotten cynic like that fellow. Ha! ha! Now, off with you to the park, and write your poem. Half past one, sharp, mind: we never wait for anybody.

MARCHBANKS [*wildly*] No: stop: you shant. I'll force it into the light.

MORELL [*puzzled*] Eh? Force what?

MARCHBANKS. I must speak to you. There is something that must be settled between us.

MORELL [*with a whimsical glance at his watch*] Now?

MARCHBANKS [*passionately*] Now. Before you leave this room. [*He retreats a few steps, and stands as if to bar Morell's way to the door*].

MORELL [*without moving, and gravely, perceiving now that there is something serious the matter*] I'm not going to leave it, my dear boy! I thought you were. [*Eugene, baffled by his firm tone, turns his back on him, writhing with anger. Morell goes to him and puts his hand on his shoulder strongly and kindly, disregarding his attempt to shake it off*]. Come: sit down quietly; and tell me what it is: And remember: we are friends, and need not fear that either of us will be anything but patient and kind to the other, whatever we may have to say.

MARCHBANKS [*twisting himself round on him*] Oh, I am not forgetting myself: I am only [*covering his face desperately with his hands*] full of horror. [*Then, dropping his hands, and thrusting his face forward fiercely at Morell, he goes on threateningly*] You shall see whether this is a time for patience and kindness. [*Morell, firm as a rock, looks indulgently at him*]. Dont look at me in that self-complacent way. You think yourself stronger than I am; but I shall stagger you if you have a heart in your breast.

MORELL [*powerfully confident*] Stagger me, my boy. Out with it.

MARCHBANKS. First –

MORELL. First?

MARCHBANKS. I love your wife.

Morell recoils, and, after staring at him for a moment in utter amazement, bursts into uncontrollable laughter. Eugene is taken aback; but not disconcerted; and he soon becomes indignant and contemptuous.

MORELL [*sitting down to have his laugh out*] Why, my dear child, of course you do. Everybody loves her: they cant help it. I like it. But [*looking up jocosely at him*] I say, Eugene: do you think yours is a case to be talked about? Youre under twenty: she's over thirty. Doesnt it look rather too like a case of calf love?

MARCHBANKS [*vehemently*] You dare say that of her! You think that way of the love she inspires! It is an insult to her!

MORELL [*rising quickly, in an altered tone*] To her! Eugene: take care. I have been patient. I hope to remain patient. But there are some things I wont allow. Dont force me to shew you the indulgence I should shew to a child. Be a man.

MARCHBANKS [*with a gesture as if sweeping something behind him*] Oh, let us put aside all that cant. It horrifies me when I think of the doses of it she has had to endure in all the weary years during which you have selfishly and blindly sacrificed her to minister to your self-sufficiency: you! [*turning on him*] who have not one thought – one sense – in common with her.

MORELL [*philosophically*] She seems to bear it pretty well. [*Looking him straight in the face*] Eugene, my boy: you are making a fool of yourself: a very great fool of yourself. Theres a piece of wholesome plain speaking for you. [*He knocks in the lesson with a nod in his old way, and posts himself on the hearth-rug, holding his hands behind him to warm them*].

MARCHBANKS. Oh, do you think I dont know all that? Do you think that the things people make fools of themselves about are any less real and true than the things they behave sensibly about? [*Morell's gaze wavers for the first time. He forgets to warm his hands, and stands listening, startled and thoughtful*]. They are more true: they are the only things that are true. You are very calm and sensible and moderate with me because you can see that I am a fool about your wife; just as no doubt that old man who was here just now is very wise over your Socialism, because he sees that you are a fool about it. [*Morell's perplexity deepens markedly. Eugene follows up his advantage, plying him fiercely with questions*]. Does that prove you wrong? Does your complacent superiority to me prove that *I* am wrong?

MORELL. Marchbanks: some devil is putting these words into your mouth. It is easy – terribly easy – to shake a man's faith in himself. To take advantage of that to break a man's spirit is devil's work. Take care of what you are doing. Take care.

MARCHBANKS [*ruthlessly*] I know. I'm doing it on purpose. I told you I should stagger you.

They confront one another threateningly for a moment. Then Morell recovers his dignity.

MORELL [*with noble tenderness*] Eugene: listen to me. Some day, I hope and trust, you will be a happy man like me.

[*Eugene chafes intolerantly, repudiating the worth of his happiness. Morell, deeply insulted, controls himself with fine forbearance, and continues steadily with great artistic beauty of delivery*] You will be married; and you will be working with all your might and valor to make every spot on earth as happy as your own home. You will be one of the makers of the Kingdom of Heaven on earth; and – who knows? – you may be a master builder where I am only a humble journeyman; for dont think, my boy, that I cannot see in you, young as you are, promise of higher powers than I can ever pretend to. I well know that it is in the poet that the holy spirit of man – the god within him – is most godlike. It should make you tremble to think of that – to think that the heavy burthen and great gift of a poet may be laid upon you.

MARCHBANKS [*unimpressed and remorseless, his boyish crudity of assertion telling sharply against Morell's oratory*] It does not make me tremble. It is the want of it in others that makes me tremble.

MORELL [*redoubling his force of style under the stimulus of his genuine feeling and Eugene's obduracy*] Then help to kindle it in them – in me – not to extinguish it. In the future, when you are as happy as I am, I will be your true brother in the faith. I will help you to believe that God has given us a world that nothing but our own folly keeps from being a paradise. I will help you to believe that every stroke of your work is sowing happiness for the great harvest that all – even the humblest – shall one day reap. And last, but trust me, not least, I will help you to believe that your wife loves you and is happy in her home. We need such help, Marchbanks: we need it greatly and always. There are so many things to make us doubt, if once we let our understanding be troubled. Even at home, we sit as if in camp, encompassed by a hostile army of doubts. Will you play the traitor and let them in on me?

MARCHBANKS [*looking round wildly*] Is it like this for her here always? A woman, with a great soul, craving for reality, truth, freedom; and being fed on metaphors, sermons, stale perorations, mere rhetoric. Do you think a woman's soul can live on your talent for preaching?

MORELL [*stung*] Marchbanks: you make it hard for me to control myself. My talent is like yours insofar as it has any real worth at all. It is the gift of finding words for divine truth.

MARCHBANKS [*impetuously*] It's the gift of the gab, nothing more and nothing less. What has your knack of fine talking to do with the truth, any more than playing the organ has? Ive never been in your church; but Ive been to your political meetings; and Ive seen you do whats called rousing the meeting to enthusiasm: that is, you excited them until they behaved exactly as if they were drunk. And their wives looked on and saw what fools they were. Oh, it's an old story: youll find it in the Bible. I imagine King David, in his fits of enthusiasm, was very like you. [*Stabbing him with the words*] 'But his wife despised him in her heart.'

MORELL [*wrathfully*] Leave my house. Do you hear? [*He advances on him threateningly*].

MARCHBANKS [*shrinking back against the couch*] Let me alone. Dont touch me. [*Morell grasps him powerfully by the lappel of his coat: he cowers down on the sofa and screams passionately*] Stop, Morell: if you strike me, I'll kill myself: I wont bear it. [*Almost in hysterics*] Let me go. Take your hand away.

MORELL [*with slow emphatic scorn*] You little snivelling, cowardly whelp. [*He releases him*]. Go, before you frighten yourself into a fit.

MARCHBANKS [*on the sofa, gasping, but relieved by the withdrawal of Morell's hand*] I'm not afraid of you: it's you who are afraid of me.

MORELL [*quietly, as he stands over him*] It looks like it, doesnt it?

MARCHBANKS [*with petulant vehemence*] Yes, it does. [*Morell turns away contemptuously. Eugene scrambles to his feet and follows him*]. You think because I shrink from being brutally handled – because [*with tears in his voice*] I can do nothing but cry with rage when I am met with violence – because I cant lift a heavy trunk down from the top of a

cab like you – because I can't fight you for your wife as a
drunken navvy would: all that makes you think I'm afraid
of you. But youre wrong. If I havnt got what you call
British pluck, I havnt British cowardice either: I'm not
afraid of a clergyman's ideas. I'll fight your ideas. I'll
rescue her from her slavery to them. I'll pit my own ideas
against them. You are driving me out of the house because
you darent let her choose between your ideas and mine.
You are afraid to let me see her again. [*Morell, angered,
turns on him. He flies to the door in involuntary dread*]. Let me
alone, I say. I'm going.

MORELL [*with cold scorn*] Wait a moment: I am not going to
touch you: dont be afraid. When my wife comes back she
will want to know why you have gone. And when she
finds that you are never going to cross our threshold again,
she will want to have that explained too. Now I dont wish
to distress her by telling her that you have behaved like a
blackguard.

MARCHBANKS [*coming back with renewed vehemence*] You shall.
You must. If you give any explanation but the true one,
you are a liar and a coward. Tell her what I said; and how
you were strong and manly, and shook me as a terrier
shakes a rat; and how I shrank and was terrified; and how
you called me a snivelling little whelp and put me out of
the house. If you dont tell her, I will: I'll write it to her.

MORELL [*puzzled*] Why do you want her to know this?

MARCHBANKS [*with lyric rapture*] Because she will understand me, and know that I understand her. If you keep
back one word of it from her – if you are not ready to lay
the truth at her feet as I am – then you will know to the
end of your days that she really belongs to me and not to
you. Goodbye. [*Going*].

MORELL [*terribly disquieted*] Stop: I will not tell her.

MARCHBANKS [*turning near the door*] Either the truth or a lie
you must tell her, if I go.

MORELL [*temporizing*] Marchbanks: it is sometimes justifi-
able –

MARCHBANKS [*cutting him short*] I know: to lie. It will be useless. Goodbye, Mr Clergyman.

    As he turns to the door, it opens and Candida enters in her housekeeping dress.

CANDIDA. Are you going, Eugene? [*Looking more observantly at him*] Well, dear me, just look at you, going out into the street in that state! You are a poet, certainly. Look at him, James! [*She takes him by the coat, and brings him forward, shewing him to Morell*]. Look at his collar! look at his tie! look at his hair! One would think somebody had been throttling you. [*Eugene instinctively rises to look round at Morell; but she pulls him back*]. Here! Stand still. [*She buttons his collar; ties his neckerchief in a bow; and arranges his hair*]. There! Now you look so nice that I think youd better stay to lunch after all, though I told you you mustnt. I will be ready in half an hour. [*She puts a final touch to the bow. He kisses her hand*]. Dont be silly.

MARCHBANKS. I want to stay, of course; unless the reverend gentleman your husband has anything to advance to the contrary.

CANDIDA. Shall he stay, James, if he promises to be a good boy and help me to lay the table?

MORELL [*shortly*] Oh yes, certainly: he had better. [*He goes to the table and pretends to busy himself with his papers there*].

MARCHBANKS [*offering his arm to Candida*] Come and lay the table. [*She takes it. They go to the door together. As they pass out he adds*] I am the happiest of mortals.

MORELL. So was I – an hour ago.

ACT II

The same day later in the afternoon. The same room. The chair for visitors has been replaced at the table. Marchbanks, alone and idle, is trying to find out how the typewriter works. Hearing someone at the door, he steals guiltily away to the window and pretends to be absorbed in the view. Miss Garnett, carrying the notebook in which she takes down Morell's letters in shorthand from his dictation, sits down at the typewriter and sets to work transcribing them, much too busy to notice Eugene. When she begins the second line she stops and stares at the machine. Something wrong evidently.

PROSERPINE. Bother! Youve been meddling with my typewriter, Mr Marchbanks; and theres not the least use in your trying to look as if you hadnt.

MARCHBANKS [*timidly*] I'm very sorry, Miss Garnett. I only tried to make it write. [*Plaintively*] But it wouldnt.

PROSERPINE. Well, youve altered the spacing.

MARCHBANKS [*earnestly*] I assure you I didn't. I didnt indeed. I only turned a little wheel. It gave a sort of click.

PROSERPINE. Oh, now I understand. [*She restores the spacing, talking volubly all the time*]. I suppose you thought it was a sort of barrel-organ. Nothing to do but turn the handle, and it would write a beautiful love letter for you straight off, eh?

MARCHBANKS [*seriously*] I suppose a machine could be made to write love letters. Theyre all the same, arnt they?

PROSERPINE [*somewhat indignantly: any such discussion, except by way of pleasantry, being outside her code of manners*] How do I know? Why do you ask me?

MARCHBANKS. I beg your pardon. I thought clever people – people who can do business and write letters and that sort of thing – always had to have love affairs to keep them from going mad.

PROSERPINE [*rising, outraged*] Mr Marchbanks! [*She looks severely at him, and marches majestically to the bookcase*].

MARCHBANKS [*approaching her humbly*] I hope I havnt

offended you. Perhaps I shouldnt have alluded to your love affairs.

PROSERPINE [*plucking a blue book from the shelf and turning sharply on him*] I havnt any love affairs. How dare you say such a thing? The idea! [*She tucks the book under her arm, and is flouncing back to her machine when he addresses her with awakened interest and sympathy*].

MARCHBANKS. Really! Oh, then you are shy, like me.

PROSERPINE. Certainly I am not shy. What do you mean?

MARCHBANKS [*secretly*] You must be: that is the reason there are so few love affairs in the world. We all go about longing for love: it is the first need of our natures, the first prayer of our hearts; but we dare not utter our longing: we are too shy. [*Very earnestly*] Oh, Miss Garnett, what would you not give to be without fear, without shame –

PROSERPINE [*scandalized*] Well, upon my word!

MARCHBANKS [*with petulant impatience*] Ah, dont say those stupid things to me: they dont deceive me: what use are they? Why are you afraid to be your real self with me? I am just like you.

PROSERPINE. Like me! Pray are you flattering me or flattering yourself? I dont feel quite sure which. [*She again rises to get back to her work*].

MARCHBANKS [*stopping her mysteriously*] Hush! I go about in search of love; and I find it in unmeasured stores in the bosoms of others. But when I try to ask for it, this horrible shyness strangles me; and I stand dumb, or worse than dumb, saying meaningless things: foolish lies. And I see the affection I am longing for given to dogs and cats and pet birds, because they come and ask for it. [*Almost whispering*] It must be asked for: it is like a ghost: it cannot speak unless it is first spoken to. [*At his usual pitch, but with deep melancholy*] All the love in the world is longing to speak; only it dare not, because it is shy! shy! shy! That is the world's tragedy. [*With a deep sigh he sits in the visitor's chair and buries his face in his hands*].

PROSERPINE [*amazed, but keeping her wits about her: her point of honor in encounters with strange young men*] Wicked people get over that shyness occasionally, dont they?

MARCHBANKS [*scrambling up almost fiercely*] Wicked people means people who have no love: therefore they have no shame. They have the power to ask love because they dont need it: they have the power to offer it because they have none to give. [*He collapses into his seat, and adds, mournfully*] But we, who have love, and long to mingle it with the love of others: we cannot utter a word. [*Timidly*] You find that, dont you?

PROSERPINE. Look here: if you dont stop talking like this, I'll leave the room, Mr Marchbanks: I really will. It's not proper.

She resumes her seat at the typewriter, opening the blue book and preparing to copy a passage from it.

MARCHBANKS [*hopelessly*] Nothing thats worth saying is proper. [*He rises, and wanders about the room in his lost way*]. I cant understand you, Miss Garnett. What am I to talk about?

PROSERPINE [*snubbing him*] Talk about indifferent things. Talk about the weather.

MARCHBANKS. Would you talk about indifferent things if a child were by, crying bitterly with hunger?

PROSERPINE. I suppose not.

MARCHBANKS. Well: *I* cant talk about indifferent things with my heart crying out bitterly in its hunger.

PROSERPINE. Then hold your tongue.

MARCHBANKS. Yes: that is what it always comes to. We hold our tongues. Does that stop the cry of your heart? for it does cry: doesnt it? It must, if you have a heart.

PROSERPINE [*suddenly rising with her hand pressed on her heart*] Oh, it's no use trying to work while you talk like that. [*She leaves her little table and sits on the sofa. Her feelings are keenly stirred*]. It's no business of yours whether my heart cries or not; but I have a mind to tell you, for all that.

MARCHBANKS. You neednt. I know already that it must.

PROSERPINE. But mind! if you ever say I said so, I'll deny it.

MARCHBANKS [*compassionately*] Yes, I know. And so you havnt the courage to tell him?

PROSERPINE [*bouncing up*] Him! Who?

MARCHBANKS. Whoever he is. The man you love. It might be anybody. The curate, Mr Mill, perhaps.

PROSERPINE [*with disdain*] Mr Mill!!! A fine man to break my heart about, indeed! I'd rather have y o u than Mr Mill.

MARCHBANKS [*recoiling*] No, really: I'm very sorry; but you mustnt think of that. I –

PROSERPINE [*testily, going to the fireplace and standing at it with her back to him*] Oh, dont be frightened: it's not you. It's not any one particular person.

MARCHBANKS. I know. You feel that you could love anybody that offered –

PROSERPINE [*turning, exasperated*] Anybody that offered! No, I do not. What do you take me for?

MARCHBANKS [*discouraged*] No use. You wont make me real answers: only those things that everybody says. [*He strays to the sofa and sits down disconsolately*].

PROSERPINE [*nettled at what she takes to be a disparagement of her manners by an aristocrat*] Oh well, if you want original conversation, youd better go and talk to yourself.

MARCHBANKS. That is what all poets do: they talk to themselves out loud; and the world overhears them. But it's horribly lonely not to hear someone else talk sometimes.

PROSERPINE. Wait until Mr Morell comes. He'll talk to you. [*Marchbanks shudders*]. Oh, you neednt make wry faces over him: he can talk better than you. [*With temper*] He'd talk your little head off. [*She is going back angrily to her place, when he, suddenly enlightened, springs up and stops her*].

MARCHBANKS. Ah! I understand now.

PROSERPINE [*reddening*] What do you understand?

MARCHBANKS. Your secret. Tell me: is it really and truly possible for a woman to love him?

PROSERPINE [*as if this were beyond all bounds*] Well!!

MARCHBANKS [*passionately*] No: answer me. I want to know: I must know. *I* cant understand it. I can see nothing in

him but words, pious resolutions, what people call goodness. You cant love that.

PROSERPINE [*attempting to snub him by an air of cool propriety*] I
simply dont know what youre talking about. I dont understand you.

MARCHBANKS [*vehemently*] You do. You lie.

PROSERPINE. Oh!

MARCHBANKS. You d o understand; and you know. [*Determined to have an answer*] Is it possible for a woman to love
him?

PROSERPINE [*looking him straight in the face*] Yes. [*He covers
his face with his hands*]. Whatever is the matter with you!
[*He takes down his hands. Frightened at the tragic mask presented
to her, she hurries past him at the utmost possible distance, keeping her eyes on his face until he turns from her and goes to the
child's chair beside the hearth, where he sits in the deepest dejection.
As she approaches the door, it opens and Burgess enters. Seeing him,
she ejaculates*] Praise heaven! here's somebody [*and feels safe
enough to resume her place at her table. She puts a fresh sheet of
paper into the typewriter as Burgess crosses to Eugene*].

BURGESS [*bent on taking care of the distinguished visitor*] Well: so
this is the way they leave you to yourself, Mr Morchbanks.
Ive come to keep you company. [*Marchbanks looks up at him
in consternation, which is quite lost on him*]. James is receivin a
deppitation in the dinin room; and Candy is hupstairs
heducating of a young stitcher gurl she's hinterested in.
[*Condolingly*] You must find it lonesome here with no one
but the typist to talk to. [*He pulls round the easy chair, and
sits down*].

PROSERPINE [*highly incensed*] He'll be all right now that he
has the advantage of your polished conversation: thats
one comfort, anyhow. [*She begins to typewrite with clattering
asperity*].

BURGESS [*amazed at her audacity*]. Hi was not addressin myself to you, young woman, that I'm awerr of.

PROSERPINE. Did you ever see worse manners, Mr
Marchbanks?

BURGESS [*with pompous severity*] Mr Morchbanks is a gentleman, and knows his place, which is more than some
people do.

PROSERPINE [*fretfully*] It's well you and I are not ladies and
gentlemen: I'd talk to you pretty straight if Mr Marchbanks wasnt here. [*She pulls the letter out of the machine so
crossly that it tears*]. There! now I've spoiled this letter!
have to be done all over again! Oh, I cant contain myself:
silly old fathead!

BURGESS [*rising, breathless with indignation*] Ho! I'm a silly ole
fat'ead, am I? Ho, indeed [*gasping*]! Hall right, my gurl!
Hall right. You just wait till I tell that to yore hemployer.
Youll see. I'll teach you: see if I dont.

PROSERPINE [*conscious of having gone too far*] I –

BURGESS [*cutting her short*] No: youve done it now. No huse
a-talking to me. I'll let you know who I am. [*Proserpine
shifts her paper carriage with a defiant bang, and disdainfully goes
on with her work*]. Dont you take no notice of her, Mr
Morchbanks. She's beneath it. [*He loftily sits down again*].

MARCHBANKS [*miserably nervous and disconcerted*] Hadnt we
better change the subject? I – I dont think Miss Garnett
meant anything.

PROSERPINE [*with intense conviction*] Oh, didnt I though,
just!

BURGESS. I wouldnt demean myself to take notice on her.
An electric bell rings twice.

PROSERPINE [*gathering up her note-book and papers*] Thats for
me. [*She hurries out*].

BURGESS [*calling after her*] Oh, we can spare you. [*Somewhat
relieved by the triumph of having the last word, and yet half inclined
to try to improve on it, he looks after her for a moment; then subsides
into his seat by Eugene, and addresses him very confidentially*].
Now we're alone, Mr Morchbanks, let me give you a
friendly int that I wouldnt give to heverybody. Ow long
ave you known my son-in-law James ere?

MARCHBANKS. I dont know. I never can remember dates.
A few months, perhaps.

BURGESS. Ever notice hennythink queer about him?

MARCHBANKS. I dont think so.

BURGESS [*impressively*] No more you wouldnt. Thats the danger on it. Well, he's mad.

MARCHBANKS. Mad!

BURGESS. Mad as a Morch 'are. You take notice on him and youll see.

MARCHBANKS [*uneasily*] But surely that is only because his opinions –

BURGESS [*touching him on the knee with his forefinger, and pressing it to hold his attention*] Thats the same what I hused to think, Mr Morchbanks. Hi thought long enough that it was only his opinions; though, mind you, hopinions becomes vurry serious things when people takes to hactin on em as e does. But thats not what I go on. [*He looks round to make sure that they are alone, and bends over to Eugene's ear*]. What do you think he sez to me this mornin in this very room?

MARCHBANKS. What?

BURGESS. He sez to me – this is as sure as we're settin here now – he sez 'I'm a fool,' he sez; 'and yore a scounderl.' Me a scounderl, mind you! And then shook ands with me on it, as if it was to my credit! Do you mean to tell me as that man's sane?

MORELL [*outside, calling to Proserpine as he opens the door*] Get all their names and addresses, Miss Garnett.

PROSERPINE [*in the distance*] Yes, Mr Morell.

Morell comes in, with the deputation's documents in his hands.

BURGESS [*aside to Marchbanks*] Yorr he is. Just you keep your heye on im and see. [*Rising momentously*] I'm sorry, James, to ave to make a complaint to you. I dont want to do it; but I feel I oughter, as a matter o right and dooty.

MORELL. Whats the matter?

BURGESS. Mr Morchbanks will bear me hout: he was a witness. [*Very solemnly*] Yore young woman so far forgot herself as to call ma a silly old fat'ead.

MORELL [*with tremendous heartiness*] Oh, now, isnt that

exactly like Prossy? She's so frank: she cant contain herself! Poor Prossy! Ha! ha!

BURGESS [*trembling with rage*] And do you hexpec me to put up with it from the like of er?

MORELL. Pooh, nonsense! you cant take any notice of it. Never mind. [*He goes to the cellaret and puts the papers into one of the drawers*].

BURGESS. Oh, Hi dont mind. Hi'm above it. But is it right? thats what I want to know. Is it right?

MORELL. Thats a question for the Church, not for the laity. Has it done you any harm? thats the question for you, eh? Of course it hasnt. Think no more of it. [*He dismisses the subject by going to his place at the table and setting to work at his correspondence*].

BURGESS [*aside to Marchbanks*] What did I tell you? Mad as a atter. [*He goes to the table and asks, with the sickly civility of a hungry man*] When's dinner, James?

MORELL. Not for a couple of hours yet.

BURGESS [*with plaintive resignation*] Gimme a nice book to read over the fire, will you, James: thur's a good chap.

MORELL. What sort of book? A good one?

BURGESS [*with almost a yell of remonstrance*] Nah-oo! Summat pleasant, just to pass the time. [*Morell takes an illustrated paper from the table and offers it. He accepts it humbly*]. Thank yer, James. [*He goes back to the big chair at the fire, and sits there at his ease, reading*].

MORELL [*as he writes*] Candida will come to entertain you presently. She has got rid of her pupil. She is filling the lamps.

MARCHBANKS [*starting up in the wildest consternation*] But that will soil her hands. I cant bear that, Morell: it's a shame. I'll go and fill them. [*He makes for the door*].

MORELL. Youd better not. [*Marchbanks stops irresolutely*]. She'd only set you to clean my boots, to save me the trouble of doing it myself in the morning.

BURGESS [*with grave disapproval*] Dont you keep a servant now, James?

MORELL. Yes: but she isnt a slave; and the house looks as if I kept three. That means that everyone has to lend a hand. It's not a bad plan: Prossy and I can talk business after breakfast while we're washing up. Washing up's no trouble when there are two people to do it.

MARCHBANKS [*tormentedly*] Do you think every woman is as coarse-grained as Miss Garnett?

BURGESS [*emphatically*] Thats quite right, Mr Morchbanks: thats quite right. She is coarse-grained.

MORELL [*quietly and significantly*] Marchbanks!

MARCHBANKS. Yes?

MORELL. How many servants does your father keep?

MARCHBANKS [*pettishly*] Oh, I dont know. [*He moves to the sofa, as if to get as far as possible from Morell's questioning, and sits down in great agony of spirit, thinking of the paraffin*].

MORELL [*very gravely*] So many that you dont know! [*More aggressively*] When theres anything coarse-grained to be done, you just ring the bell and throw it on to somebody else, eh?

MARCHBANKS. Oh, dont torture me. You dont even ring the bell. But your wife's beautiful fingers are dabbling in paraffin oil while you sit here comfortably preaching about it: everlasting preaching! preaching! words! words! words!

BURGESS [*intensely appreciating this retort*] Har, har! Devil a better! [*Radiantly*] Ad you there, James, straight.

Candida comes in, well aproned, with a reading lamp trimmed, filled, and ready for lighting. She places it on the table near Morell, ready for use.

CANDIDA [*brushing her finger tips together with a slight twitch of her nose*] If you stay with us, Eugene, I think I will hand over the lamps to you.

MARCHBANKS. I will stay on condition that you hand over all the rough work to me.

CANDIDA. Thats very gallant; but I think I should like to see how you do it first. [*Turning to Morell*] James: youve not been looking after the house properly.

MORELL. What have I done – or not done – my love?

CANDIDA [*with serious vexation*] My own particular pet scrubbing brush has been used for blackleading. [*A heart-breaking wail bursts from Marchbanks. Burgess looks round, amazed. Candida hurries to the sofa*]. Whats the matter? Are you ill, Eugene?

MARCHBANKS. No: not ill. Only horror! horror! horror! [*He bows his head on his hands*].

BURGESS [*shocked*] What! Got the orrors, Mr Morchbanks! Oh, thats bad, at your age. You must leave it off grajally.

CANDIDA [*reassured*] Nonsense, papa! It's only poetic horror, isnt it, Eugene [*petting him*]?

BURGESS [*abashed*] Oh, poetic orror is it? I beg your pardon, I'm shore. [*He turns to the fire again, deprecating his hasty conclusion*].

CANDIDA. What is it, Eugene? the scrubbing brush? [*He shudders*] Well, there! never mind. [*She sits down beside him*]. Wouldnt you like to present me with a nice new one, with an ivory back inlaid with mother-of-pearl?

MARCHBANKS [*softly and musically, but sadly and longingly*] No, not a scrubbing brush, but a boat: a tiny shallop to sail away in, far from the world, where the marble floors are washed by the rain and dried by the sun; where the south wind dusts the beautiful green and purple carpets. Or a chariot! to carry us up into the sky, where the lamps are stars, and dont need to be filled with paraffin oil every day.

MORELL [*harshly*] And where there is nothing to do but to be idle, selfish, and useless.

CANDIDA [*jarred*] Oh James! how could you spoil it all?

MARCHBANKS [*firing up*] Yes, to be idle, selfish, and useless: that is, to be beautiful and free and happy: hasnt every man desired that with all his soul for the woman he loves? Thats my ideal: whats yours, and that of all the dreadful people who live in these hideous rows of houses? Sermons and scrubbing brushes! With you to preach the sermon and your wife to scrub.

CANDIDA [*quaintly*] He cleans the boots, Eugene. You will
have to clean them tomorrow for saying that about him.

MARCHBANKS. Oh, dont talk about boots! Your feet should
be beautiful on the mountains.

CANDIDA. My feet would not be beautiful on the Hackney
Road without boots.

BURGESS [*scandalized*] Come, Candy! dont be vulgar. Mr
Morchbanks aint accustomed to it. Youre givin him the
orrors again. I mean the poetic ones.

*Morell is silent. Apparently he is busy with his letters: really he
is puzzling with misgiving over his new and alarming experience
that the surer he is of his moral thrusts, the more swiftly and
effectively Eugene parries them. To find himself beginning to fear
a man whom he does not respect afflicts him bitterly.*

Miss Garnett comes in with a telegram.

PROSERPINE [*handing the telegram to Morell*] Reply paid.
The boy's waiting. [*To Candida, coming back to her machine
and sitting down*] Maria is ready for you now in the kitchen,
Mrs Morell [*Candida rises*]. The onions have come.

MARCHBANKS [*convulsively*] Onions!

CANDIDA. Yes, onions. Not even Spanish ones: nasty little
red onions. You shall help me to slice them. Come
along.

*She catches him by the wrist and runs out, pulling him after
her. Burgess rises in consternation, and stands aghast on the
hearth-rug, staring after them.*

BURGESS. Candy didnt oughter andle a hearl's nevvy like
that. It's goin too fur with it. Lookee ere, James: do e
often git taken queer like that?

MORELL [*shortly, writing a telegram*] I dont know.

BURGESS [*sentimentally*] He talks very pretty. I awlus had a
turn for a bit of poetry. Candy takes arter me that-a-way.
Huster make me tell er fairy stories when she was only
a little kiddy not that igh [*indicating a stature of two feet or
thereabouts*].

MORELL [*preoccupied*] Ah, indeed. [*He blots the telegram and
goes out*].

PROSERPINE. Used you to make the fairy stories up out of your own head?

Burgess, not deigning to reply, strikes an attitude of the haughtiest disdain on the hearth-rug.

PROSERPINE [*calmly*] I should never have supposed you had it in you. By the way, I'd better warn you, since youve taken such a fancy to Mr Marchbanks. He's mad.

BURGESS. Mad! What! Im too!!

PROSERPINE. Mad as a March hare. He did frighten me, I can tell you, just before you came in that time. Havent you noticed the queer things he says?

BURGESS. So thats what the poetic orrors means. Blame me if it didnt come into my ed once or twyst that he was a bit horff is chump! [*He crosses the room to the door, lifting up his voice as he goes*]. Well, this is a pretty sort of asylum for a man to be in, with no one but you to take care of him!

PROSERPINE [*as he passes her*] Yes, what a dreadful thing it would be if anything happened to you!

BURGESS [*loftily*] Dont you haddress no remarks to me. Tell your hemployer that Ive gone into the gorden for a smoke.

PROSERPINE [*mocking*] Oh!

Before Burgess can retort, Morell comes back.

BURGESS [*sentimentally*] Goin for a turn in the gording to smoke, James.

MORELL [*brusquely*] Oh, all right, all right. [*Burgess goes out pathetically in the character of a weary old man. Morell stands at the table, turning over his papers, and adding, across to Proserpine, half humorously, half absently*] Well, Miss Prossy, why have you been calling my father-in-law names?

PROSERPINE [*blushing fiery red, and looking quickly up at him, half scared, half reproachful*] I – [*She bursts into tears*].

MORELL [*with tender gaiety, leaning across the table towards her, and consoling her*] Oh, come! come! come! Never mind, Pross: he is a silly old fathead, isnt he?

With an explosive sob, she makes a dash at the door, and vanishes, banging it. Morell, shaking his head resignedly, sighs, and goes wearily to his chair, where he sits down and sets to work, looking old and careworn.

Candida comes in. She has finished her household work and taken off the apron. She at once notices his dejected appearance, and posts herself quietly at the visitors' chair, looking down at him attentively. She says nothing.

MORELL [*looking up, but with his pen raised ready to resume his work*] Well? Where is Eugene?

CANDIDA. Washing his hands in the scullery under the tap. He will make an excellent cook if he can only get over his dread of Maria.

MORELL [*shortly*] Ha! No doubt. [*He begins writing again*].

CANDIDA [*going nearer, and putting her hand down softly on his to stop him as she says*] Come here, dear. Let me look at you. [*He drops his pen and yields himself to her disposal. She makes him rise, and brings him a little away from the table, looking at him critically all the time*]. Turn your face to the light. [*She places him facing the window*]. My boy is not looking well. Has he been overworking?

MORELL. Nothing more than usual.

CANDIDA. He looks very pale, and grey, and wrinkled, and old. [*His melancholy deepens: and she attacks it with wilful gaiety*] Here: [*pulling him towards the easy chair*] youve done enough writing for today. Leave Prossy to finish it. Come and talk to me.

MORELL. But —

CANDIDA [*insisting*] Yes, I must be talked to. [*She makes him sit down, and seats herself on the carpet beside his knee*]. Now [*patting his hand*] youre beginning to look better already. Why must you go out every night lecturing and talking? I hardly have one evening a week with you. Of course what you say is all very true; but it does no good: they dont mind what you say to them one little bit. They think they agree with you; but whats the use of their agreeing with you if they go and do just the opposite of what you tell them the moment your back is turned? Look at our congregation at St Dominic's! Why do they come to hear you

talking about Christianity every Sunday? Why, just because theyve been so full of business and money-making
for six days that they want to forget all about it and have
a rest on the seventh; so that they can go back fresh and
make money harder than ever! You positively help them
at it instead of hindering them.

MORELL [*with energetic seriousness*] You know very well,
Candida, that I often blow them up soundly for that. And
if there is nothing in their churchgoing but rest and diver-
sion, why dont they try something more amusing? more
self-indulgent? There must be some good in the fact that
they prefer St Dominic's to worse places on Sundays.

CANDIDA. Oh, the worse places arnt open; and even if they
were, they darent be seen going to them. Besides, James
dear, you preach so splendidly that it's as good as a play for
them. Why do you think the women are so enthusiastic?

MORELL [*shocked*] Candida!

CANDIDA. Oh, *I* know. You silly boy: you think it's your
Socialism and your religion; but if it were that, theyd do
what you tell them instead of only coming to look at you.
They all have Prossy's complaint.

MORELL. Prossy's complaint! What do you mean, Candida?

CANDIDA. Yes, Prossy, and all the other secretaries you ever
had. Why does Prossy condescend to wash up the things,
and to peel potatoes and abase herself in all manner of
ways for six shillings a week less than she used to get in a
city office? She's in love with you, James: thats the reason.
Theyre all in love with you. And you are in love with
preaching because you do it so beautifully. And you think
it's all enthusiasm for the kingdom of Heaven on earth;
and so do they. You dear silly!

MORELL. Candida: what dreadful! what soul-destroying
cynicism! Are you jesting? Or – can it be? – are you jealous?

CANDIDA [*with curious thoughtfulness*] Yes, I feel a little jealous sometimes.

MORELL [*incredulously*] Of Prossy?

CANDIDA [*laughing*] No, no, no, no. Not jealous of anybody.

Jealous for somebody else, who is not loved as he ought to be.

MORELL. Me?

CANDIDA. You! Why, youre spoiled with love and worship: you get far more than is good for you. No: I mean Eugene.

MORELL [*startled*] Eugene!

CANDIDA. It seems unfair that all the love should go to you, and none to him; although he needs it so much more than you do. [*A convulsive movement shakes him in spite of himself*]. Whats the matter? Am I worrying you?

MORELL [*hastily*] Not at all. [*Looking at her with troubled intensity*] You know that I have perfect confidence in you, Candida.

CANDIDA. You vain thing! Are you so sure of your irresistible attractions?

MORELL. Candida: you are shocking me. I never thought of my attractions. I thought of your goodness, of your purity. That is what I confide in.

CANDIDA. What a nasty uncomfortable thing to say to me! Oh, you a r e a clergyman, James: a thorough clergyman!

MORELL [*turning away from her, heart-stricken*] So Eugene says.

CANDIDA [*with lively interest, leaning over to him with her arms on his knee*] Eugene's always right. He's a wonderful boy: I have grown fonder and fonder of him all the time I was away. Do you know, James, that though he has not the least suspicion of it himself, he is ready to fall madly in love with me?

MORELL [*grimly*] Oh, he has no suspicion of it himself, hasnt he?

CANDIDA. Not a bit. [*She takes her arms from his knee, and turns thoughtfully, sinking into a more restful attitude with her hands in her lap*]. Some day he will know: when he is grown up and experienced, like you. And he will know that I must have known. I wonder what he will think of me then.

MORELL. No evil, Candida. I hope and trust, no evil.

CANDIDA [*dubiously*] That will depend.

MORELL [*bewildered*] Depend!

CANDIDA [*looking at him*] Yes: it will depend on what happens to him. [*He looks vacantly at her*]. Dont you see? It will depend on how he comes to learn what love really is. I mean on the sort of woman who will teach it to him.

MORELL [*quite at a loss*] Yes. No. I dont know what you mean.

CANDIDA [*explaining*] If he learns it from a good woman, then it will be all right: he will forgive me.

MORELL. Forgive?

CANDIDA. But suppose he learns it from a bad woman, as so many men do, especially poetic men, who imagine all women are angels! Suppose he only discovers the value of love when he has thrown it away and degraded himself in his ignorance! Will he forgive me then, do you think?

MORELL. Forgive you for what?

CANDIDA [*realizing how stupid he is, and a little disappointed, though quite tenderly so*] Dont you understand? [*He shakes his head. She turns to him again, so as to explain with the fondest intimacy*]. I mean, will he forgive me for not teaching him myself? For abandoning him to the bad women for the sake of my goodness, of my purity, as you call it? Ah, James, how little you understand me, to talk of your confidence in my goodness and purity! I would give them both to poor Eugene as willingly as I would give my shawl to a beggar dying of cold, if there were nothing else to restrain me. Put your trust in my love for you, James; for if that went, I should care very little for your sermons: mere phrases that you cheat yourself and others with every day. [*She is about to rise*].

MORELL. His words!

CANDIDA [*checking herself quickly in the act of getting up*] Whose words?

MORELL. Eugene's.

CANDIDA [*delighted*] He is always right. He understands you; he understands me; he understands Prossy; and you, darling, you understand nothing. [*She laughs, and kisses him to console him. He recoils as if stabbed, and springs up*].

MORELL. How can you bear to do that when – Oh, Candida [*with anguish in his voice*] I had rather you had plunged a grappling iron into my heart than given me that kiss.

CANDIDA [*amazed*] My dear: whats the matter?

MORELL [*frantically waving her off*] Dont touch me.

CANDIDA. James!!!

 They are interrupted by the entrance of Marchbanks with Burgess, who stop near the door, staring.

MARCHBANKS. Is anything the matter?

MORELL [*deadly white, putting an iron constraint on himself*] Nothing but this: that either you were right this morning, or Candida is mad.

BURGESS [*in loudest protest*] What! Candy mad too! Oh, come! come! come! [*He crosses the room to the fireplace, protesting as he goes, and knocks the ashes out of his pipe on the bars*].

 Morell sits down at his table desperately, leaning forward to hide his face, and interlacing his fingers rigidly to keep them steady.

CANDIDA [*to Morell, relieved and laughing*] Oh, youre only shocked! Is that all? How conventional all you unconventional people are! [*She sits gaily on the arm of the chair*].

BURGESS. Come: be'ave yourself, Candy. Whatll Mr Morchbanks think of you?

CANDIDA. This comes of James teaching me to think for myself, and never to hold back out of fear of what other people may think of me. It works beautifully as long as I think the same things as he does. But now! because I have just thought something different! look at him! Just look! [*She points to Morell, greatly amused*].

 Eugene looks, and instantly presses his hand on his heart, as if some pain had shot through it. He sits down on the sofa like a man witnessing a tragedy.

BURGESS [*on the hearth-rug*] Well, James, you certnly haint as himpressive lookin as usu'l.

MORELL [*with a laugh which is half a sob*] I suppose not. I beg all your pardons: I was not conscious of making a fuss. [*Pulling himself together*] Well, well, well, well, well! [*He sets to work at his papers again with resolute cheerfulness*].

CANDIDA [*going to the sofa and sitting beside Marchbanks, still in a bantering humor*] Well, Eugene: why are you so sad? Did the onions make you cry?

MARCHBANKS [*aside to her*] It is your cruelty. I hate cruelty. It is a horrible thing to see one person make another suffer.

CANDIDA [*petting him ironically*] Poor boy! have I been cruel? Did I make it slice nasty little red onions?

MARCHBANKS [*earnestly*] Oh, stop, stop: I dont mean myself. You have made him suffer frightfully. I feel his pain in my own heart. I know that it is not your fault: it is something that must happen; but dont make light of it. I shudder when you torture him and laugh.

CANDIDA [*incredulously*] *I* torture James! Nonsense, Eugene: how you exaggerate! Silly! [*She rises and goes to the table, a little troubled*]. Dont work any more, dear. Come and talk to us.

MORELL [*affectionately but bitterly*] Ah no: *I* cant talk. I can only preach.

CANDIDA [*caressing his hand*] Well, come and preach.

BURGESS [*strongly remonstrating*] Aw no, Candy. Ang it all!

Lexy Mill comes in, anxious and important.

LEXY [*hastening to shake hands with Candida*] How do you do, Mrs Morell? So glad to see you back again.

CANDIDA. Thank you, Lexy. You know Eugene, dont you?

LEXY. Oh yes. How do you do, Marchbanks?

MARCHBANKS. Quite well, thanks.

LEXY [*to Morell*] Ive just come from the Guild of St Matthew. They are in the greatest consternation about your telegram.

CANDIDA. What did you telegraph about, James?

LEXY [*to Candida*] He was to have spoken for them tonight. Theyve taken the large hall in Mare Street and spent a lot of money on posters. Morell's telegram was to say he couldnt come. It came on them like a thunderbolt.

CANDIDA [*surprised, and beginning to suspect something wrong*] Given up an engagement to speak!

BURGESS. Fust time in his life, I'll bet. Aint it, Candy?

LEXY [*to Morell*] They decided to send an urgent telegram to you asking whether you could not change your mind. Have you received it?

MORELL [*with restrained impatience*] Yes, yes: I got it.

LEXY. It was reply paid.

MORELL. Yes, I know. I answered it. I cant go.

CANDIDA. But why, James?

MORELL [*almost fiercely*] Because I dont choose. These people forget that I am a man: they think I am a talking machine to be turned on for their pleasure every evening of my life. May I not have one night at home, with my wife, and my friends?

They are all amazed at this outburst, except Eugene. His expression remains unchanged.

CANDIDA. Oh, James, you mustnt mind what I said about that. And if you dont go youll have an attack of bad conscience tomorrow.

LEXY [*intimidated, but urgent*] I know, of course, that they make the most unreasonable demands on you. But they have been telegraphing all over the place for another speaker; and they can get nobody but the President of the Agnostic League.

MORELL [*promptly*] Well, an excellent man. What better do they want?

LEXY. But he always insists so powerfully on the divorce of Socialism from Christianity. He will undo all the good we have been doing. Of course you know best; but – [*he shrugs his shoulders and wanders to the hearth beside Burgess*].

CANDIDA [*coaxingly*] Oh, do go, James. We'll all go.

BURGESS [*grumblingly*] Look ere, Candy! I say! Lets stay at home by the fire, comfortable. He wont need to be more'n a couple-o-hour away.

CANDIDA. Youll be just as comfortable at the meeting. We'll all sit on the platform and be great people.

MARCHBANKS [*terrified*] Oh please dont let us go on the platform. No: everyone will stare at us: I couldnt. I'll sit at the back of the room.

CANDIDA. Dont be afraid. Theyll be too busy looking at James to notice you.

MORELL. Prossy's complaint, Candida! Eh?

CANDIDA [*gaily*] Yes: Prossy's complaint.

BURGESS [*mystified*] Prossy's complaint! What are you talkin about, James?

MORELL [*not heeding him, rises; goes to the door; and holds it open, calling in a commanding tone*] Miss Garnett.

PROSERPINE [*in the distance*] Yes, Mr Morell. Coming.

They all wait, except Burgess, who turns stealthily to Lexy.

BURGESS. Listen ere, Mr Mill. Whats Prossy's complaint? Whats wrong with er?

LEXY [*confidentially*] Well, I dont exactly know; but she spoke very strangely to me this morning. I'm afraid she's a little out of her mind sometimes.

BURGESS [*overwhelmed*] Why, it must be catchin! Four in the same ouse!

PROSERPINE [*appearing on the threshold*] What is it, Mr Morell?

MORELL. Telegraph to the Guild of St Matthew that I am coming.

PROSERPINE [*surprised*] Dont they expect you?

MORELL[*peremptorily*] Do as I tell you.

Proserpine, frightened, sits down at her typewriter, and obeys. Morell, now unaccountably resolute and forceful, goes across to Burgess. Candida watches his movements with growing wonder and misgiving.

MORELL. Burgess: you dont want to come.

BURGESS. Oh, dont put it like that, James. It's ony that it aint Sunday, you know.

MORELL. I'm sorry. I thought you might like to be introduced to the chairman. He's on the Works Committee of the County Council, and has some influence in the matter of contracts. [*Burgess wakes up at once*]. Youll come?

BURGESS [*with enthusiasm*] Cawrse I'll come, James. Aint it awlus a pleasure to ear you!

MORELL [*turning to Prossy*] I shall want you to take some

notes at the meeting, Miss Garnett, if you have no other engagement. [*She nods, afraid to speak*]. You are coming, Lexy, I suppose?

LEXY. Certainly.

CANDIDA. We're all coming, James.

MORELL. No: you are not coming; and Eugene is not coming. You will stay here and entertain him – to celebrate your return home. [*Eugene rises, breathless*].

CANDIDA. But, James –

MORELL [*authoritatively*] I insist. You do not want to come; and he does not want to come. [*Candida is about to protest*]. Oh, dont concern yourselves: I shall have plenty of people without you: your chairs will be wanted by unconverted people who have never heard me before.

CANDIDA [*troubled*] Eugene: wouldn't you like to come?

MORELL. I should be afraid to let myself go before Eugene: he is so critical of sermons. [*Looking at him*] He knows I am afraid of him: he told me as much this morning. Well, I shall shew him how much afraid I am by leaving him here in your custody, Candida.

MARCHBANKS [*to himself, with vivid feeling*] Thats brave. Thats beautiful.

CANDIDA [*with anxious misgiving*] But – but – Is anything the matter, James? [*Greatly troubled*] I cant understand –

MORELL [*taking her tenderly in his arms and kissing her on the forehead*] Ah, I thought it was *I* who couldnt understand, dear.

ACT III

*Past ten in the evening. The curtains are drawn, and the lamps lighted.
The typewriter is in its case: the large table has been cleared and
tidied: everything indicates that the day's work is over.*

*Candida and Marchbanks are sitting by the fire. The reading lamp
is on the mantelshelf above Marchbanks, who is in the small chair,
reading aloud. A little pile of manuscripts and a couple of volumes
of poetry are on the carpet beside him. Candida is in the easy chair.
The poker, a light brass one, is upright in her hand. Leaning back
and looking intently at the point of it, with her feet stretched towards
the blaze, she is in a waking dream, miles away from her surroundings and completely oblivious of Eugene.*

MARCHBANKS [*breaking off in his recitation*] Every poet that
 ever lived has put that thought into a sonnet. He must: he
 cant help it. [*He looks to her for assent, and notices her absorp-
 tion in the poker*]. Havnt you been listening? [*No response*].
 Mrs Morell!

CANDIDA [*starting*] Eh?

MARCHBANKS. Havnt you been listening?

CANDIDA [*with a guilty excess of politeness*] Oh yes. It's very
 nice. Go on, Eugene. I'm longing to hear what happens
 to the angel.

MARCHBANKS [*letting the manuscript drop from his hand to the
 floor*] I beg your pardon for boring you.

CANDIDA. But you are not boring me, I assure you. Please
 go on. Do, Eugene.

MARCHBANKS. I finished the poem about the angel quarter
 of an hour ago. Ive read you several things since.

CANDIDA [*remorsefully*] I'm so sorry, Eugene. I think the
 poker must have hypnotized me. [*She puts it down*].

MARCHBANKS. It made me horribly uneasy.

CANDIDA. Why didnt you tell me? I'd have put it down at
 once.

MARCHBANKS. I was afraid of making you uneasy too. It
 looked as if it were a weapon. If I were a hero of old I

141

should have laid my drawn sword between us. If Morell had come in he would have thought you had taken up the poker because there was no sword between us.

CANDIDA [*wondering*] What? [*With a puzzled glance at him*] I cant quite follow that. Those sonnets of yours have perfectly addled me. Why should there be a sword between us?

MARCHBANKS [*evasively*] Oh, never mind. [*He stoops to pick up the manuscript*].

CANDIDA. Put that down again, Eugene. There are limits to my appetite for poetry: even your poetry. Youve been reading to me for more than two hours, ever since James went out. I want to talk.

MARCHBANKS [*rising, scared*] No: I mustnt talk. [*He looks round him in his lost way, and adds, suddenly*] I think I'll go out and take a walk in the park. [*He makes for the door*].

CANDIDA. Nonsense: it's closed long ago. Come and sit down on the hearth-rug, and talk moonshine as you usually do. I want to be amused. Dont you want to?

MARCHBANKS [*half in terror, half enraptured*] Yes.

CANDIDA. Then come along. [*She moves her chair back a little to make room*].

He hesitates; then timidly stretches himself on the hearth-rug, face upwards, and throws back his head across her knees, looking up at her.

MARCHBANKS. Oh, Ive been so miserable all the evening, because I was doing right. Now I'm doing wrong; and I'm happy.

CANDIDA [*tenderly amused at him*] Yes: I'm sure you feel a great grown-up wicked deceiver. Quite proud of yourself, arnt you?

MARCHBANKS [*raising his hand quickly and turning a little to look round at her*] Take care. I'm ever so much older than you, if you only knew. [*He turns quite over on his knees, with his hands clasped and his arms on her lap, and speaks with growing impulse, his blood beginning to stir*]. May I say some wicked things to you?

CANDIDA [*without the least fear or coldness, and with perfect respect for his passion, but with a touch of her wise-hearted maternal humor*] No. But you may say anything you really and truly feel. Anything at all, no matter what it is. I am not afraid, so long as it is your real self that speaks, and not a mere attitude: a gallant attitude, or a wicked attitude, or even a poetic attitude. I put you on your honor and truth. Now say whatever you want to.

MARCHBANKS [*the eager expression vanishing utterly from his lips and nostrils as his eyes light up with pathetic spirituality*] Oh, now I cant say anything: all the words I know belong to some attitude or other – all except one.

CANDIDA. What one is that?

MARCHBANKS [*softly, losing himself in the music of the name*] Candida, Candida, Candida, Candida, Candida. I must say that now, because you have put me on my honor and truth; and I never think or feel Mrs Morell: it is always Candida.

CANDIDA. Of course. And what have you to say to Candida?

MARCHBANKS. Nothing but to repeat your name a thousand times. Dont you feel that every time is a prayer to you?

CANDIDA. Doesnt it make you happy to be able to pray?

MARCHBANKS. Yes, very happy.

CANDIDA. Well, that happiness is the answer to your prayer. Do you want anything more?

MARCHBANKS. No: I have come into Heaven, where want is unknown.

Morell comes in. He halts on the threshold, and takes in the scene at a glance.

MORELL [*grave and self-contained*] I hope I dont disturb you.

Candida starts up violently, but without the smallest embarrassment, laughing at herself. Eugene, capsized by her sudden movement, recovers himself without rising, and sits on the rug hugging his ankles, also quite unembarrassed.

CANDIDA. Oh, James, how you startled me! I was so taken up with Eugene that I didnt hear your latchkey. How did the meeting go off? Did you speak well?

MORELL. I have never spoken better in my life.

CANDIDA. That was first rate! How much was the collection?

MORELL. I forgot to ask.

CANDIDA [*to Eugene*] He must have spoken splendidly, or he would never have forgotten that. [*To Morell*] Where are all the others?

MORELL. They left long before I could get away: I thought I should never escape. I believe they are having supper somewhere.

CANDIDA [*in her domestic business tone*] Oh, in that case, Maria may go to bed. I'll tell her. [*She goes out to the kitchen*].

MORELL [*looking sternly down at Marchbanks*] Well?

MARCHBANKS [*squatting grotesquely on the hearth-rug, and actually at ease with Morell: even impishly humorous*] Well?

MORELL. Have you anything to tell me?

MARCHBANKS. Only that I have been making a fool of myself here in private whilst you have been making a fool of yourself in public.

MORELL. Hardly in the same way, I think.

MARCHBANKS [*eagerly, scrambling up*] The very, very, very same way. I have been playing the Good Man. Just like you. When you began your heroics about leaving me here with Candida –

MORELL [*involuntarily*] Candida!

MARCHBANKS. Oh yes: Ive got that far. But dont be afraid. Heroics are infectious: I caught the disease from you. I swore not to say a word in your absence that I would not not have said a month ago in your presence.

MORELL. Did you keep your oath?

MARCHBANKS [*suddenly perching himself on the back of the easy chair*] It kept itself somehow until about ten minutes ago. Up to that moment I went on desperately reading to her – reading my own poems – anybody's poems – to stave off a conversation. I was standing outside the gate of Heaven, and refusing to go in. Oh, you cant think how heroic it was, and how uncomfortable! Then –

MORELL [*steadily controlling his suspense*] Then?

MARCHBANKS [*prosaically slipping down into a quite ordinary attitude on the seat of the chair*] Then she couldnt bear being read to any longer.

MORELL. And you approached the gate of Heaven at last?

MARCHBANKS. Yes.

MORELL. Well? [*Fiercely*] Speak, man: have you no feeling for me?

MARCHBANKS [*softly and musically*] Then she became an angel; and there was a flaming sword that turned every way, so that I couldnt go in; for I saw that that gate was really the gate of Hell.

MORELL [*triumphantly*] She repulsed you!

MARCHBANKS [*rising in wild scorn*] No, you fool: if she had done that I should never have seen that I was in Heaven already. Repulsed me! You think that would have saved us! virtuous indignation! Oh, you are not worthy to live in the same world with her. [*He turns away contemptuously to the other side of the room*].

MORELL [*who has watched him quietly without changing his place*] Do you think you make yourself more worthy by reviling me, Eugene?

MARCHBANKS. Here endeth the thousand and first lesson. Morell: I dont think much of your preaching after all: I believe I could do it better myself. The man I want to meet is the man that Candida married.

MORELL. The man that –? Do you mean me?

MARCHBANKS. I dont mean the Reverend James Mavor Morell, moralist and windbag. I mean the real man that the Reverend James must have hidden somewhere inside his black coat: the man that Candida loved. You cant make a woman like Candida love you by merely buttoning your collar at the back instead of in front.

MORELL [*boldly and steadily*] When Candida promised to marry me, I was the same moralist and windbag you now see. I wore my black coat; and my collar was buttoned behind instead of in front. Do you think she would have loved me any the better for being insincere in my profession?

MARCHBANKS [*on the sofa, hugging his ankles*] Oh, she forgave you, just as she forgives me for being a coward, and a weakling, and what you call a snivelling little whelp and all the rest of it. [*Dreamily*] A woman like that has divine insight: she loves our souls, and not our follies and vanities and illusions, nor our collars and coats, nor any other of the rags and tatters we are rolled up in. [*He reflects on this for an instant: then turns intently to question Morell*]. What I want to know is how you got past the flaming sword that stopped me.

MORELL. Perhaps because I was not interrupted at the end of ten minutes.

MARCHBANKS [*taken aback*] What!

MORELL. Man can climb to the highest summits; but he cannot dwell there long.

MARCHBANKS [*springing up*] It's false: there can he dwell for ever, and there only. It's in the other moment that he can find no rest, no sense of the silent glory of life. Where would you have me spend my moments, if not on the summits?

MORELL. In the scullery, slicing onions and filling lamps.

MARCHBANKS. Or in the pulpit, scrubbing cheap earthenware souls?

MORELL. Yes, that too. It was there that I earned my golden moment, and the right, in that moment, to ask her to love me. *I* did not take the moment on credit; nor did I use it to steal another man's happiness.

MARCHBANKS [*rather disgustedly, trotting back towards the fireplace*] I have no doubt you conducted the transaction as honestly as if you were buying a pound of cheese. [*He stops on the brink of the hearth-rug, and adds, thoughtfully, to himself, with his back turned to Morell*] *I* could only go to her as a beggar.

MORELL [*staring*] A beggar dying of cold! asking for her shawl!

MARCHBANKS [*turning, surprised*] Thank you for touching up my poetry. Yes, if you like: a beggar dying of cold, asking for her shawl.

MORELL [*excitedly*] And she refused. Shall I tell you why she refused? I can tell you, on her own authority. It was because of –

MARCHBANKS. She didnt refuse.

MORELL. Not!

MARCHBANKS. She offered me all I chose to ask for: her shawl, her wings, the wreath of stars on her head, the lilies in her hand, the crescent moon beneath her feet –

MORELL [*seizing him*] Out with the truth, man: my wife is my wife: I want no more of your poetic fripperies. I know well that if I have lost her love and you have gained it, no law will bind her.

MARCHBANKS [*quaintly, without fear or resistance*] Catch me by the shirt collar, Morell: she will arrange it for me afterwards as she did this morning. [*With quiet rapture*] I shall feel her hands touch me.

MORELL. You young imp, do you know how dangerous it is to say that to me? Or [*with a sudden misgiving*] has something made you brave?

MARCHBANKS. I'm not afraid now. I disliked you before: that was why I shrank from your touch. But I saw today – when she tortured you – that you love her. Since then I have been your friend: you may strangle me if you like.

MORELL [*releasing him*] Eugene: if that is not a heartless lie – if you have a spark of human feeling left in you – will you tell me what has happened during my absence?

MARCHBANKS. What happened! Why, the flaming sword [*Morell stamps with impatience*] – Well, in plain prose, I loved her so exquisitely that I wanted nothing more than the happiness of being in such love. And before I had time to come down from the highest summits, you came in.

MORELL [*suffering deeply*] So it is still unsettled. Still the misery of doubt.

MARCHBANKS. Misery! I am the happiest of men. I desire

nothing now but her happiness. [*In a passion of sentiment*] Oh, Morell, let us both give her up. Why should she have to choose between a wretched little nervous disease like me, and a pig-headed parson like you? Let us go on a pilgrimage, you to the east and I to the west, in search of a worthy lover for her: some beautiful archangel with purple wings –

MORELL. Some fiddlestick! Oh, if she is mad enough to leave me for you, who will protect her? who will help her? who will work for her? who will be a father to her children? [*He sits down distractedly on the sofa, with his elbows on his knees and his head propped on his clenched fists*].

MARCHBANKS [*snapping his fingers wildly*] She does not ask those silly questions. It is she who wants somebody to protect, to help, to work for: somebody to give her children to protect, to help and to work for. Some grown up man who has become as a little child again. Oh, you fool, you fool, you triple fool! I am the man, Morell: I am the man. [*He dances about excitedly, crying*] You dont understand what a woman is. Send for her, Morell: send for her and let her choose between – [*The door opens and Candida enters. He stops as if petrified*].

CANDIDA [*amazed, on the threshold*] What on earth are you at, Eugene?

MARCHBANKS [*oddly*] James and I are having a preaching match; and he is getting the worst of it.

Candida looks quickly round at Morell. Seeing that he is distressed, she hurries down to him, greatly vexed.

CANDIDA. You have been annoying him. Now I wont have it, Eugene: do you hear? [*She puts her hand on Morell's shoulder, and quite forgets her wifely tact in her anger*]. My boy shall not be worried: I will protect him.

MORELL [*rising proudly*] Protect!

CANDIDA [*not heeding him: to Eugene*] What have you been saying?

MARCHBANKS [*appalled*] Nothing. I –

CANDIDA. Eugene! Nothing?

MARCHBANKS [*piteously*] I mean – I – I'm very sorry. I wont do it again: indeed I wont. I'll let him alone.

MORELL [*indignantly, with an aggressive movement towards Eugene*] Let me alone! You young –

CANDIDA [*stopping him*] Sh!–no: let me deal with him, James.

MARCHBANKS. Oh, youre not angry with me, are you?

CANDIDA [*severely*] Yes I am: very angry. I have a good mind to pack you out of the house.

MORELL [*taken aback by Candida's vigor, and by no means relishing the position of being rescued by her from another man*] Gently, Candida, gently. I am able to take care of myself.

CANDIDA [*petting him*] Yes, dear: of course you are. But you musnt be annoyed and made miserable.

MARCHBANKS [*almost in tears, turning to the door*] I'll go.

CANDIDA. Oh, you neednt go: I cant turn you out at this time of night. [*Vehemently*] Shame on you! For shame!

MARCHBANKS [*desperately*] But what have I done?

CANDIDA. I know what you have done: as well as if I had been here all the time. Oh, it was unworthy! You are like a child: you cannot hold your tongue.

MARCHBANKS. I would die ten times over sooner than give you a moment's pain.

CANDIDA [*with infinite contempt for this puerility*] Much good your dying would do me!

MORELL. Candida, my dear: this altercation is hardly quite seemly. It is a matter between two men; and I am the right person to settle it.

CANDIDA. Two men! Do you call that a man! [*To Eugene*] You bad boy!

MARCHBANKS [*gathering a whimsically affectionate courage from the scolding*] If I am to be scolded like a boy, I must make a boy's excuse. He began it. And he's bigger than I am.

CANDIDA [*losing confidence a little as her concern for Morell's dignity takes the alarm*] That cant be true. [*To Morell*] You didnt begin it, James, did you?

MORELL [*contemptuously*] No.

MARCHBANKS [*indignant*] Oh!

MORELL [*to Eugene*] You began it: this morning. [*Candida,

instantly connecting this with his mysterious allusion in the after-noon to something told him by Eugene in the morning, looks at him with quick suspicion. Morell proceeds, with the emphasis of offended superiority] But your other point is true. I am certainly the bigger of the two, and, I hope, the stronger, Candida. So you had better leave the matter in my hands.

CANDIDA [*again soothing him*] Yes, dear; but – [*troubled*] I dont understand about this morning.

MORELL [*gently snubbing her*] You need not understand, my dear.

CANDIDA. But James, I [*the street bell rings*] – Oh bother! Here they all come. [*She goes out to let them in*].

MARCHBANKS [*running to Morell*] Oh, Morell, isnt it dreadful? She's angry with us: she hates me. What shall I do?

MORELL [*with quaint desperation, walking up and down the middle of the room*] Eugene: my head is spinning round. I shall begin to laugh presently.

MARCHBANKS [*following him anxiously*] No, no: she'll think Ive thrown you into hysterics. Dont laugh.

Boisterous voices and laughter are heard approaching. Lexy Mill, his eyes sparkling, and his bearing denoting unwonted eleva-tion of spirit, enters with Burgess, who is greasy and self-com-placent, but has all his wits about him. Miss Garnett, with her smartest hat and jacket on, follows them; but though her eyes are brighter than before, she is evidently a prey to misgiving. She places herself with her back to her typewriting table, with one hand on it to steady herself, passing the other across her forehead as if she were a little tired and giddy. Marchbanks relapses into shyness and edges away into the corner near the window, where Morell's books are.

LEXY [*exhilarated*] Morell: I m u s t congratulate you. [*Grasp-ing his hand*] What a noble, splendid, inspired address you gave us! You surpassed yourself.

BURGESS. So you did, James. It fair kep me awake to the lars' word. Didnt it, Miss Gornett?

PROSERPINE [*worriedly*] Oh, I wasnt minding you: I was trying to make notes. [*She takes out her note-book, and looks at her stenography, which nearly makes her cry*].

MORELL. Did I go too fast, Pross?

PROSERPINE. Much too fast. You know I cant do more than ninety words a minute. [*She relieves her feelings by throwing her note-book angrily beside her machine, ready for use next morning*].

MORELL [*soothingly*] Oh well, well, never mind, never mind, never mind. Have you all had supper?

LEXY. Mr Burgess has been kind enough to give us a really splendid supper at the Belgrave.

BURGESS [*with effusive magnanimity*] Dont mention it, Mr Mill. [*Modestly*] Youre arty welcome to my little treat.

PROSERPINE. We had champagne. I never tasted it before. I feel quite giddy.

MORELL [*surprised*] A champagne supper! That was very handsome. Was it my eloquence that produced all this extravagance?

LEXY [*rhetorically*] Your eloquence, and Mr Burgess's goodness of heart. [*With a fresh burst of exhilaration*] And what a very fine fellow the chairman is, Morell! He came to supper with us.

MORELL [*with long drawn significance, looking at Burgess*] O-o-o-h! the chairman. Now I understand.

Burgess covers with a deprecatory cough a lively satisfaction with his own diplomatic cunning. Lexy folds his arms and leans against the head of the sofa in a high-spirited attitude after nearly losing his balance. Candida comes in with glasses, lemons, and a jug of hot water on a tray.

CANDIDA. Who will have some lemonade? You know our rules: total abstinence. [*She puts the tray on the table, and takes up the lemon squeezer, looking enquiringly round at them*].

MORELL. No use, dear. Theyve all had champagne. Pross has broken her pledge.

CANDIDA [*to Proserpine*] You dont mean to say youve been drinking champagne!

PROSERPINE [*stubbornly*] Yes I do. I'm only a beer teetotaller, not a champagne teetotaller. I dont like beer. Are there any letters for me to answer, Mr Morell?

MORELL. No more tonight.

PROSERPINE. Very well. Goodnight, everybody.

LEXY [*gallantly*] Had I not better see you home, Miss Garnett?

PROSERPINE. No thank you. I shant trust myself with anybody tonight. I wish I hadn't taken any of that stuff. [*She takes uncertain aim at the door; dashes at it; and barely escapes without disaster*].

BURGESS [*indignantly*] Stuff indeed! That gurl dunno what champagne is! Pommery and Greeno at twelve and six a bottle. She took two glasses amost straight horff.

MORELL [*anxious about her*] Go and look after her, Lexy.

LEXY [*alarmed*] But if she should really be – Suppose she began to sing in the street, or anything of that sort.

MORELL. Just so: she may. Thats why youd better see her safely home.

CANDIDA. Do, Lexy: theres a good fellow. [*She shakes his hand and pushes him gently to the door*].

LEXY. It's evidently my duty to go. I hope it may not be necessary. Goodnight, Mrs Morell. [*To the rest*] Goodnight. [*He goes. Candida shuts the door*].

BURGESS. He was gushin with hextra piety hisself arter two sips. People carnt drink like they huseter. [*Bustling across to the hearth*] Well, James: it's time to lock up. Mr Morchbanks: shall I ave the pleasure of your company for a bit o the way ome?

MARCHBANKS [*affrightedly*] Yes: I'd better go. [*He hurries towards the door; but Candida places herself before it, barring his way*].

CANDIDA [*with quiet authority*] You sit down. Youre not going yet.

MARCHBANKS [*quailing*] No: I – I didnt mean to. [*He sits down abjectly on the sofa*].

CANDIDA. Mr Marchbanks will stay the night with us, papa.

BURGESS. Oh well, I'll say goodnight. So long, James. [*He shakes hands with Morell, and goes over to Eugene*]. Make em give you a nightlight by your bed, Mr Morchbanks: itll comfort you if you wake up in the night with a touch of that complaint of yores. Goodnight.

MARCHBANKS. Thank you: I will. Goodnight, Mr Burgess. [*They shake hands. Burgess goes to the door*].

CANDIDA [*intercepting Morell, who is following Burgess*] Stay here, dear: I'll put on papa's coat for him. [*She goes out with Burgess*].

MARCHBANKS [*rising and stealing over to Morell*] Morell: theres going to be a terrible scene. Arnt you afraid?

MORELL. Not in the least.

MARCHBANKS. I never envied you your courage before. [*He puts his hand appealingly on Morell's forearm*]. Stand by me, wont you?

MORELL [*casting him off resolutely*] Each for himself, Eugene. She must choose between us now.

    Candida returns. Eugene creeps back to the sofa like a guilty schoolboy.

CANDIDA [*between them, addressing Eugene*] Are you sorry?

MARCHBANKS [*earnestly*] Yes. Heartbroken.

CANDIDA. Well, then, you are forgiven. Now go off to bed like a good little boy: I want to talk to James about you.

MARCHBANKS [*rising in great consternation*] Oh, I cant do that, Morell. I must be here. I'll not go away. Tell her.

CANDIDA [*her suspicions confirmed*] Tell me what? [*His eyes avoid hers furtively. She turns and mutely transfers the question to Morell*].

MORELL [*bracing himself for the catastrophe*] I have nothing to tell her, except [*here his voice deepens to a measured and mournful tenderness*] that she is my greatest treasure on earth – if she is really mine.

CANDIDA [*coldly, offended by his yielding to his orator's instinct and treating her as if she were the audience at the Guild of St Matthew*] I am sure Eugene can say no less, if that is all.

MARCHBANKS [*discouraged*] Morell: she's laughing at us.

MORELL [*with a quick touch of temper*] There is nothing to laugh at. Are you laughing at us, Candida?

CANDIDA [*with quiet anger*] Eugene is very quick-witted, James. I hope I am going to laugh; but I am not sure that I am not going to be very angry. [*She goes to the fireplace, and stands there leaning with her arms on the mantelpiece, and her foot on the fender, whilst Eugene steals to Morell and plucks him by the sleeve*].

MARCHBANKS [*whispering*] Stop, Morell. Dont let us say anything.

MORELL [*pushing Eugene away without deigning to look at him*] I hope you dont mean that as a threat, Candida.

CANDIDA [*with emphatic warning*] Take care, James. Eugene: I asked you to go. Are you going?

MORELL [*putting his foot down*] He shall not go. I wish him to remain.

MARCHBANKS. I'll go. I'll do whatever you want. [*He turns to the door*].

CANDIDA. Stop! [*He obeys*]. Didnt you hear James say he wished you to stay? James is master here. Dont you know that?

MARCHBANKS [*flushing with a young poet's rage against tyranny*] By what right is he master?

CANDIDA [*quietly*] Tell him, James.

MORELL [*taken aback*] My dear: I dont know of any right that makes me master. I assert no such right.

CANDIDA [*with infinite reproach*] You dont know! Oh, James! James! [*To Eugene, musingly*] I wonder do you understand, Eugene! [*He shakes his head helplessly, not daring to look at her*]. No: youre too young. Well, I give you leave to stay: to stay and learn. [*She comes away from the hearth and places herself between them*]. Now, James! whats the matter? Come: tell me.

MARCHBANKS [*whispering tremulously across to him*] Dont.

CANDIDA. Come. Out with it!

MORELL [*slowly*] I meant to prepare your mind carefully, Candida, so as to prevent misunderstanding.

CANDIDA. Yes, dear: I am sure you did. But never mind: I shant misunderstand.

MORELL. Well – er – [*he hesitates, unable to find the long explanation which he supposed to be available*].

CANDIDA. Well?

MORELL [*blurting it out baldly*] Eugene declares that you are in love with him.

MARCHBANKS [*frantically*] No, no, no, no, never. I did not, Mrs Morell: it's not true. I said I loved you. I said I understood you, and that he couldnt. And it was not after what passed there before the fire that I spoke: it was not, on my word. It was this morning.

CANDIDA [*enlightened*] This morning!

MARCHBANKS. Yes. [*He looks at her, pleading for credence, and then adds simply*] That was what was the matter with my collar.

CANDIDA. Your collar? [*Suddenly taking in his meaning she turns to Morell, shocked*]. Oh, James: did you – [*she stops*]?

MORELL [*ashamed*] You know, Candida, that I have a temper to struggle with. And he said [*shuddering*] that you despised me in your heart.

CANDIDA [*turning quickly on Eugene*] Did you say that?

MARCHBANKS [*terrified*] No.

CANDIDA [*almost fiercely*] Then James has just told me a falsehood. Is that what you mean?

MARCHBANKS. No, no: I – I – [*desperately*] it was David's wife. And it wasnt at home: it was when she saw him dancing before all the people.

MORELL [*taking the cue with a debater's adroitness*] Dancing before all the people, Candida; and thinking he was moving their hearts by his mission when they were only suffering from – Prossy's complaint. [*She is about to protest: he raises his hand to silence her*]. Dont try to look indignant, Candida –

CANDIDA. Try!

MORELL [*continuing*] Eugene was right. As you told me a few hours after, he is always right. He said nothing that you did not say far better yourself. He is the poet, who sees everything; and I am the poor parson, who understands nothing.

CANDIDA [*remorsefully*] Do you mind what is said by a foolish boy, because I said something like it in jest?

MORELL. That foolish boy can speak with the inspiration of a child and the cunning of a serpent. He has claimed that you belong to him and not to me; and, rightly or wrongly, I have come to fear that it may be true. I will not go about tortured with doubts and suspicions. I will not live with you and keep a secret from you. I will not suffer the intolerable degradation of jealousy. We have agreed – he and I – that you shall choose between us now. I await your decision.

CANDIDA [*slowly recoiling a step, her heart hardened by his rhetoric in spite of the sincere feeling behind it*] Oh! I am to choose am I? I suppose it is quite settled that I must belong to one or the other.

MORELL [*firmly*] Quite. You must choose definitely.

MARCHBANKS [*anxiously*] Morell: you dont understand. She means that she belongs to herself.

CANDIDA [*turning to him*] I mean that, and a good deal more, Master Eugene, as you will both find out presently. And pray, my lords and masters, what have you to offer for my choice? I am up for auction, it seems. What do you bid, James?

MORELL [*reproachfully*] Cand – [*He breaks down: his eyes and throat fill with tears: the orator becomes a wounded animal*]. I cant speak –

CANDIDA [*impulsively going to him*] Ah, dearest –

MARCHBANKS [*in wild alarm*] Stop: it's not fair. You musnt shew her that you suffer, Morell. I am on the rack too; but I am not crying.

MORELL [*rallying all his forces*] Yes: you are right. It is not for pity that I am bidding. [*He disengages himself from Candida*].

CANDIDA [*retreating, chilled*] I beg your pardon, James: I did not mean to touch you. I am waiting to hear your bid.

MORELL [*with great humility*] I have nothing to offer you but my strength for your defence, my honesty for your surety, my ability and industry for your livelihood, and my authority and position for your dignity. That is all it becomes a man to offer to a woman.

CANDIDA [*quite quietly*] And you, Eugene? What do you offer?

MARCHBANKS. My weakness. My desolation. My heart's need.

CANDIDA [*impressed*] Thats a good bid, Eugene. Now I know how to make my choice.

She pauses and looks curiously from one to the other, as if weighing them. Morell, whose lofty confidence has changed into heartbreaking dread at Eugene's bid, loses all power of concealing his anxiety. Eugene, strung to the highest tension, does not move a muscle.

MORELL [*in a suffocated voice: the appeal bursting from the depths of his anguish*] Candida!

MARCHBANKS [*aside, in a flash of contempt*] Coward!

CANDIDA [*significantly*] I give myself to the weaker of the two.

Eugene divines her meaning at once: his face whitens like steel in a furnace.

MORELL [*bowing his head with the calm of collapse*] I accept your sentence, Candida.

CANDIDA. Do you understand, Eugene?

MARCHBANKS. Oh, I feel I'm lost. He cannot bear the burden.

MORELL [*incredulously, raising his head and voice with comic abruptness*] Do you mean me, Candida?

CANDIDA [*smiling a little*] Let us sit and talk comfortably over it like three friends. [*To Morell*] Sit down, dear. [*Morell, quite lost, takes the chair from the fireside: the children's chair*]. Bring me that chair, Eugene. [*She indicates the easy chair. He fetches it silently, even with something like cold strength, and places it next Morell, a little behind him. She sits down. He takes the visitor's chair himself, and sits, inscrutable. When they are all settled she begins, throwing a spell of quietness on them by her calm, sane, tender tone*]. You remember what you told me about yourself, Eugene: how nobody has cared for you since your old

nurse died: how those clever fashionable sisters and successful brothers of yours were your mother's and father's pets:
how miserable you were at Eton: how your father is trying
to starve you into returning to Oxford: how you have had
to live without comfort or welcome or refuge: always lonely,
and nearly always disliked and misunderstood, poor boy!

MARCHBANKS [*faithful to the nobility of his lot*] I had my
books. I had Nature. And at last I met you.

CANDIDA. Never mind that just at present. Now I want you
to look at this other boy here: my boy! spoiled from his
cradle. We go once a fortnight to see his parents. You
should come with us, Eugene, to see the pictures of the
hero of that household. James as a baby! the most wonderful of all babies. James holding his first school prize, won
at the ripe age of eight! James as the captain of his eleven!
James in his first frock coat! James under all sorts of glorious circumstances! You know how strong he is (I hope he
didnt hurt you): how clever he is: how happy. [*With
deepening gravity*] Ask James's mother and his three sisters
what it cost to save James the trouble of doing anything
but be strong and clever and happy. Ask me what it costs
to be James's mother and three sisters and wife and
mother to his children all in one. Ask Prossy and Maria
how troublesome the house is even when we have no visitors to help us to slice the onions. Ask the tradesmen who
want to worry James and spoil his beautiful sermons who
it is that puts them off. When there is money to give, he
gives it: when there is money to refuse, I refuse it. I build
a castle of comfort and indulgence and love for him, and
stand sentinel always to keep little vulgar cares out. I
make him master here, though he does not know it, and
could not tell you a moment ago how it came to be so.
[*With sweet irony*] And when he thought I might go away
with you, his only anxiety was – what should become of
me! And to tempt me to stay he offered me [*leaning forward to stroke his hair caressingly at each phrase*] his strength
for my defence! his industry for my livelihood! his dignity

for my position! his – [*relenting*] ah, I am mixing up your beautiful cadences and spoiling them, am I not, darling? [*She lays her cheek fondly against his*].

MORELL [*quite overcome, kneeling beside her chair and embracing her with boyish ingenuousness*] It's all true, every word. What I am you have made me with the labor of your hands and the love of your heart. You are my wife, my mother, my sisters: you are the sum of all loving care to me.

CANDIDA [*in his arms, smiling, to Eugene*] Am I your mother and sister to you, Eugene?

MARCHBANKS [*rising with a fierce gesture of disgust*] Ah, never. Out, then, into the night with me!

CANDIDA [*rising quickly*] You are not going like that, Eugene?

MARCHBANKS [*with the ring of a man's voice – no longer a boy's – in the words*] I know the hour when it strikes. I am impatient to do what must be done.

MORELL [*who has also risen*] Candida: dont let him do anything rash.

CANDIDA [*confident, smiling at Eugene*] Oh, there is no fear. He has learnt to live without happiness.

MARCHBANKS. I no longer desire happiness: life is nobler than that. Parson James: I give you my happiness with both hands: I love you because you have filled the heart of the woman I loved. Goodbye. [*He goes towards the door*].

CANDIDA. One last word. [*He stops, but without turning to her. She goes to him*]. How old are you, Eugene?

MARCHBANKS. As old as the world now. This morning I was eighteen.

CANDIDA. Eighteen! Will you, for my sake, make a little poem out of the two sentences I am going to say to you? And will you promise to repeat it to yourself whenever you think of me?

MARCHBANKS [*without moving*] Say the sentences.

CANDIDA. When I am thirty, she will be forty-five. When I am sixty, she will be seventy-five.

MARCHBANKS [*turning to her*] In a hundred years, we shall be the same age. But I have a better secret than that in my heart. Let me go now. The night outside grows impatient.

CANDIDA. Goodbye. [*She takes his face in her hands; and as he divines her intention and falls on his knees, she kisses his forehead. Then he flies out into the night. She turns to Morell, holding out her arms to him.*] Ah, James!

They embrace. But they do not know the secret in the poet's heart.

THE MAN OF DESTINY
1896

THE MAN OF DESTINY

The twelfth of May, 1796, in north Italy, at Tavazzano, on the road from Lodi to Milan. The afternoon sun is blazing serenely over the plains of Lombardy, treating the Alps with respect and the ant-hills with indulgence, neither disgusted by the basking of the swine in the villages nor hurt by its cool reception in the churches, but ruthlessly disdainful of two hordes of mischievous insects which are the French and Austrian armies. Two days before, at Lodi, the Austrians tried to prevent the French from crossing the river by the narrow bridge there; but the French, commanded by a general aged 27, Napoleon Bonaparte, who does not respect the rules of war, rushed the fireswept bridge, supported by a tremendous cannonade in which the young general assisted with his own hands. Cannonading is his technical speciality: he has been trained in the artillery under the old régime, and made perfect in the military arts of shirking his duties, swindling the paymaster over travelling expenses, and dignifying war with the noise and smoke of cannon, as depicted in all military portraits. He is, however, an original observer, and has perceived, for the first time since the invention of gunpowder, that a cannon ball, if it strikes a man, will kill him. To a thorough grasp of this remarkable discovery he adds a highly evolved faculty for physical geography and for the calculation of times and distances. He has prodigious powers of work, and a clear realistic knowledge of human nature in public affairs, having seen it exhaustively tested in that department during the French Revolution. He is imaginative without illusions, and creative without religion, loyalty, patriotism or any of the common ideals. Not that he is incapable of these ideals: on the contrary, he has swallowed them all in his boyhood, and now, having a keen dramatic faculty, is extremely clever at playing upon them by the arts of the actor and stage manager. Withal, he is no spoiled child. Poverty, ill-luck, the shifts of impecunious shabby-gentility, repeated failure as a would-be author, humiliation as a rebuffed time server, reproof and punishment as an incompetent and dishonest officer, an escape from dismissal from the service so narrow that if the emigration of the nobles had not raised the value of even the most rascally lieutenant to the famine price of a general he would have been swept contemptuously from the army: these trials have ground his conceit out of him, and forced him to be self-sufficient and to understand that to such men as he is the world will give nothing that he cannot take from it by force. In this the world is not free from cowardice and folly; for Napoleon, as a merciless cannonader of political rubbish, is making himself useful: indeed, it is even now impossible to live in England without sometimes feeling how much that country lost in not being conquered by him as well as by Julius Cæsar.

However, on this May afternoon in 1796, it is early days with him. He has but recently been promoted general, partly by using his wife to seduce the Directory (then governing France); partly by the scarcity of officers caused by the emigration as aforesaid; partly by his faculty of knowing a country, with all its roads, rivers, hills and valleys, as he knows the palm of his hand; and largely by that new faith of his in the efficacy of firing cannons at people. His army is, as to discipline, in a state which has so greatly shocked some modern writers before whom the following story has been enacted, that they, impressed with the later glory of 'L'Empereur', have altogether refused to credit it. But Napoleon is not L'Empereur yet: his men call him Le Petit Caporal, as he is still in the stage of gaining influence over them by displays of pluck. He is not in a position to force his will on them in orthodox military fashion by the cat o' nine tails. The French Revolution, which has escaped suppression solely through the monarchy's habits of being at least four years in arrear with its soldiers in the matter of pay, has substituted for that habit, as far as possible, the habit of not paying at all, except in promises and patriotic flatteries which are not compatible with martial law of the Prussian type. Napoleon has therefore approached the Alps in command of men without money, in rags, and consequently indisposed to stand much discipline, especially from upstart generals. This circumstance, which would have embarrassed an idealist soldier, has been worth a thousand cannon to Napoleon. He has said to his army 'You have patriotism and courage; but you have no money, no clothes, and hardly anything to eat. In Italy there are all these things, and glory as well, to be gained by a devoted army led by a general who regards loot as the natural right of the soldier. I am such a general. En avant, mes enfants!' The result has entirely justified him. The army conquers Italy as the locusts conquered Cyprus. They fight all day and march all night, covering impossible distances and appearing in incredible places, not because every soldier carries a field marshal's baton in his knapsack, but because he hopes to carry at least half a dozen silver forks there next day.

It must be understood, by the way, that the French army does not make war on the Italians. It is there to rescue them from the tyranny of their Austrian conquerors, and confer republican institutions on them; so that in incidentally looting them it merely makes free with the property of its friends, who ought to be grateful to it, and perhaps would be if ingratitude were not the proverbial failing of their country. The Austrians, whom it fights, are a thoroughly respectable regular army, well disciplined, commanded by gentlemen versed in orthodox campaigning: at the head of them Beaulieu, practising the classic art of war under orders from Vienna, and getting horribly beaten by Napoleon, who acts on his own responsibility in defiance of professional precedents or orders from Paris. Even when the Austrians win a battle, all that is necessary is to wait until their routine obliges them to return to their quarters for afternoon tea, so to speak, and win it back again from them: a course pursued later on with brilliant success at Marengo. On the whole, with his foe handicapped by Austrian statesmanship, classic generalship, and the exigencies of the aristocratic social structure of Viennese society, Napoleon finds it possible to be irresistible without working heroic miracles. The world, however, likes miracles and heroes, and is quite incapable of conceiving the action of such forces as academic militarism or Viennese drawing-roomism. Hence it has already begun to manufacture 'L'Empereur', and thus to make it difficult for the romanticists of a hundred years later to credit the hitherto unrecorded little scene now in question at Tavazzano.

The best quarters at Tavazzano are at a little inn, the first house reached by travellers passing through the place from Milan to Lodi. It stands in a vineyard; and its principal room, a pleasant refuge from the summer heat, is open so widely at the back to this vineyard that it is almost a large veranda. The bolder children, much excited by the alarums and excursions of the past few days, and by an irruption of French troops at six o'clock, know that the French commander has quartered himself in this room, and are divided between a craving to peep in at the front windows, and a mortal dread of the sentinel, a young gentleman-soldier who, having no natural moustache, has had a most ferocious one painted on his face with boot blacking by his sergeant. As his heavy uniform, like all the uniforms of that day, is designed for parade without the least reference to his health or comfort, he perspires profusely in the sun; and his painted moustache has run in little streaks down his chin and round his neck, except where it has dried in stiff japanned flakes and had its sweeping outline chipped off in grotesque little bays and headlands, making him unspeakably ridiculous in the eye of History a hundred years later, but monstrous and horrible to the contemporary north Italian infant, to whom nothing would seem more natural than that he should relieve the monotony of his guard by pitchforking a stray child up on his bayonet, and eating it uncooked. Nevertheless one girl of bad character, in whom an instinct of privilege with soldiers is already stirring, does peep in at the safest window for a moment before a glance and a clink from the sentinel sends her flying. Most of what she sees she has seen before: the vineyard at the back, with the old winepress and a cart among the vines; the door close on her right leading to the street entry; the landlord's best sideboard, now in full action for dinner, further back on the same side; the fireplace on the other side with a couch near it; another door, leading to the inner rooms, between it and the vineyard; and the table in the middle set out with a repast of Milanese risotto, cheese, grapes, bread, olives, and a big wickered flask of red wine.

The landlord, Giuseppe Grandi, she knows well. He is a swarthy vivacious shrewdly cheerful black-curled bullet headed grinning little innkeeper of 40. Naturally an excellent host, he is in the highest spirits this evening at his good fortune in having as his guest the French commander to protect him against the license of the troops. He actually sports a pair of gold earrings which would otherwise have been hidden carefully under the winepress with his little equipment of silver plate.

Napoleon, sitting facing her on the further side of the table, she sees for the first time. He is working hard, partly at his meal, which he has discovered how to dispatch in ten minutes by attacking all the courses simultaneously (this practise is the beginning of his downfall), and partly at a military map on which he from time to time marks the position of the forces by taking a grapeskin from his mouth and planting it on the map with his thumb like a wafer. There is no revolutionary untidiness about his dress or person; but his elbow has displaced most of

the dishes and glasses; and his long hair trails into the risotto when he
forgets it and leans more intently over the map.

GIUSEPPE. Will your excellency –

NAPOLEON [*intent on his map, but cramming himself mechanically
with his left hand*] Dont talk. I'm busy.

GIUSEPPE [*with perfect goodhumor*] Excellency: I obey.

NAPOLEON. Some red ink.

GIUSEPPE. Alas! excellency, there is none.

NAPOLEON [*with Corsican facetiousness*] Kill something and
bring me its blood.

GIUSEPPE [*grinning*] There is nothing but your excellency's
horse, the sentinel, the lady upstairs, and my wife.

NAPOLEON. Kill your wife.

GIUSEPPE. Willingly, your excellency; but unhappily I am
not strong enough. She would kill me.

NAPOLEON. That will do equally well.

GIUSEPPE. Your excellency does me too much honor.
[*Stretching his hand towards the flask*] Perhaps some wine will
answer your excellency's purpose.

NAPOLEON [*hastily protecting the flask, and becoming quite serious*]
Wine! No: that would be waste. You are all the same:
waste! waste! waste! [*He marks the map with gravy, using his
fork as a pen*]. Clear away. [*He finishes his wine; pushes back his
chair; and uses his napkin, stretching his legs and leaning back,
but still frowning and thinking*].

GIUSEPPE [*clearing the table and removing the things to a tray on
the sideboard*] Every man to his trade, excellency. We innkeepers have plenty of cheap wine: we think nothing of
spilling it. You great generals have plenty of cheap blood:
you think nothing of spilling it. Is it not so, excellency?

NAPOLEON. Blood costs nothing: wine costs money. [*He
rises and goes to the fireplace*].

GIUSEPPE. They say you are careful of everything except
human life, excellency.

NAPOLEON. Human life, my friend, is the only thing that
takes care of itself. [*He throws himself at his ease on the couch*].

GIUSEPPE [*admiring him*] Ah, excellency, what fools we all are beside you! If I could only find out the secret of your success!

NAPOLEON. You would make yourself Emperor of Italy, eh?

GIUSEPPE. Too troublesome, excellency: I leave all that to you. Besides, what would become of my inn if I were Emperor? See how you enjoy looking on at me whilst I keep the inn for you and wait on you! Well, I shall enjoy looking on at you whilst you become Emperor of Europe, and govern the country for me [*As he chatters, he takes the cloth off deftly without removing the map, and finally takes the corners in his hands and the middle in his mouth, to fold it up*].

NAPOLEON. Emperor of Europe, eh? Why only Europe?

GIUSEPPE. Why, indeed? Emperor of the world, excellency! Why not? [*He folds and rolls up the cloth, emphasizing his phrase by the steps of the process*]. One man is like another [*fold*]: one country is like another [*fold*]: one battle is like another. [*At the last fold, he slaps the cloth on the table and deftly rolls it up, adding, by way of peroration*] Conquer one: conquer all. [*He takes the cloth to the sideboard, and puts it in a drawer*].

NAPOLEON. And govern for all; fight for all; be everybody's servant under cover of being everybody's master, Giuseppe.

GIUSEPPE [*at the sideboard*] Excellency?

NAPOLEON. I forbid you to talk to me about myself.

GIUSEPPE [*coming to the foot of the couch*] Pardon. Your excellency is so unlike other great men. It is the subject they like best.

NAPOLEON. Well, talk to me about the subject they like next best, whatever that may be.

GIUSEPPE [*unabashed*] Willingly, your excellency. Has your excellency by any chance caught a glimpse of the lady upstairs?

NAPOLEON [*sitting up promptly*] How old is she?

GIUSEPPE. The right age, excellency.

NAPOLEON. Do you mean seventeen or thirty?

GIUSEPPE. Thirty, excellency.

NAPOLEON. Goodlooking?

GIUSEPPE. I cannot see with your excellency's eyes: every man must judge that for himself. In my opinion, excellency, a fine figure of a lady. [*Slyly*] Shall I lay the table for her collation here?

NAPOLEON [*brusquely, rising*] No: lay nothing here until the officer for whom I am waiting comes back. [*He looks at his watch, and takes to walking to and fro between the fireplace and the vineyard*].

GIUSEPPE [*with conviction*] Excellency: believe me, he has been captured by the accursed Austrians. He dare not keep you waiting if he were at liberty.

NAPOLEON [*turning at the edge of the shadow of the veranda*] Giuseppe: if that turns out to be true, it will put me into such a temper that nothing short of hanging you and your whole household, including the lady upstairs, will satisfy me.

GIUSEPPE. We are all cheerfully at your excellency's disposal, except the lady. I cannot answer for her; but no lady could resist you, General.

NAPOLEON [*sourly, resuming his march*] Hm! You will never be hanged. There is no satisfaction in hanging a man who does not object to it.

GIUSEPPE [*sympathetically*] Not the least in the world, excellency: is there? [*Napoleon again looks at his watch, evidently growing anxious*]. Ah, one can see that you are a great man, General: you know how to wait. If it were a corporal now, or a sub-lieutenant, at the end of three minutes he would be swearing, fuming, threatening, pulling the house about our ears.

NAPOLEON. Giuseppe: your flatteries are insufferable. Go and talk outside. [*He sits down again at the table, with his jaws in his hands, and his elbows propped on the map, poring over it with a troubled expression*].

GIUSEPPE. Willingly, your excellency. You shall not be disturbed. [*He takes up the tray and prepares to withdraw*].

NAPOLEON. The moment he comes back, send him to me.

GIUSEPPE. Instantaneously, your excellency.

A LADY'S VOICE [*calling from some distant part of the inn*] Giusep-pe! [*The voice is very musical, and the two final notes make an ascending interval*].

NAPOLEON [*startled*] Who's that?

GIUSEPPE. The lady, excellency.

NAPOLEON. The lady upstairs?

GIUSEPPE. Yes, excellency. The strange lady.

NAPOLEON. Strange? Where does she come from?

GIUSEPPE [*with a shrug*] Who knows? She arrived here just before your excellency in a hired carriage belonging to the Golden Eagle at Borghetto. By herself, excellency. No servants. A dressing bag and a trunk: that is all. The postillion says she left a horse at the Golden Eagle. A charger, with military trappings.

NAPOLEON. A woman with a charger! French or Austrian?

GIUSEPPE. French, excellency.

NAPOLEON. Her husband's charger, no doubt. Killed at Lodi, poor fellow.

THE LADY'S VOICE [*the two final notes now making a peremptory descending interval*] Giuseppe!

NAPOLEON [*rising to listen*] Thats not the voice of a woman whose husband was killed yesterday.

GIUSEPPE. Husbands are not always regretted, excellency. [*Calling*] Coming, lady, coming. [*He makes for the inner door*].

NAPOLEON [*arresting him with a strong hand on his shoulder*] Stop. Let her come.

VOICE. Giuseppe!! [*impatiently*].

GIUSEPPE. Let me go, excellency. It is my point of honor as an innkeeper to come when I am called. I appeal to you as a soldier.

A MAN'S VOICE [*outside, at the inn door, shouting*] Here, someone. Hollo! Landlord! Where are you? [*Somebody raps vigorously with a whip on a bench in the passage*].

NAPOLEON [*suddenly becoming the commanding officer again and throwing Giuseppe off*] My man at last. [*Pointing to the inner door*] Go. Attend to your business: the lady is calling you.

[*He goes to the fireplace and stands with his back to it with a determined military air*].

GIUSEPPE [*with bated breath, snatching up his tray*] Certainly, excellency. [*He hurries out by the inner door*].

THE MAN'S VOICE [*impatiently*] Are you all asleep here?

The other door is kicked rudely open. A dusty sub-lieutenant bursts into the room. He is a tall chuckle-headed young man of 24, with the complexion and style of a man of rank, and a self-assurance on that ground which the French Revolution has failed to shake in the smallest degree. He has a thick silly lip, an eager credulous eye, an obstinate nose, and a loud confident voice. A young man without fear, without reverence, without imagination, without sense, hopelessly insusceptible to the Napoleonic or any other idea, stupendously egotistical, eminently qualified to rush in where angels fear to tread, yet of a vigorous babbling vitality which bustles him into the thick of things. He is just now boiling with vexation, attributable by a superficial observer to his impatience at not being promptly attended to by the staff of the inn, but in which a more discerning eye can perceive a certain moral depth, indicating a more permanent and momentous grievance. On seeing Napoleon, he is sufficiently taken aback to check himself and salute; but he does not betray by his manner any of that prophetic consciousness of Marengo and Austerlitz, Waterloo and St Helena, or the Napoleonic pictures of Delaroche and Meissonier, which later ages expect from him.

NAPOLEON [*watch in hand*] Well, sir, you have come at last. Your instructions were that I should arrive here at six, and find you waiting for me with my mail from Paris and with despatches. It is now twenty minutes to eight. You were sent on this service as a hard rider with the fastest horse in the camp. You arrive a hundred minutes late, on foot. Where is your horse?

THE LIEUTENANT [*moodily pulling off his gloves and dashing them with his cap and whip on the table*] Ah! where indeed? Thats just what I should like to know, General. [*With emotion*] You dont know how fond I was of that horse.

NAPOLEON [*angrily sarcastic*] Indeed! [*With sudden misgiving*] Where are the letters and despatches?

THE LIEUTENANT [*importantly, rather pleased than otherwise at having some remarkable news*] I dont know.

NAPOLEON [*unable to believe his ears*] You dont know!

LIEUTENANT. No more than you do, General. Now I suppose I shall be court-martialled. Well, I dont mind being court-martialled; but [*with solemn determination*] I tell you, General, if ever I catch that innocent looking youth, I'll spoil his beauty, the slimy little liar! I'll make a picture of him. I'll –

NAPOLEON [*advancing from the hearth to the table*] What innocent looking youth? Pull yourself together, sir, will you; and give an account of yourself.

LIEUTENANT [*facing him at the opposite side of the table, leaning on it with his fists*] Oh, I'm all right, General: I'm perfectly ready to give an account of myself. I shall make the court-martial thoroughly understand that the fault was not mine. Advantage has been taken of the better side of my nature; and I'm not ashamed of it. But with all respect to you as my commanding officer, General, I say again that if ever I set eyes on that son of Satan, I'll –

NAPOLEON [*angrily*] So you said before.

LIEUTENANT [*drawing himself upright*] I say it again. Just wait until I catch him. Just wait: thats all. [*He folds his arms resolutely, and breathes hard, with compressed lips*].

NAPOLEON. I am waiting, sir. For your explanation.

LIEUTENANT [*confidently*] Youll change your tone, General, when you hear what has happened to me.

NAPOLEON. Nothing has happened to you, sir: you are alive and not disabled. Where are the papers entrusted to you?

LIEUTENANT. Nothing happened to me! Nothing!! He swore eternal brotherhood with me. Was that nothing? He said my eyes reminded him of his sister's eyes. Was that nothing? He cried – actually cried – over the story of my separation from Angelica. Was that nothing? He paid for both bottles of wine, though he only ate bread and grapes himself. Perhaps you call that nothing. He gave me his pistols and his horse and his despatches – most important despatches – and let me go away with them. [*Triumphantly, seeing that he has reduced Napoleon to blank stupefaction*] Was that nothing?

NAPOLEON [*enfeebled by astonishment*] What did he do that for?

LIEUTENANT [*as if the reason were obvious*] To shew his confidence in me, of course. [*Napoleon's jaw does not exactly drop; but its hinges become nerveless*]. And I was worthy of his confidence: I brought them all back honorably. But would you believe it? when I trusted him with my pistols, and my horse, and my despatches –

NAPOLEON. What the devil did you do that for?

LIEUTENANT. I'm telling you: to shew my confidence in him. And he betrayed it! abused it! never came back again! The thief! the swindler! the heartless treacherous little blackguard! You call that nothing, I suppose. But look here, General: [*again resorting to the table with his fists for greater emphasis*] you may put up with this outrage from the Austrians if you like; but speaking for myself personally, I tell you that if ever I catch –

NAPOLEON [*turning on his heel in disgust and irritably resuming his march to and fro*] Yes: you have said that more than once already.

LIEUTENANT [*excitedly*] More than once! I'll say it fifty times; and whats more, I'll do it. Youll see, General. I'll shew my confidence in him, so I will. I'll –

NAPOLEON. Yes, yes, sir: no doubt you will. What kind of man was he?

LIEUTENANT. Well, I should think you ought to be able to tell from his conduct the kind of man he was.

NAPOLEON. Psha! What was he like?

LIEUTENANT. Like! He was like – well, well, you ought to have just seen the fellow: that will give you a notion of what he was like. He wont be like it five minutes after I catch him; for I tell you that if ever –

NAPOLEON [*shouting furiously for the innkeeper*] Giuseppe! [*To the Lieutenant, out of all patience*] Hold your tongue, sir, if you can.

LIEUTENANT [*plaintively*] I warn you it's no use trying to put the blame on me. How was I to know the sort of fellow he was? [*He takes a chair from between the sideboard and the outer door; places it near the table; and sits down*]. If you only knew how hungry and tired I am, youd have more consideration.

GIUSEPPE [*returning*] What is it, excellency?

NAPOLEON [*struggling with his temper*] Take this – this officer. Feed him; and put him to bed, if necessary. When he is in his right mind again, find out what has happened to him and bring me word. [*To the Lieutenant*] Consider yourself under arrest, sir.

LIEUTENANT [*with sulky stiffness*] I was prepared for that. It takes a gentleman to understand a gentleman. [*He throws his sword on the table*].

GIUSEPPE [*with sympathetic concern*] Have you been attacked by the Austrians, lieutenant? Dear! dear! dear!

LIEUTENANT [*contemptuously*] Attacked! I could have broken his back between my finger and thumb. I wish I had, now. No: it was by appealing to the better side of my nature: thats what I cant get over. He said he'd never met a man he liked so much as me. He put his handkerchief round my neck because a gnat bit me, and my stock was chafing it. Look! [*He pulls a handkerchief from his stock. Giuseppe takes it and examines it*].

GIUSEPPE [*to Napoleon*] A lady's handkerchief, excellency. [*He smells it*]. Perfumed.

NAPOLEON. Eh? [*He takes it and looks at it attentively*]. Hm! [*He smells it*]. Ha! [*He walks thoughtfully across the room, looking at the handkerchief, which he finally sticks in the breast of his coat*].

LIEUTENANT. Good enough for him, anyhow. I noticed that he had a woman's hands when he touched my neck, with his coaxing fawning ways, the mean effeminate little hound. [*Lowering his voice with thrilling intensity*] But mark my words, General. If ever –

THE LADY'S VOICE [*outside, as before*] Giuseppe!

LIEUTENANT [*petrified*] What was that?

GIUSEPPE. Only a lady upstairs, lieutenant, calling me.

LIEUTENANT. Lady!

VOICE. Giuseppe, Giuseppe: where are you?

LIEUTENANT [*murderously*] Give me that sword. [*He snatches up the sword and draws it*].

GIUSEPPE [*rushing forward and seizing his right arm*] What are you thinking of, lieutenant? It's a lady: dont you hear? It's a woman's voice.

LIEUTENANT. It's his voice, I tell you. Let me go. [*He breaks away, and rushes to the edge of the veranda, where he posts himself, sword in hand, watching the door like a cat watching a mousehole*].

It opens; and the Strange Lady steps in. She is tall and extraordinarily graceful, with a delicately intelligent, apprehensive, questioning face: perception in the brow, sensitiveness in the nostrils, character in the chin: all keen, refined, and original. She is very feminine, but by no means weak: the lithe tender figure is hung on a strong frame: the hands and feet, neck and shoulders, are useful vigorous members, of full size in proportion to her stature, which perceptibly exceeds that of Napoleon and the innkeeper, and leaves her at no disadvantage with the lieutenant. Only, her elegance and radiant charm keep the secret of her size and strength. She is not, judging by her dress, an admirer of the latest fashions of the Directory; or perhaps she uses up her old dresses for travelling. At all events she wears no jacket with extravagant lappels, no Greco-Tallien sham chiton, nothing, indeed, that the Princesse de Lamballe might not have worn. Her dress of flowered silk is long waisted, with a Watteau pleat behind, but with the paniers reduced to mere rudiments, as she is too tall for them. It is cut low in the neck where it is eked out by a creamy fichu. She is fair, with golden brown hair and grey eyes.

She enters with the self-possession of a woman accustomed to the privileges of rank and beauty. The innkeeper, who has excellent natural manners, is highly appreciative of her. Napoleon is smitten self-conscious. His color deepens: he becomes stiffer and less at ease than before. She is advancing in an infinitely well bred manner to pay her respects to him when the lieutenant pounces on her and seizes her right wrist. As she recognizes him, she becomes deadly pale.

There is no mistaking her expression: a revelation of some fatal error, utterly unexpected, has suddenly appalled her in the midst of tranquillity, security, and victory. The next moment a wave of angry color rushes up from beneath the creamy fichu and drowns her whole face. One can see that she is blushing all over her body. Even the lieutenant, ordinarily incapable of observation, can see a thing when it is painted red for him. Interpreting the blush as the involuntary confession of black deceit confronted with its victim, he addresses her in a loud crow of retributive triumph.

LIEUTENANT. So Ive got you, my lad. So youve disguised yourself, have you? [*In a voice of thunder, releasing her wrist*] Take off that skirt.

GIUSEPPE [*remonstrating*] Oh, lieutenant!

LADY [*affrighted, but highly indignant at his having dared to touch her*] Gentlemen: I appeal to you. [*To Napoleon*] You, sir, are an officer: a general. You will protect me will you not?

LIEUTENANT. Never mind him, General. Leave me to deal with him.

NAPOLEON. With him! With whom, sir? Why do you treat this lady in such a fashion?

LIEUTENANT. Lady! He's a man! the man I shewed my confidence in. [*Raising his sword*] Here, you –

LADY [*running behind Napoleon and in her agitation clasping to her breast the arm which he extends before her as a fortification*] Oh, thank you, General. Keep him away.

NAPOLEON. Nonsense, sir. This is certainly a lady [*she suddenly drops his arm and blushes again*]; and you are under arrest. Put down your sword, sir, instantly.

LIEUTENANT. General: I tell you he's an Austrian spy. He passed himself off on me as one of General Masséna's staff this afternoon; and now he's passing himself off on you as a woman. Am I to believe my own eyes or not?

LADY. General: it must be my brother. He is on General Masséna's staff. He is very like me.

LIEUTENANT [*his mind giving way*] Do you mean to say that youre not your brother, but your sister? the sister who was so like me? who had my beautiful blue eyes? It's a lie: your eyes are not like mine: theyre exactly like your own.

NAPOLEON [*with contained exasperation*] Lieutenant: will you obey my orders and leave the room, since you are convinced at last that this is no gentleman?

LIEUTENANT. Gentleman! I should think not. No gentleman would have abused my confid –

NAPOLEON [*out of all patience*] That will do, sir: do you hear? Will you leave the room? I order you to leave the room.

LADY. Oh pray let me go instead.

NAPOLEON [*drily*] Excuse me, madam. With all possible respect for your brother, I do not yet understand what an officer on General Masséna's staff wants with my letters. I have some questions to put to you.

GIUSEPPE [*discreetly*] Come, lieutenant. [*He opens the door*].

LIEUTENANT. I'm off. General: take warning by me: be on your guard against the better side of your nature. [*To the lady*] Madam: my apologies. I thought you were the same person, only of the opposite sex; and that naturally misled me.

LADY [*recovering her good humor*] It was not your fault was it? I'm so glad youre not angry with me any longer, lieutenant. [*She offers her hand*].

LIEUTENANT [*bending gallantly to kiss it*] Oh, madam, not the lea – [*Checking himself and looking at it*] You have your brother's hand. And the same sort of ring!

LADY [*sweetly*] We are twins.

LIEUTENANT. That accounts for it. [*He kisses her hand*]. A thousand pardons. I didnt mind about the despatches at all: thats more the General's affair than mine: it was the abuse of my confidence through the better side of my nature. [*Taking his cap, gloves and whip from the table and going*] Youll excuse my leaving you, General, I hope. Very sorry, I'm sure. [*He talks himself out of the room. Giuseppe follows him and shuts the door*].

NAPOLEON [*looking after them with concentrated irritation*] Idiot! *The Strange Lady smiles sympathetically. He comes frowning*

*down the room between the table and the fireplace, all his awkward-
ness gone now that he is alone with her.*

LADY. How can I thank you, General, for your protection?

NAPOLEON [*turning on her suddenly*] My despatches: come!
[*He puts out his hand for them*].

LADY. General! [*She involuntarily puts her hand on her fichu as if
to protect something there*].

NAPOLEON. You tricked that blockhead out of them. You
disguised yourself as a man. I want my despatches. They
are there in the bosom of your dress, under your hands.

LADY [*quickly removing her hands*] Oh, how unkindly you are
speaking to me! [*She takes her handkerchief from her fichu*] You
frighten me. [*She touches her eyes as if to wipe away a tear*].

NAPOLEON. I see you dont know me, madam, or you would
save yourself the trouble of pretending to cry.

LADY [*producing an effect of smiling through her tears*] Yes, I do
know you. You are the famous General Buonaparte. [*She
gives the name a marked Italian pronunciation; Bwawna-parr-te*].

NAPOLEON [*angrily, with the French pronunciation*] Bonaparte,
madam, Bonaparte. The papers, if you please.

LADY. But I assure you – [*He snatches the handkerchief rudely*].
General! [*indignantly*].

NAPOLEON [*taking the other handkerchief from his breast*] You
lent one of your handkerchiefs to my lieutenant when you
robbed him. [*He looks at the two handkerchiefs*]. They match
one another. [*He smells them*]. The same scent. [*He flings
them down on the table*]. I am waiting for my despatches. I
shall take them, if necessary, with as little ceremony as I
took the handkerchief.

LADY [*in dignified reproof*] General: do you threaten women?

NAPOLEON [*bluntly*] Yes.

LADY [*disconcerted, trying to gain time*] But I dont understand.
I –

NAPOLEON. You understand perfectly. You came here
because your Austrian employers calculated that I was six
leagues away. I am always to be found where my enemies
dont expect me. You have walked into the lion's den.

THE MAN OF DESTINY

Come! you are a brave woman. Be a sensible one: I have
no time to waste. The papers. [*He advances a step ominously*].

LADY [*breaking down in the childish rage of impotence, and throwing
herself in tears on the chair left beside the table by the lieutenant*] *I*
brave! How little you know! I have spent the day in an
agony of fear. I have a pain here from the tightening of
my heart at every suspicious look, every threatening movement. Do you think everyone is as brave as you? Oh, why
will not you brave people do the brave things? Why do you
leave them to us, who have no courage at all? I'm not
brave: I shrink from violence: danger makes me miserable.

NAPOLEON [*interested*] Then why have you thrust yourself
into danger?

LADY. Because there is no other way: I can trust nobody
else. And now it is all useless: all because of you, who have
no fear because you have no heart, no feeling, no – [*She
breaks off, and throws herself on her knees*]. Ah, General, let me
go: let me go without asking any questions. You shall
have your despatches and letters: I swear it.

NAPOLEON [*holding out his hand*] Yes: I am waiting for them.
*She gasps, daunted by his ruthless promptitude into despair of
moving him by cajolery. She looks up perplexedly at him, racking
her brains for some device to outwit him. He meets her regard
inflexibly.*

LADY [*rising at last with a quiet little sigh*] I will get them for
you. They are in my room. [*She turns to the door*].

NAPOLEON. I shall accompany you, madam.

LADY [*drawing herself up with a noble air of offended delicacy*] I
cannot permit you, General, to enter my chamber.

NAPOLEON. Then you shall stay here, madam, whilst I have
your chamber searched for my papers.

LADY [*spitefully, openly giving up her plan*] You may save yourself the trouble. They are not there.

NAPOLEON. No: I have already told you where they are
[*pointing to her breast*].

LADY [*with pretty piteousness*] General: I only want to keep
one little private letter. Only one. Let me have it.

NAPOLEON [*cold and stern*] Is that a reasonable demand, madam?

LADY [*encouraged by his not refusing point-blank*] No: but that is why you must grant it. Are your own demands reasonable? thousands of lives for the sake of your victories, your ambitions, your destiny! And what I ask is such a little thing. And I am only a weak woman, and you a brave man. [*She looks at him with her eyes full of tender pleading, and is about to kneel to him again*].

NAPOLEON [*brusquely*] Get up, get up. [*He turns moodily away and takes a turn across the room, pausing for a moment to say, over his shoulder*] Youre talking nonsense; and you know it. [*She sits down submissively on the couch. When he turns and sees her despair, he feels that his victory is complete, and that he may now indulge in a little play with his victim. He comes back and sits beside her. She looks alarmed and moves a little away from him; but a ray of rallying hope beams from her eye. He begins like a man enjoying some secret joke*]. How do you know I am a brave man?

LADY [*amazed*] You! General Buonaparte [*Italian pronunciation*].

NAPOLEON. Yes, I, General Bonaparte [*emphasizing the French pronunciation*].

LADY. Oh, how can you ask such a question? you! who stood only two days ago at the bridge at Lodi, with the air full of death, fighting a duel with cannons across the river! [*Shuddering*]. Oh, you do brave things.

NAPOLEON. So do you.

LADY. I! [*With a sudden odd thought*] Oh! Are you a coward?

NAPOLEON [*laughing grimly and slapping his knees*] That is the one question you must never ask a soldier. The sergeant asks after the recruit's height, his age, his wind, his limb, but never after his courage.

LADY [*as if she had found it no laughing matter*] Ah, you can laugh at fear. Then you dont know what fear is.

NAPOLEON. Tell me this. Suppose you could have got that letter by coming to me over the bridge at Lodi the day before yesterday! Suppose there had been no other way, and that this was a sure way – if only you escaped the cannon! [*She shudders and covers her eyes for a moment with her hands*]. Would you have been afraid?

LADY. Oh, horribly afraid, agonizingly afraid. [*She presses her hand on her heart*]. It hurts only to imagine it.

NAPOLEON [*inflexibly*] Would you have come for the despatches?

LADY [*overcome by the imagined horror*] Dont ask me. I must have come.

NAPOLEON. Why?

LADY. Because I must. Because there would have been no other way.

NAPOLEON [*with conviction*] Because you would have wanted my letter enough to bear your fear. [*He rises suddenly, and deliberately poses for an oration*]. There is only one universal passion: fear. Of all the thousand qualities a man may have, the only one you will find as certainly in the youngest drummer boy in my army as in me, is fear. It is fear that makes men fight: it is indifference that makes them run away: fear is the mainspring of war. Fear! I know fear well, better than you, better than any woman. I once saw a regiment of good Swiss soldiers massacred by a mob in Paris because I was afraid to interfere: I felt myself a coward to the tips of my toes as I looked on at it. Seven months ago I revenged my shame by pounding that mob to death with cannon balls. Well, what of that? Has fear ever held a man back from anything he really wanted – or a woman either? Never. Come with me; and I will shew you twenty thousand cowards who will risk death every day for the price of a glass of brandy. And do you think there are no women in the army, braver than the men, though their lives are worth more? Psha! I think nothing of your fear or your bravery. If you had had to come across to me at Lodi, you would not have been afraid: once on the bridge, every other feeling would have gone down before the necessity – the n e c e s s i t y – for making your way to my side and getting what you wanted.

And now, suppose you had done all this! suppose you had come safely out with that letter in your hand, knowing that when the hour came, your fear had tightened, not your heart, but your grip of your own purpose! that it had ceased to be fear, and had become strength, penetration, vigilance, iron resolution! how would you answer then if you were asked whether you were a coward?

LADY [*rising*] Ah, you are a hero, a real hero.

NAPOLEON. Pooh! theres no such thing as a real hero. [*He strolls about the room, making light of her enthusiasm, but by no means displeased with himself for having evoked it*].

LADY. Ah yes, there is. There is a difference between what you call my bravery and yours. You wanted to win the battle of Lodi for yourself and not for anyone else, didnt you?

NAPOLEON. Of course. [*Suddenly recollecting himself*] Stop: no. [*He pulls himself piously together, and says, like a man conducting a religious service*] I am only the servant of the French republic, following humbly in the footsteps of the heroes of classical antiquity. I win battles for humanity: for my country, not for myself.

LADY [*disappointed*] Oh, then you are only a womanish hero after all. [*She sits down again, all her enthusiasm gone*].

NAPOLEON [*greatly astonished*] Womanish!

LADY [*listlessly*] Yes, like me. [*With deep melancholy*] Do you think that if I wanted those despatches only for myself, I dare venture into a battle for them? No: if that were all, I should not have the courage to ask to see you at your hotel, even. My courage is mere slavishness: it is of no use to me for my own purposes. It is only through love, through pity, through the instinct to save and protect someone else, that I can do the things that terrify me.

NAPOLEON [*contemptuously*] Pshaw [*He turns slightingly away from her*].

LADY. Aha! now you see that I'm not really brave. [*Relapsing into petulant listlessness*] But what right have you to despise me if you only win your battles for others? for your

country! through patriotism! That is what I call womanish: it is so like a Frenchman!

NAPOLEON [*furiously*] I am no Frenchman.

LADY [*innocently*] I thought you said you won the battle of
Lodi for your country, General Bu – shall I pronounce it
in Italian or French?

NAPOLEON. You are presuming on my patience, madam. I
was born a French subject, but not in France.

LADY [*affecting a marked access of interest in him*] You were not
born a subject at all, I think.

NAPOLEON [*greatly pleased*] Eh? Eh? You think not.

LADY. I am sure of it.

NAPOLEON. Well, well, perhaps not. [*The self-complacency of
his assent catches his own ear. He stops short, reddening. Then,
composing himself into a solemn attitude, modelled on the heroes of
classical antiquity, he takes a high moral tone*]. But we must not
live for ourselves alone, little one. Never forget that we
should always think of others, and work for others, and
lead and govern them for their own good. Self-sacrifice is
the foundation of all true nobility of character.

LADY [*again relaxing her attitude with a sigh*] Ah, it is easy to
see that you have never tried it, General.

NAPOLEON [*indignantly, forgetting all about Brutus and Scipio*]
What do you mean by that speech, madam?

LADY. Havnt you noticed that people always exaggerate the
value of the things they havnt got? The poor think they
need nothing but riches to be quite happy and good.
Everybody worships truth, purity, unselfishness, for the
same reason: because they have no experience of them.
Oh, if they only knew!

NAPOLEON [*with angry derision*] If they only knew! Pray do
you know?

LADY. Yes. I had the misfortune to be born good. [*Glancing
up at him for a moment*] And it is a misfortune, I can tell you,
General. I really am truthful and unselfish and all the rest
of it; and it's nothing but cowardice; want of character;
want of being really, strongly, positively oneself.

NAPOLEON. Ha? [*turning to her quickly with a flash of strong interest*].

LADY [*earnestly, with rising enthusiasm*] What is the secret of your power? Only that you believe in yourself. You can fight and conquer for yourself and for nobody else. You are not afraid of your own destiny. You teach us what we all might be if we had the will and courage; and that [*suddenly sinking on her knees before him*] is why we all begin to worship you. [*She kisses his hands*].

NAPOLEON [*embarrassed*] Tut! tut! Pray rise, madam.

LADY. Do not refuse my homage: it is your right. You will be Emperor of France —

NAPOLEON [*hurriedly*] Take care. Treason!

LADY [*insisting*] Yes, Emperor of France; then of Europe; perhaps of the world. I am only the first subject to swear allegiance. [*Again kissing his hand*] My Emperor!

NAPOLEON [*overcome, raising her*] Pray! pray! No, no: this is folly. Come: be calm, be calm. [*Petting her*] There! there! my girl.

LADY [*struggling with happy tears*] Yes, I know it is an impertinence in me to tell you what you must know far better than I do. But you are not angry with me, are you?

NAPOLEON. Angry! No, no: not a bit, not a bit. Come: you are a very clever and sensible and interesting woman. [*He pats her on the cheek*] Shall we be friends?

LADY [*enraptured*] Your friend! You will let me be your friend! Oh! [*She offers him both her hands with a radiant smile*]. You see: I shew my confidence in you.

This incautious echo of the lieutenant undoes her. Napoleon starts: his eyes flash: he utters a yell of rage.

NAPOLEON. What!!!

LADY. Whats the matter?

NAPOLEON. Shew your confidence in me! So that I may shew my confidence in you in return by letting you give me the slip with the despatches, eh? Ah, Dalila, Dalila, you have been trying your tricks on me; and I have been as gross a gull as my jackass of a lieutenant. [*Menacingly*]

Come: the despatches. Quick: I am not to be trifled with now.

LADY [*flying round the couch*] General –

NAPOLEON. Quick, I tell you. [*He passes swiftly up the middle of the room and intercepts her as she makes for the vineyard*].

LADY [*at bay, confronting him and giving way to her temper*] You dare address me in that tone.

NAPOLEON. Dare!

LADY. Yes dare. Who are you that you should presume to speak of me in that coarse way. Oh, the vile, vulgar Corsican adventurer comes out in you very easily.

NAPOLEON [*beside himself*] You she devil! [*Savagely*] Once more, and only once, will you give me those papers or shall I tear them from you? – by force!

LADY. Tear them from me: by force!

As he glares at her like a tiger about to spring, she crosses her arms on her breast in the attitude of a martyr. The gesture and pose instantly awaken his theatrical instinct: he forgets his rage in the desire to shew her that in acting, too, she has met her match. He keeps her a moment in suspense; then suddenly clears up his countenance; puts his hands behind him with provoking coolness; looks at her up and down a couple of times; takes a pinch of snuff; wipes his fingers carefully and puts up his handkerchief, her heroic pose becoming more and more ridiculous all the time.

NAPOLEON [*at last*] Well?

LADY [*disconcerted, but with her arms still crossed devotedly*] Well: what are you going to do?

NAPOLEON. Spoil your attitude.

LADY. You brute! [*Abandoning the attitude, she comes to the end of the couch, where she turns with her back to it, leaning against it and facing him with her hands behind her*].

NAPOLEON. Ah, thats better. Now listen to me. I like you. Whats more, I value your respect.

LADY. You value what you have not got, then.

NAPOLEON. I shall have it presently. Now attend to me. Suppose I were to allow myself to be abashed by the respect due to your sex, your beauty, your heroism and all the rest of it! Suppose I, with nothing but such sentimental stuff to stand between these muscles of mine and those papers which you have about you, and which I want and mean to have! suppose I, with the prize within my grasp, were to falter and sneak away with my hands empty; or, what would be worse, cover up my weakness by playing the magnanimous hero, and sparing you the violence I dared not use! would you not despise me from the depths of your woman's soul? Would any woman be such a fool? Well, Bonaparte can rise to the situation and act like a woman when it is necessary. Do you understand?

The lady, without speaking, stands upright, and takes a packet of papers from her bosom. For a moment she has an intense impulse to dash them in his face. But her good breeding cuts her off from any vulgar method of relief. She hands them to him politely, only averting her head. The moment he takes them, she hurries across to the other side of the room; sits down; and covers her face with her hands.

NAPOLEON [*gloating over the papers*] Aha! Thats right. Thats right. [*Before he opens them, he looks at her and says*] Excuse me. [*He sees that she is hiding her face*]. Very angry with me, eh? [*He unties the packet, the seal of which is already broken, and puts it on the table to examine its contents*].

LADY [*quietly, taking down her hands and shewing that she is not crying, but only thinking*] No. You were right. But I am sorry for you.

NAPOLEON [*pausing in the act of taking the uppermost paper from the packet*] Sorry for me! Why?

LADY. I am going to see you lose your honor.

NAPOLEON. Hm! Nothing worse than that? [*He takes up the paper*].

LADY. And your happiness.

NAPOLEON. Happiness! Happiness is the most tedious thing in the world to me. Should I be what I am if I cared for happiness? Anything else?

LADY. Nothing.

NAPOLEON. Good.

LADY. Except that you will cut a very foolish figure in the eyes of France.

NAPOLEON [*quickly*] What? [*The hand unfolding the paper involuntarily stops. The lady looks at him enigmatically in tranquil silence. He throws the letter down and breaks out into a torrent of scolding*]. What do you mean? Eh? Are you at your tricks again? Do you think I dont know what these papers contain? I'll tell you. First, my information as to Beaulieu's retreat. There are only two things he can do – leather-brained idiot that he is! – shut himself up in Mantua or violate the neutrality of Venice by taking Peschiera. You are one of the old Leather-brain's spies: he has discovered that he has been betrayed, and has sent you to intercept the information at all hazards. As if that could save him from me, the old fool! The other papers are only my private letters from Paris, of which you know nothing.

LADY [*prompt and businesslike*] General: let us make a fair division. Take the information your spies have sent you about the Austrian army; and give me the Paris correspondence. That will content me.

NAPOLEON [*his breath taken away by the coolness of the proposal*] A fair di – [*he gasps*]. It seems to me, madam, that you come to regard my letters as your own property, of which I am trying to rob you.

LADY [*earnestly*] No: on my honor I ask for no letter of yours: not a word that has been written by you or to you. That packet contains a stolen letter: a letter written by a woman to a man: a man not her husband: a letter that means disgrace, infamy –

NAPOLEON. A love letter?

LADY [*bitter-sweetly*] What else but a love letter could stir up so much hate?

NAPOLEON. Why is it sent to me? To put the husband in my power, eh?

LADY. No, no: it can be of no use to you: I swear that it will cost you nothing to give it to me. It has been sent to you out of sheer malice: solely to injure the woman who wrote it.

NAPOLEON. Then why not send it to her husband instead of to me?

LADY [*completely taken aback*] Oh! [*Sinking back into the chair*] I – I dont know. [*She breaks down*].

NAPOLEON. Aha! I thought so: a little romance to get the papers back. Per Bacco, I cant help admiring you. I wish I could lie like that. It would save me a great deal of trouble.

LADY [*wringing her hands*] Oh, how *I* wish I really had told you some lie! You would have believed me then. The truth is the one thing nobody will believe.

NAPOLEON [*with coarse familiarity, treating her as if she were a vivandière*] Capital! Capital! [*He puts his hands behind him on the table, and lifts himself on to it, sitting with his arms akimbo and his legs wide apart*] Come: I am a true Corsican in my love for stories. But I could tell them better than you if I set my mind to it. Next time you are asked why a letter compromising a wife should not be sent to her husband, answer simply that the husband wouldnt read it. Do you suppose, you goose, that a man wants to be compelled by public opinion to make a scene, to fight a duel, to break up his household, to injure his career by a scandal, when he can avoid it all by taking care not to know?

LADY [*revolted*] Suppose that packet contained a letter about your own wife?

NAPOLEON [*offended, coming off the table*] You are impertinent, madam.

LADY [*humbly*] I beg your pardon. Cæsar's wife is above suspicion.

NAPOLEON [*with a deliberate assumption of superiority*] You have committed an indiscretion. I pardon you. In future, do not permit yourself to introduce real persons in your romances.

LADY [*politely ignoring a speech which is to her only a breach of good manners*] General: there really is a woman's letter there. [*Pointing to the packet*] Give it to me.

NAPOLEON [*with brute conciseness*] Why?

LADY. She is an old friend: we were at school together. She

has written to me imploring me to prevent the letter falling into your hands.

NAPOLEON. Why has it been sent to me?

LADY. Because it compromises the director Barras.

NAPOLEON [*frowning, and evidently startled*] Barras! [*Haughtily*] Take care, madam. The director Barras is my attached personal friend.

LADY [*nodding placidly*] Yes. You became friends through your wife.

NAPOLEON. Again! Have I not forbidden you to speak of my wife? [*She keeps looking curiously at him, taking no account of the rebuke. More and more irritated, he drops his haughty manner, of which he is himself somewhat impatient, and says suspiciously, lowering his voice*] Who is this woman with whom you sympathize so deeply?

LADY. Oh, General! How could I tell you that?

NAPOLEON [*ill humoredly, beginning to walk about again in angry perplexity*] Ay, ay: stand by one another. You are all the same, you women.

LADY [*indignantly*] We are not all the same, any more than you are. Do you think that if *I* loved another man, I should pretend to go on loving my husband, or be afraid to tell him or all the world? But this woman is not made that way. She governs men by cheating them; and they like it, and let her govern them. [*She turns her back to him in disdain*].

NAPOLEON [*not attending to her*] Barras? Barras? [*Very threateningly, his face darkening*] Take care. Take care: do you hear? You may go too far.

LADY [*innocently turning her face to him*] Whats the matter?

NAPOLEON. What are you hinting at? Who is this woman?

LADY [*meeting his angry searching gaze with tranquil indifference as she sits looking up at him*] A vain, silly, extravagant creature, with a very able and ambitious husband who knows her through and through: knows that she has lied to him about her age, her income, her social position, about everything that silly women lie about: knows that she is incapable of fidelity to any principle or any person; and yet cannot help loving her – cannot help his man's instinct to make use of her for his own advancement with Barras.

NAPOLEON [*in a stealthy coldly furious whisper*] This is your revenge, you she cat, for having had to give me the letters.

LADY. Nonsense! Or do you mean that you are that sort of man?

NAPOLEON [*exasperated, clasps his hands behind him, his fingers twitching, and says, as he walks irritably away from her to the fireplace*] This woman will drive me out of my senses. [*To her*] Begone.

LADY [*seated immovably*] Not without that letter.

NAPOLEON. Begone, I tell you. [*Walking from the fireplace to the vineyard and back to the table*] You shall have no letter. I dont like you. Youre a detestable woman, and as ugly as Satan. I dont choose to be pestered by strange women. Be off. [*He turns his back on her. In quiet amusement, she leans her cheek on her hand and laughs at him. He turns again, angrily mocking her*]. Ha! ha! ha! What are you laughing at?

LADY. At you, General. I have often seen persons of your sex getting into a pet and behaving like children; but I never saw a really great man do it before.

NAPOLEON [*brutally, flinging the words in her face*] Psha! Flattery! Flattery! Coarse, impudent flattery!

LADY [*springing up with a bright flush in her cheeks*] Oh, you are too bad. Keep your letters. Read the story of your own dishonor in them; and much good may they do. Goodbye. [*She goes indignantly towards the inner door*].

NAPOLEON. My own – ! Stop. Come back. Come back, I order you. [*She proudly disregards his savagely peremptory tone and continues on her way to the door. He rushes at her; seizes her by the arm; and drags her back*]. Now, what do you mean? Explain. Explain. I tell you, or – [*threatening her. She looks at him with unflinching defiance*]. Rrrr! you obstinate devil, you. [*Throwing her arm away*] Why cant you answer a civil question?

LADY [*deeply offended by his violence*] Why do you ask me? You have the explanation.

NAPOLEON. Where?

LADY [*pointing to the letters on the table*] There. You have only
to read it.

*He snatches the packet up; hesitates; looks at her suspiciously;
and throws it down again.*

NAPOLEON. You seem to have forgotten your solicitude for
the honor of your old friend.

LADY. I do not think she runs any risk now. She does not
quite understand her husband.

NAPOLEON. I am to read the letter then? [*He stretches out
his hand as if to take up the packet again, with his eye on
her*].

LADY. I do not see how you can very well avoid doing so
now. [*He instantly withdraws his hand*]. Oh, dont be afraid.
You will find many interesting things in it.

NAPOLEON. For instance?

LADY. For instance, a duel with Barras, a domestic scene, a
broken household, a public scandal, a checked career, all
sorts of things.

NAPOLEON. Hm! [*He looks at her; takes up the packet and looks
at it, pursing his lips and balancing it in his hand; looks at her
again; passes the packet into his left hand and puts it behind his
back, raising his right to scratch the back of his head as he turns
and goes up to the edge of the vineyard, where he stands for a
moment looking out into the vines, deep in thought. The lady
watches him in silence, somewhat slightingly. Suddenly he turns
and comes back again, full of force and decision*]. I grant your
request, madam. Your courage and resolution deserved
to succeed. Take the letters for which you have fought so
well; and remember henceforth that you found the vile
vulgar Corsican adventurer as generous to the vanquished
after the battle as he was resolute in the face of the enemy
before it. [*He offers her the packet*].

LADY [*without taking it, looking hard at him*] What are you at
now, I wonder? [*He dashes the packet furiously to the floor*].
Aha! Ive spoilt that attitude, I think. [*She makes him a
pretty mocking curtsey*].

NAPOLEON [*snatching it up again*] Will you take the letters and be gone [*advancing and thrusting them upon her*]?

LADY [*escaping round the table*] No: I dont want your letters.

NAPOLEON. Ten minutes ago, nothing else would satisfy you.

LADY [*keeping the table carefully between them*] Ten minutes ago you had not insulted me beyond all bearing.

NAPOLEON. I – [*swallowing his spleen*] I apologize.

LADY [*coolly*] Thanks. [*With forced politeness he offers her the packet across the table. She retreats a step out of its reach and says*] But dont you want to know whether the Austrians are at Mantua or Peschiera?

NAPOLEON. I have already told you that I can conquer my enemies without the aid of spies, madam.

LADY. And the letter? dont you want to read that?

NAPOLEON. You have said that it is not addressed to me. I am not in the habit of reading other people's letters. [*He again offers the packet*].

LADY. In that case there can be no objection to your keeping it. All I wanted was to prevent your reading it. [*Cheerfully*] Good afternoon, General. [*She turns coolly towards the inner door*].

NAPOLEON [*angrily flinging the packet on the couch*] Heaven grant me patience! [*He goes determinedly to the door, and places himself before it*]. Have you any sense of personal danger? Or are you one of those women who like to be beaten black and blue?

LADY. Thank you, General: I have no doubt the sensation is very voluptuous; but I had rather not. I simply want to go home: thats all. I was wicked enough to steal your despatches; but you have got them back; and you have forgiven me, because [*delicately reproducing his rhetorical cadence*] you are as generous to the vanquished after the battle as you are resolute in the face of the enemy before it. Wont you say goodbye to me? [*She offers her hand sweetly*].

NAPOLEON [*repulsing the advance with a gesture of concentrated rage, and opening the door to call fiercely*] Giuseppe! [*Louder*]

Giuseppe! [*He bangs the door to, and comes to the middle of the room. The lady goes a little way into the vineyard to avoid him*].

GIUSEPPE [*appearing at the door*] Excellency?

NAPOLEON. Where is that fool?

GIUSEPPE. He has had a good dinner, according to your instructions, excellency, and is now doing me the honor to gamble with me to pass the time.

NAPOLEON. Send him here. Bring him here. Come with him. [*Giuseppe, with unruffled readiness, hurries off. Napoleon turns curtly to the lady, saying*] I must trouble you to remain some moments longer, madam. [*He comes to the couch*].

She comes from the vineyard along the opposite side of the room to the sideboard, and posts herself there, leaning against it, watching him. He takes the packet from the couch and deliberately buttons it carefully into his breast pocket, looking at her meanwhile with an expression which suggests that she will soon find out the meaning of his proceedings, and will not like it. Nothing more is said until the Lieutenant arrives followed by Giuseppe, who stands modestly in attendance at the table. The Lieutenant, without cap, sword or gloves, and much improved in temper and spirit by his meal, chooses the lady's side of the room, and waits, much at his ease, for Napoleon to begin.

NAPOLEON. Lieutenant.

LIEUTENANT [*encouragingly*] General.

NAPOLEON. I cannot persuade this lady to give me much information; but there can be no doubt that the man who tricked you out of your charge was, as she admitted to you, her brother.

LIEUTENANT [*triumphantly*] What did I tell you, General! What did I tell you!

NAPOLEON. You must find that man. Your honor is at stake; and the fate of the campaign, the destiny of France, of Europe, of humanity, perhaps, may depend on the information those despatches contain.

LIEUTENANT. Yes, I suppose they really are rather serious [*as if this hardly occurred to him before*].

NAPOLEON [*energetically*] They are so serious, sir, that if you do not recover them, you will be degraded in the presence of your regiment.

LIEUTENANT. Whew! The regiment wont like that, I can tell you.

NAPOLEON. Personally I am sorry for you. I would willingly hush up the affair if it were possible. But I shall be called to account for not acting on the despatches. I shall have to prove to all the world that I never received them, no matter what the consequences may be to you. I am sorry; but you see that I cannot help myself.

LIEUTENANT [*goodnaturedly*] Oh, dont take it to heart, General: it's really very good of you. Never mind what happens to me: I shall scrape through somehow; and we'll beat the Austrians for you, despatches or no despatches. I hope you wont insist on my starting off on a wild goose chase after the fellow now. I havent a notion where to look for him.

GIUSEPPE [*deferentially*] You forget, Lieutenant: he has your horse.

LIEUTENANT [*starting*] I forgot that. [*Resolutely*] I'll go after him, General: I'll find that horse if it's alive anywhere in Italy. And I shant forget the despatches: never fear. Giuseppe: go and saddle one of those mangy old post-horses of yours while I get my cap and sword and things. Quick march. Off with you [*bustling him*].

GIUSEPPE. Instantly, Lieutenant, instantly. [*He disappears in the vineyard, where the light is now reddening with the sunset*].

LIEUTENANT [*looking about him on his way to the inner door*] By the way, General, did I give you my sword or did I not? Oh, I remember now. [*Fretfully*] It's all that nonsense about putting a man under arrest: one never knows where to find – [*he talks himself out of the room*].

LADY [*still at the sideboard*] What does all this mean, General?

NAPOLEON. He will not find your brother.

LADY. Of course not. Theres no such person.

NAPOLEON. The despatches will be irrecoverably lost.

LADY. Nonsense! They are inside your coat.

NAPOLEON. You will find it hard, I think, to prove that wild statement. [*The lady starts. He adds, with clinching emphasis*] Those papers are lost.

LADY [*anxiously, advancing to the corner of the table*] And that unfortunate young man's career will be sacrificed?

NAPOLEON. His career! The fellow is not worth the gunpowder it would cost to have him shot. [*He turns contemptuously and goes to the hearth, where he stands with his back to her*].

LADY [*wistfully*] You are very hard. Men and women are nothing to you but things to be used, even if they are broken in the use.

NAPOLEON [*turning on her*] Which of us has broken this fellow? I or you? Who tricked him out of the despatches? Did you think of his career then?

LADY [*conscience-stricken*] Oh, I never thought of that. It was wicked of me; but I couldnt help it, could I? How else could I have got the papers? [*Supplicating*] General: you will save him from disgrace.

NAPOLEON [*laughing sourly*] Save him yourself, since you are so clever: it was you who ruined him. [*With savage intensity*] I hate a bad soldier.

He goes out determinedly through the vineyard. She follows him a few steps with an appealing gesture, but is interrupted by the return of the Lieutenant, gloved and capped, with his sword on, ready for the road. He is crossing to the outer door when she intercepts him.

LADY. Lieutenant.

LIEUTENANT [*importantly*] You musnt delay me, you know. Duty, madam, duty.

LADY [*imploringly*] Oh, sir, what are you going to do to my poor brother?

LIEUTENANT. Are you very fond of him?

LADY. I should die if anything happened to him. You must spare him. [*The Lieutenant shakes his head gloomily*]. Yes, yes: you must: you shall: he is not fit to die. Listen to me. If I tell you where to find him – if I undertake to place him in your hands a prisoner, to be delivered up by you to General

Bonaparte – will you promise me on your honor as an officer and a gentleman not to fight with him or treat him unkindly in any way?

LIEUTENANT. But suppose he attacks me. He has my pistols.

LADY. He is too great a coward.

LIEUTENANT. I dont feel so sure about that. He's capable of anything.

LADY. If he attacks you, or resists you in any way, I release you from your promise.

LIEUTENANT. My promise! I didnt mean to promise. Look here: youre as bad as he is: youve taken an advantage of me through the better side of my nature. What about my horse?

LADY. It is part of the bargain that you are to have your horse and pistols back.

LIEUTENANT. Honor bright?

LADY. Honor bright. [*She offers her hand*].

LIEUTENANT [*taking it and holding it*] All right: I'll be as gentle as a lamb with him. His sister's a very pretty woman. [*He attempts to kiss her*].

LADY [*slipping away from him*] Oh, Lieutenant! You forget: your career is at stake – the destiny of Europe – of humanity.

LIEUTENANT. Oh, bother the destiny of humanity! [*Making for her*] Only a kiss.

LADY [*retreating round the table*] Not until you have regained your honor as an officer. Remember: you have not captured my brother yet.

LIEUTENANT [*seductively*] Youll tell me where he is, wont you?

LADY. I have only to send him a certain signal; and he will be here in quarter of an hour.

LIEUTENANT. He's not far off, then.

LADY. No: quite close. Wait here for him: when he gets my message he will come here at once and surrender himself to you. You understand?

LIEUTENANT [*intellectually overtaxed*] Well, it's a little complicated; but I daresay it will be all right.

LADY. And now, whilst youre waiting, dont you think you had better make terms with the General?

LIEUTENANT. Oh, look here: this is getting frightfully complicated. What terms?

LADY. Make him promise that if you catch my brother he will consider that you have cleared your character as a soldier. He will promise anything you ask on that condition.

LIEUTENANT. Thats not a bad idea. Thank you: I think I'll try it.

LADY. Do. And mind, above all things, dont let him see how clever you are.

LIEUTENANT. I understand. He'd be jealous.

LADY. Dont tell him anything except that you are resolved to capture my brother or perish in the attempt. He wont believe you. Then you will produce my brother –

LIEUTENANT [*interrupting as he masters the plot*] And have the laugh at him! I say: what a jolly clever woman you are! [*Shouting*] Giuseppe!

LADY. Sh! Not a word to Giuseppe about me. [*She puts her finger on her lips. He does the same. They look at one another warningly. Then, with a ravishing smile, she changes the gesture into wafting him a kiss, and runs out through the inner door. Electrified, he bursts into a volley of chuckles*].

Giuseppe comes back by the outer door.

GIUSEPPE. The horse is ready, Lieutenant.

LIEUTENANT. I'm not going just yet. Go and find the General and tell him I want to speak to him.

GIUSEPPE [*shaking his head*] That will never do, Lieutenant.

LIEUTENANT. Why not?

GIUSEPPE. In this wicked world a general may send for a lieutenant; but a lieutenant must not send for a general.

LIEUTENANT. Oh, you think he wouldnt like it. Well, perhaps youre right: one has to be awfully particular about that sort of thing now we're a republic.

Napoleon reappears, advancing from the vineyard, buttoning the breast of his coat, pale and full of gnawing thoughts.

GIUSEPPE [*unconscious of Napoleon's approach*] Quite true,

Lieutenant, quite true. You are all like innkeepers now in France: you have to be polite to everybody.

NAPOLEON [*putting his hand on Giuseppe's shoulder*] And that destroys the whole value of politeness, eh?

LIEUTENANT. The very man I wanted! See here, General; suppose I catch that fellow for you!

NAPOLEON [*with ironical gravity*] You will not catch him, my friend.

LIEUTENANT. Aha! you think so; but youll see. Just wait. Only, if I do catch him and hand him over to you, will you cry quits? Will you drop all this about degrading me in the presence of my regiment? Not that *I* mind, you know; but still no regiment likes to have all the other regiments laughing at it.

NAPOLEON [*a cold ray of humor striking pallidly across his gloom*] What shall we do with this officer, Giuseppe? Everything he says is wrong.

GIUSEPPE [*promptly*] Make him a general, excellency; and then everything he says will be right.

LIEUTENANT [*crowing*] Haw-aw! [*He throws himself ecstatically on the couch to enjoy the joke*].

NAPOLEON [*laughing and pinching Giuseppe's ear*] You are thrown away in this inn, Giuseppe. [*He sits down and places Giuseppe before him like a schoolmaster with a pupil*]. Shall I take you away with me and make a man of you?

GIUSEPPE [*shaking his head rapidly and repeatedly*] No no no no no no no. All my life long people have wanted to make a man of me. When I was a boy, our good priest wanted to make a man of me by teaching me to read and write. Then the organist at Melegnano wanted to make a man of me by teaching me to read music. The recruiting sergeant would have made a man of me if I had been a few inches taller. But it always meant making me work; and I am too lazy for that, thank Heaven! So I taught myself to cook and became an innkeeper; and now I keep servants to do the work, and have nothing to do myself except talk, which suits me perfectly.

NAPOLEON [*looking at him thoughtfully*] You are satisfied?

GIUSEPPE [*with cheerful conviction*] Quite, excellency.

NAPOLEON. And you have no devouring devil inside you who must be fed with action and victory: gorged with them night and day: who makes you pay, with the sweat of your brain and body, weeks of Herculean toil for ten minutes of enjoyment: who is at once your slave and your tyrant, your genius and your doom: who brings you a crown in one hand and the oar of a galley slave in the other: who shews you all the kingdoms of the earth and offers to make you their master on condition that you become their servant! have you nothing of that in you?

GIUSEPPE. Nothing of it! Oh, I assure you, excellency, my devouring devil is far worse than that. He offers me no crowns and kingdoms: he expects to get everything for nothing: sausages! omelettes! grapes! cheese! polenta! wine! three times a day, excellency: nothing less will content him.

LIEUTENANT. Come: drop it, Giuseppe: youre making me feel hungry again.

Giuseppe, with an apologetic shrug, retires from the conversation.

NAPOLEON [*turning to the Lieutenant with sardonic politeness*] I hope *I* have not been making you feel ambitious.

LIEUTENANT. Not at all: I dont fly so high. Besides, I'm better as I am: men like me are wanted in the army just now. The fact is, the Revolution was all very well for civilians; but it wont work in the army. You know what soldiers are, General: they will have men of family for their officers. A subaltern must be a gentleman, because he's so much in contact with the men. But a general, or even a colonel, may be any sort of riff-raff if he understands his job well enough. A lieutenant is a gentleman: all the rest is chance. Why, who do you suppose won the battle of Lodi? I'll tell you. My horse did.

NAPOLEON [*rising*] Your folly is carrying you too far, sir. Take care.

LIEUTENANT. Not a bit of it. You remember all that red-hot cannonade across the river: the Austrians blazing away

at you to keep you from crossing, and you blazing away at
them to keep them from setting the bridge on fire? Did
you notice where I was then?

NAPOLEON. I am sorry. I am afraid I was rather occupied
at the moment.

GIUSEPPE [*with eager admiration*] They say you jumped off
your horse and worked the big guns with your own hands,
General.

LIEUTENANT. That was a mistake: an officer should never
let himself down to the level of his men. [*Napoleon looks at
him dangerously, and begins to walk tigerishly to and fro*]. But
you might have been firing away at the Austrians still if
we cavalry fellows hadnt found the ford and got across and
turned old Beaulieu's flank for you. You know you didnt
dare give the order to charge the bridge until you saw us
on the other side. Consequently, I say that whoever found
that ford won the battle of Lodi. Well, who found it? I
was the first man to cross; and I know. It was my horse
that found it. [*With conviction, as he rises from the couch*] That
horse is the true conqueror of the Austrians.

NAPOLEON [*passionately*] You idiot: I'll have you shot for
losing those despatches: I'll have you blown from the
mouth of a cannon: nothing less could make any impression
on you. [*Baying at him*] Do you hear? Do you understand?

*A French officer enters unobserved, carrying his sheathed sabre
in his hand.*

LIEUTENANT [*unabashed*] If I dont capture him, General.
Remember the if.

NAPOLEON. If!! Ass: there is no such man.

THE OFFICER [*suddenly stepping between them and speaking in
the unmistakable voice of the Strange Lady*] Lieutenant: I am
your prisoner. [*She offers him her sabre*].

*Napoleon gazes at her for a moment thunderstruck; then seizes
her by the wrist and drags her roughly to him, looking closely and
fiercely at her to satisfy himself as to her identity: for it now begins
to darken rapidly into night, the red glow over the vineyard giving
way to clear starlight.*

NAPOLEON. Pah! [*He flings her hand away with an exclamation of disgust, and turns his back on them with his hand in his breast, his brow lowering, and his toes twitching*].

LIEUTENANT [*triumphantly, taking the sabre*] No such man! eh, General? [*To the Lady*] I say: wheres my horse?

LADY. Safe at Borghetto, waiting for you, Lieutenant.

NAPOLEON [*turning on them*] Where are the despatches?

LADY. You would never guess. They are in the most unlikely place in the world. Did you meet my sister here, any of you?

LIEUTENANT. Yes. Very nice woman. She's wonderfully like you; but of course she's better-looking.

LADY [*mysteriously*] Well, do you know that she is a witch?

GIUSEPPE [*in terror, crossing himself*] Oh, no, no, no. It is not safe to jest about such things. I cannot have it in my house, excellency.

LIEUTENANT. Yes, drop it. Youre my prisoner, you know. Of course I dont believe in any such rubbish; but still its not a proper subject for joking.

LADY. But this is very serious. My sister has bewitched the General. [*Giuseppe and the lieutenant recoil from Napoleon*]. General: open your coat: you will find the despatches in the breast of it. [*She puts her hand quickly on his breast*]. Yes: there they are: I can feel them. Eh? [*She looks up into his face half coaxingly, half mockingly*]. Will you allow me, General? [*She takes a button as if to unbutton his coat, and pauses for permission*].

NAPOLEON [*inscrutably*] If you dare.

LADY. Thank you. [*She opens his coat and takes out the despatches*]. There! [*To Giuseppe, shewing him the despatches*] See!

GIUSEPPE [*flying to the outer door*] No, in heaven's name! Theyre bewitched.

LADY [*turning to the lieutenant*] Here, Lieutenant: you are not afraid of them.

LIEUTENANT [*retreating*] Keep off. [*Seizing the hilt of the sabre*] Keep off, I tell you.

LADY [*to Napoleon*] They belong to you, General. Take them.

GIUSEPPE. Dont touch them, excellency. Have nothing to do with them.

LIEUTENANT. Be careful, General: be careful.

GIUSEPPE. Burn them. And burn the witch too.

LADY [*to Napoleon*] Shall I burn them?

NAPOLEON [*thoughtfully*] Yes, burn them. Giuseppe: go and fetch a light.

GIUSEPPE [*trembling and stammering*] Do you mean go alone? in the dark! with a witch in the house?

NAPOLEON. Psha! Youre a poltroon. [*To the lieutenant*] Oblige me by going, Lieutenant.

LIEUTENANT [*remonstrating*] Oh, I say, General! No, look here, you know: nobody can say I'm a coward after Lodi. But to ask me to go into the dark by myself without a candle after such an awful conversation is a little too much. How would you like to do it yourself?

NAPOLEON [*irritably*] You refuse to obey my order?

LIEUTENANT [*resolutely*] Yes I do. It's not reasonable. But I'll tell you what I'll do. If Giuseppe goes, I'll go with him and protect him.

NAPOLEON [*to Giuseppe*] There! will that satisfy you? Be off, both of you.

GIUSEPPE [*humbly, his lips trembling*] W-willingly, your excellency. [*He goes reluctantly towards the inner door*]. Heaven protect me! [*To the lieutenant*] After you, Lieutenant.

LIEUTENANT. Youd better go first: I dont know the way.

GIUSEPPE. You cant miss it. Besides [*imploringly, laying his hand on his sleeve*] I am only a poor innkeeper: you are a man of family.

LIEUTENANT. Theres something in that. Here: you neednt be in such a fright. Take my arm. [*Giuseppe does so*]. Thats the way. [*They go out, arm in arm*].

It is now starry night. The Lady throws the packet on the table and seats herself at her ease on the couch, enjoying the sensation of freedom from petticoats.

LADY. Well, General: Ive beaten you.

NAPOLEON [*walking about*] You are guilty of indelicacy: of

unwomanliness. Is that costume proper?

LADY. It seems to me much the same as yours.

NAPOLEON. Psha! I blush for you.

LADY [*naïvely*] Yes: soldiers blush so easily. [*He growls and turns away. She looks mischievously at him, balancing the despatches in her hand*]. Wouldn't you like to read these before theyre burnt, General? You must be dying with curiosity. Take a peep. [*She throws the packet on the table, and turns her face away from it*]. I wont look.

NAPOLEON. I have no curiosity whatever, madam. But since you are evidently burning to read them, I give you leave to do so.

LADY. Oh, Ive read them already.

NAPOLEON [*starting*] What!

LADY. I read them the first thing after I rode away on that poor lieutenant's horse. So you see I know whats in them; and you dont.

NAPOLEON. Excuse me: I read them when I was out there in the vineyard ten minutes ago.

LADY. Oh! [*Jumping up*] Oh, General: Ive not beaten you after all. I do admire you so. [*He laughs and pats her cheek*]. This time, really and truly without shamming, I do you homage [*kissing his hand*].

NAPOLEON [*quickly withdrawing it*] Brr! Dont do that. No more witchcraft.

LADY. I want to say something to you; only you would misunderstand it.

NAPOLEON. Need that stop you?

LADY. Well, it is this. I adore a man who is not afraid to be mean and selfish.

NAPOLEON [*indignantly*] I am neither mean nor selfish.

LADY. Oh, you dont appreciate yourself. Besides, I dont really mean meanness and selfishness.

NAPOLEON. Thank you. I thought perhaps you did.

LADY. Well, of course I do. But what I mean is a certain strong simplicity about you.

NAPOLEON. Thats better.

LADY. You didnt want to read the letters; but you were curious about what was in them. So you went into the garden and read them when no one was looking, and then came back and pretended you hadnt. Thats the meanest thing I ever knew any man do; but it exactly fulfilled your purpose; and so you werent a bit afraid or ashamed to do it.

NAPOLEON [*abruptly*] Where did you pick up all these vulgar scruples? this [*with contemptuous emphasis*] conscience of yours? I took you for a lady: an aristocrat. Was your grandfather a shopkeeper, pray?

LADY. No: he was an Englishman.

NAPOLEON. That accounts for it. The English are a nation of shopkeepers. Now I understand why youve beaten me.

LADY. Oh, I havnt beaten you. And I'm not English.

NAPOLEON. Yes you are: English to the backbone. Listen to me: I will explain the English to you.

LADY [*eagerly*] Do. [*With a lively air of anticipating an intellectual treat, she sits down on the couch and composes herself to listen to him. Secure of his audience, he at once nerves himself for a performance. He considers a little before he begins; so as to fix her attention by a moment of suspense. His style is at first modelled on Talma's in Corneille's Cinna; but it is somewhat lost in the darkness, and Talma presently gives way to Napoleon, the voice coming through the gloom with startling intensity*].

NAPOLEON. There are three sorts of people in the world: the low people, the middle people, and the high people. The low people and the high people are alike in one thing: they have no scruples, no morality. The low are beneath morality, the high above it. I am not afraid of either of them; for the low are unscrupulous without knowledge, so that they make an idol of me; whilst the high are unscrupulous without purpose, so that they go down before my will. Look you: I shall go over all the mobs and all the courts of Europe as a plough goes over a field. It is the middle people who are dangerous: they have both knowledge and purpose. But they, too, have their weak point. They are full of scruples: chained hand and foot by their morality and respectability.

LADY. Then you will beat the English; for all shopkeepers are middle people.

NAPOLEON. No, because the English are a race apart. No Englishman is too low to have scruples: no Englishman is high enough to be free from their tyranny. But every Englishman is born with a certain miraculous power that makes him master of the world. When he wants a thing, he never tells himself that he wants it. He waits patiently until there comes into his mind, no one knows how, a burning conviction that it is his moral and religious duty to conquer those who possess the thing he wants. Then he becomes irresistible. Like the aristocrat, he does what pleases him and grabs what he covets: like the shopkeeper, he pursues his purpose with the industry and steadfastness that come from strong religious conviction and deep sense of moral responsibility. He is never at a loss for an effective moral attitude. As the great champion of freedom and national independence, he conquers and annexes half the world, and calls it Colonization. When he wants a new market for his adulterated Manchester goods, he sends a missionary to teach the natives the Gospel of Peace. The natives kill the missionary: he flies to arms in defence of Christianity; fights for it; conquers for it; and takes the market as a reward from heaven. In defence of his island shores, he puts a chaplain on board his ship; nails a flag with a cross on it to his top-gallant mast; and sails to the ends of the earth, sinking, burning, and destroying all who dispute the empire of the seas with him. He boasts that a slave is free the moment his foot touches British soil; and he sells the children of his poor at six years of age to work under the lash in his factories for sixteen hours a day. He makes two revolutions, and then declares war on our one in the name of law and order. There is nothing so bad or so good that you will not find Englishmen doing it; but you will never find an Englishman in the wrong. He does everything on principle. He fights you on patriotic principles; he robs you on business principles; he enslaves you on imperial principles; he bullies you on manly principles; he supports his king on royal principles and cuts off his king's head on republican principles. His watchword is always Duty; and he never forgets that the nation which lets its duty get on the opposite side to its interest is lost. He –

LADY. W-w-w-w-w-wh! Do stop a moment. I want to know how you make me out to be English at this rate.

NAPOLEON [*dropping his rhetorical style*] It's plain enough. You wanted some letters that belonged to me. You have spent the morning in stealing them: yes, stealing them, by highway robbery. And you have spent the afternoon in putting me in the wrong about them: in assuming that it was *I* who wanted to steal your letters: in explaining that it all came about through my meanness and selfishness, and your goodness, your devotion, your self-sacrifice. Thats English.

LADY. Nonsense! I am sure I am not a bit English. The English are a very stupid people.

NAPOLEON. Yes, too stupid sometimes to know when theyre beaten. But I grant that your brains are not English. You see, though your grandfather was an Englishman, your grandmother was – what? A Frenchwoman?

LADY. Oh no. An Irishwoman.

NAPOLEON [*quickly*] Irish! [*Thoughtfully*] Yes: I forgot the Irish. An English army led by an Irish general: that might be a match for a French army led by an Italian general. [*He pauses, and adds, half jestingly, half moodily*] At all events, you have beaten me; and what beats a man first will beat him last. [*He goes meditatively into the moonlit vineyard and looks up*].

　　She steals out after him. She ventures to rest her hand on his shoulder, overcome by the beauty of the night and emboldened by its obscurity.

LADY [*softly*] What are you looking at?

NAPOLEON [*pointing up*] My star.

LADY. You believe in that?

NAPOLEON. I do.

They look at it for a moment, she leaning a little on his shoulder.

LADY. Do you know that the English say that a man's star is not complete without a woman's garter?

NAPOLEON [*scandalized: abruptly shaking her off and coming back into the room*] Pah! The hypocrites! If the French said that, how they would hold up their hands in pious horror! [*He goes to the inner door and holds it open, shouting*] Hallo! Giuseppe! Wheres that light, man? [*He comes between the table and the sideboard, and moves the second chair to the table, beside his own*]. We have still to burn the letter. [*He takes up the packet*].

Giuseppe comes back, pale and still trembling, carrying in one hand a branched candlestick with a couple of candles alight, and a broad snuffers tray in the other.

GIUSEPPE [*piteously, as he places the light on the table*] Excellency: what were you looking up at just now? Out there! [*He points across his shoulder to the vineyard, but is afraid to look round*].

NAPOLEON [*unfolding the packet*] What is that to you?

GIUSEPPE. Because the witch is gone: vanished; and no one saw her go out.

LADY [*coming behind him from the vineyard*] We were watching her riding up to the moon on your broomstick, Giuseppe. You will never see her again.

GIUSEPPE. Gesu Maria! [*He crosses himself and hurries out*].

NAPOLEON [*throwing down the letters in a heap on the table*] Now! [*He sits down at the table in the chair which he has just placed*].

LADY. Yes; but you know you have THE letter in your pocket. [*He smiles; takes a letter from his pocket; and tosses it on top of the heap. She holds it up and looks at him, saying*] About Cæsar's wife.

NAPOLEON. Cæsar's wife is above suspicion. Burn it.

LADY [*taking up the snuffers and holding the letter to the candle flame with it*] I wonder would Cæsar's wife be above suspicion if she saw us here together!

NAPOLEON [*echoing her, with his elbows on the table and his cheeks on his hands, looking at the letter*] I wonder!

The Strange Lady puts the letter down alight on the snuffers tray, and sits down beside Napoleon, in the same attitude, elbows on table, cheeks on hands, watching it burn. When it is burnt, they simultaneously turn their eyes and look at one another. The curtains steals down and hides them.

YOU NEVER CAN TELL
1897

YOU NEVER CAN TELL

ACT I

In a dentist's operating room on a fine August morning in 1896. *It is the best sitting room of a furnished lodging in a terrace on the sea front at a watering place on the coast of Torbay in Devon. The operating chair, with a gas pump and cylinder beside it, is half way between the centre of the room and one of the corners. If you could look into the room through the window facing the chair, you would see the fireplace in the middle of the wall opposite you, with the door beside it to your left, a dental surgeon's diploma in a frame above the mantelshelf, an easy chair on the hearth, and a neat stool and bench, with vice, tools, and a mortar and pestle, in a corner to the right. In the wall on your left is a broad window looking on the sea. Beneath it a writing table with a blotter and a diary on it, and a chair. Also a sofa, farther along. A cabinet of instruments is handy to the operating chair. The furniture, carpet, and wallpaper are those of a mid-Victorian drawing room, formally bright and festive, not for everyday use.*

Two persons just now occupy the room. One of them, a very pretty woman in miniature, her tiny figure dressed with the daintiest gaiety, is hardly eighteen yet. This darling little creature clearly does not belong to the room, or even to the country; for her complexion, though very delicate, has been burnt biscuit colour by some warmer sun than England's. She has a glass of water in her hand, and a rapidly clearing cloud of Spartan endurance on her small firm set mouth and quaintly squared eyebrows.

The dentist, contemplating her with the self-satisfaction of a successful operator, is a young man of thirty or thereabouts. He does not give the impression of being much of a workman: the professional manner of the newly set-up dentist in search of patients is underlain by a thoughtless pleasantry which betrays the young gentleman, still unsettled and in search of amusing adventures. He is not without gravity of demeanor; but the strained nostrils stamp it as the gravity of the humorist. His eyes are clear, alert, of sceptically moderate size, and yet a little rash; his forehead is an excellent one, with plenty of room behind it: his nose and chin are cavalierly handsome. On the whole, an attractive noticeable beginner, of whose prospects a man of business might form a tolerably favorable estimate.

THE YOUNG LADY [*handing him the glass*] Thank you. [*In spite of the biscuit complexion she has not the slightest foreign accent*].

THE DENTIST [*putting it down on the ledge of his cabinet of instruments*] That was my first tooth.

THE YOUNG LADY [*aghast*] Your first! Do you mean to say that you began practising on me?

THE DENTIST. Every dentist has to begin with somebody.

THE YOUNG LADY. Yes: somebody in a hospital, not people who pay.

THE DENTIST [*laughing*] Oh, the hospital doesnt count. I only meant my first tooth in private practice. Why didnt you let me give you gas?

THE YOUNG LADY. Because you said it would be five shillings extra.

THE DENTIST [*shocked*] Oh, dont say that. It makes me feel as if I had hurt you for the sake of five shillings.

THE YOUNG LADY [*with cool insolence*] Well, so you have. [*She gets up*] Why shouldnt you? it's your business to hurt people. [*It amuses him to be treated in this fashion: he chuckles secretly as he proceeds to clean and replace his instruments. She shakes her dress into order: looks inquisitively about her; and goes to the broad window*]. You have a good view of the sea from your rooms! Are they expensive?

THE DENTIST. Yes.

THE YOUNG LADY. You dont own the whole house, do you?

THE DENTIST. No.

THE YOUNG LADY. I thought not. [*Tilting the chair which stands at the writing-table and looking critically at it as she spins it round on one leg*] Your furniture isnt quite the latest thing, is it?

THE DENTIST. It's my landlord's.

THE YOUNG LADY. Does he own that toothache chair [*pointing to the operating chair*].

THE DENTIST. No: I have that on the hire-purchase system.

THE YOUNG LADY [*disparagingly*] I thought so. [*Looking*

about in search of further conclusions] I suppose you havnt been here long?

THE DENTIST. Six weeks. Is there anything else you would like to know?

THE YOUNG LADY [*the hint quite lost on her*] Any family?

THE DENTIST. I am not married.

THE YOUNG LADY. Of course not: anybody can see that. I meant sisters and mother and that sort of thing.

THE DENTIST. Not on the premises.

THE YOUNG LADY. Hm! If youve been here six weeks, and mine was your first tooth, the practice cant be very large, can it?

THE DENTIST. Not as yet. [*He shuts the cabinet, having tidied up everything*].

THE YOUNG LADY. Well, good luck! [*She takes out her purse*]. Five shillings, you said it would be?

THE DENTIST. Five shillings.

THE YOUNG LADY [*producing a crown piece*] Do you charge five shillings for everything?

THE DENTIST. Yes.

THE YOUNG LADY. Why?

THE DENTIST. It's my system. I'm whats called a five shilling dentist.

THE YOUNG LADY. How nice! Well, here! [*holding up the crown piece*] a nice new five-shilling piece! your first fee! Make a hole in it with the thing you drill people's teeth with; and wear it on your watch-chain.

THE DENTIST. Thank you.

THE PARLORMAID [*appearing at the door*] The young lady's brother, sir.

A handsome man in miniature, obviously the young lady's twin, comes in eagerly. He wears a suit of terra cotta cashmere, the elegantly cut frock coat lined in brown silk, and carries in his hand a brown tall hat and tan gloves to match. He has his sister's delicate biscuit complexion, and is built on the same scale; but he is elastic and strong in muscle, decisive in movement, unexpectedly deeptoned and trenchant in speech, and with perfect manners and a finished personal style which might be envied by a man twice his age. Suavity and self-possession are points of honor with him; and though this, rightly considered, is only a mode of boyish self-consciousness, its effect is none the less staggering to his elders, and would be quite insufferable in a less prepossessing youth. He is promptitude itself, and has a question ready the moment he enters.

THE YOUNG GENTLEMAN. Am I in time?

THE YOUNG LADY. No: it's all over.

THE YOUNG GENTLEMAN. Did you howl?

THE YOUNG LADY. Oh, something awful. Mr Valentine: this is my brother Phil. Phil: this is Mr Valentine, our new dentist. [*Valentine and Phil bow to one another. She proceeds, all in one breath*] He's only been here six weeks and he's a bachelor the house isnt his and the furniture is the landlord's but the professional plant is hired he got my tooth out beautifully at the first go and he and I are great friends.

PHILIP. Been asking a lot of questions?

THE YOUNG LADY [*as if incapable of doing such a thing*] Oh no.

PHILIP. Glad to hear it. [*To Valentine*] So good of you not to mind us, Mr Valentine. The fact is, weve never been in England before; and our mother tells us that the people here simply wont stand us. Come and lunch with us.

Valentine, bewildered by the leaps and bounds with which their acquaintanceship is proceeding, gasps, but has no time to reply, as the conversation of the twins is swift and continuous.

THE YOUNG LADY. Oh, do, Mr Valentine.

PHILIP. At the Marine Hotel: half past one.

THE YOUNG LADY. We shall be able to tell mamma that a respectable Englishman has promised to lunch with us.

PHILIP. Say no more, Mr Valentine: youll come.

VALENTINE. Say no more! I havnt said anything. May I ask whom I have the pleasure of entertaining? It's really quite impossible for me to lunch at the Marine Hotel with two perfect strangers.

THE YOUNG LADY [*flippantly*] Ooooh! what bosh! One patient in six weeks! What difference does it make to you?

PHILIP [*maturely*] No, Dolly: my knowledge of human nature

confirms Mr Valentine's judgment. He is right. Let me introduce Miss Dorothy Clandon, commonly called Dolly. [*Valentine bows to Dolly. She nods to him*]. I'm Philip Clandon. We're from Madeira, but perfectly respectable so far.

VALENTINE. Clandon! Are you related to –

DOLLY [*unexpectedly crying out in despair*] Yes we are.

VALENTINE [*astonished*] I beg your pardon?

DOLLY. Oh, we are, we are. It's all over, Phil: they know all about us in England. [*To Valentine*] Oh, you cant think how maddening it is to be related to a celebrated person, and never be valued anywhere for our own sakes.

VALENTINE. But excuse me: the gentleman I was thinking of is not celebrated.

DOLLY AND PHILIP [*staring at him*] Gentleman!

VALENTINE. Yes. I was going to ask whether you were by any chance a daughter of Mr Densmore Clandon of Newbury Hall.

DOLLY [*vacantly*] No.

PHILIP. Well, come, Dolly: how do you know youre not?

DOLLY [*cheered*] Oh, I forgot. Of course. Perhaps I am.

VALENTINE. Dont you know?

PHILIP. Not in the least.

DOLLY. It's a wise child –

PHILIP [*cutting her short*] Sh! [*Valentine starts nervously; for the sound made by Phil, though but momentary, is like cutting a sheet of silk in two with a flash of lightning. It is the result of long practice in checking Dolly's indiscretions*]. The fact is, Mr Valentine, we are the children of the celebrated Mrs Lanfrey Clandon, an authoress of great repute – in Madeira. No household is complete without her works. We came to England to get away from them. They are called the Twentieth Century Treatises.

DOLLY. Twentieth Century Cooking.

PHILIP. Twentieth Century Creeds.

DOLLY. Twentieth Century Clothing.

PHILIP. Twentieth Century Conduct.

DOLLY. Twentieth Century Children.

PHILIP. Twentieth Century Parents.

DOLLY. Cloth limp, half a dollar.

PHILIP. Or mounted on linen for hard family use, two dollars. No family should be without them. Read them, Mr Valentine: theyll improve your mind.

DOLLY. But not til weve gone, please.

PHILIP. Quite so: we prefer people with unimproved minds. Our own minds have successfully resisted all our mother's efforts to improve them.

VALENTINE [*dubiously*] Hm!

DOLLY [*echoing him inquiringly*] Hm? Phil: he prefers people whose minds are improved.

PHILIP. In that case we shall have to introduce him to the other member of the family: the Woman of the Twentieth Century: our sister Gloria!

DOLLY [*dithyrambically*] Nature's masterpiece!

PHILIP. Learning's daughter!

DOLLY. Madeira's pride!

PHILIP. Beauty's paragon!

DOLLY [*suddenly descending to prose*] Bosh! No complexion.

VALENTINE [*desperately*] May I have a word?

PHILIP [*politely*] Excuse us. Go ahead.

DOLLY [*very nicely*] So sorry.

VALENTINE [*attempting to take them paternally*] I really must give a hint to you young people –

DOLLY [*breaking out again*] Oh come! I like that. How old are you?

PHILIP. Over thirty.

DOLLY. He's not.

PHILIP [*confidently*] He is.

DOLLY [*emphatically*] Twenty-seven.

PHILIP [*imperturbably*] Thirty-three.

DOLLY. Stuff.

PHILIP [*to Valentine*] I appeal to you, Mr Valentine.

VALENTINE [*remonstrating*] Well, really – [*resigning himself*] Thirty-one.

PHILIP [*to Dolly*] You were wrong.

DOLLY. So were you.

PHILIP [*suddenly conscientious*] We're forgetting our manners, Dolly.

DOLLY [*remorseful*] Yes, so we are.

PHILIP [*apologetic*] We interrupted you, Mr Valentine.

DOLLY. You were going to improve our minds, I think.

VALENTINE. The fact is, your –

PHILIP [*anticipating him*] Our manners?

DOLLY. Our appearance?

VALENTINE [*ad misericordiam*] Oh do let me speak.

DOLLY. The old story. We talk too much.

PHILIP. We do. Shut up, both. [*He seats himself on the arm of the operating chair*].

DOLLY. Mum! [*She sits down in the writing-table chair, and closes her lips with the tips of her fingers*].

VALENTINE. Thank you. [*He brings the stool from the bench in the corner; places it between them; and sits down with a judicial air. They attend to him with extreme gravity. He addresses himself first to Dolly*]. Now may I ask, to begin with, have you ever been in an English seaside resort before? [*She shakes her head slowly and solemnly. He turns to Phil, who shakes his head quickly and expressively*]. I thought so. Well, Mr Clandon, our acquaintance has been short; but it has been voluble; and I have gathered enough to convince me that you are neither of you capable of conceiving what life in an English seaside resort is. Believe me, it's not a question of manners and appearance. In those respects we enjoy a freedom unknown in Madeira [*Dolly shakes her head vehemently*]. Oh yes, I assure you. Lord de Cresci's sister bicycles in knickerbockers; and the rector's wife advocates dress reform and wears hygienic boots. [*Dolly furtively looks at her own shoe: Valentine catches her in the act, and deftly adds*] No, thats not the sort of boot I mean. [*Dolly's shoe vanishes*]. We dont bother much about dress and manners in England, because, as a nation, we dont dress well and weve no manners. But – and now will you excuse my frankness? [*They nod*]. Thank you. Well, in a seaside resort theres one thing you

must have before anybody can afford to be seen going
about with you; and thats a father, alive or dead. Am I
to infer that you have omitted that indispensable part of
your social equipment ? [*They confirm him by melancholy nods*].
Then I'm sorry to say that if you are going to stay here for
any length of time, it will be impossible for me to accept
your kind invitation to lunch. [*He rises with an air of finality,
and replaces the stool by the bench*].

PHILIP [*rising with grave politeness*] Come, Dolly. [*He gives her
his arm*].

DOLLY. Good morning. [*They go together to the door with perfect
dignity*].

VALENTINE [*overwhelmed with remorse*] Oh stop! stop! [*They
halt and turn, arm in arm*]. You make me feel a perfect
beast.

DOLLY. Thats your conscience: not us.

VALENTINE [*energetically, throwing off all pretence of a professional
manner*] My conscience! My conscience has been my ruin.
Listen to me. Twice before I have set up as a respectable
medical practitioner in various parts of England. On both
occasions I acted conscientiously, and told my patients the
brute truth instead of what they wanted to be told. Result,
ruin. Now Ive set up as a dentist, a five shilling dentist; and
Ive done with conscience for ever. This is my last chance.
I spent my last sovereign on moving in; and I havnt paid a
shilling of rent yet. I'm eating and drinking on credit; my
landlord is as rich as a Jew and as hard as nails; and Ive
made five shillings in six weeks. If I swerve by a hair's
breadth from the straight line of the most rigid respectability, I'm done for. Under such circumstances is it fair to ask
me to lunch with you when you dont know your own
father ?

DOLLY. After all, our grandfather is a canon of Lincoln
Cathedral.

VALENTINE [*like a castaway mariner who sees a sail on the horizon*]
What! Have you a grandfather ?

DOLLY. Only one.

VALENTINE. My dear good young friends, why on earth
didnt you tell me that before? A canon of Lincoln! That
makes it all right, of course. Just excuse me while I change
my coat. [*He reaches the door in a bound and vanishes*].

*Dolly and Phil stare after him, and then at one another. Missing
their audience, they discard their style at once.*

PHILIP [*throwing away Dolly's arm and coming ill-humoredly
towards the operating chair*] That wretched bankrupt ivory
snatcher makes a compliment of allowing us to stand him
a lunch: probably the first square meal he has had for
months. [*He gives the chair a kick, as if it were Valentine*].

DOLLY. It's too beastly. I wont stand it any longer, Phil.
Here in England everybody asks whether you have a father
the very first thing.

PHILIP. I wont stand it either. Mamma must tell us who he
was.

DOLLY. Or who he is. He may be alive.

PHILIP. I hope not. No man alive shall father me.

DOLLY. He might have a lot of money, though.

PHILIP. I doubt it. My knowledge of human nature leads
me to believe that if he had a lot of money he wouldnt
have got rid of his affectionate family so easily. Anyhow,
let's look at the bright side of things. Depend on it, he's
dead.

·*He goes to the hearth and stands with his back to the fireplace.
The parlormaid appears.*

THE PARLORMAID. Two ladies for you, miss. Your mother
and sister, miss, I think.

*Mrs Clandon and Gloria come in. Mrs Clandon is a veteran of
the Old Guard of the Women's Rights movement which had for its
Bible John Stuart Mill's treatise on The Subjection of Women.
She has never made herself ugly or ridiculous by affecting masculine
waistcoats, collars, and watchchains, like some of her old comrades
who had more aggressiveness than taste; and she is too militant an
Agnostic to care to be mistaken for a Quaker. She therefore dresses in
as businesslike a way as she can without making a guy of herself,
ruling out all attempt at sex attraction and imposing respect on*

frivolous mankind and fashionable womankind. She belongs to the forefront of her own period (say 1860–80) in a jealously assertive attitude of character and intellect, and in being a woman of cultivated interests rather than passionately developed personal affections. Her voice and ways are entirely kindly and humane; and she lends herself conscientiously to the occasional demonstrations of fondness by which her children mark their esteem for her; but displays of personal sentiment secretly embarrass her; passion in her is humanitarian rather than human; she feels strongly about social questions and principles, not about persons. Only, one observes that this reasonableness and intense personal privacy, which leaves her relations with Gloria and Phil much as they might be between her and the children of any other woman, breaks down in the case of Dolly. Though almost every word she addresses to her is necessarily in the nature of a remonstrance for some breach of decorum, the tenderness in her voice is unmistakable; and it is not surprising that years of such remonstrance have left Dolly hopelessly spoiled.

Gloria, who is hardly past twenty, is a much more formidable person than her mother. She is the incarnation of haughty highmindedness, raging with the impatience of a mettlesome dominative character paralysed by the inexperience of her youth, and unwillingly disciplined by the constant danger of ridicule from her irreverent juniors. Unlike her mother, she is all passion; and the conflict of her passion with her obstinate pride and intense fastidiousness results in a freezing coldness of manner. In an ugly woman all this would be repulsive; but Gloria is attractive. A dangerous girl, one would say, if the moral passions were not also marked, and even nobly marked, in a fine brow. Her tailormade skirt-and-jacket dress, of saffron brown cloth, seems conventional when her back is turned; but it displays in front a blouse of sea-green silk which scatters its conventionality with one stroke, and sets her apart as effectually as the twins from the ordinary run of fashionable seaside humanity.

Mrs Clandon comes a little way into the room looking round to see who is present. Gloria, who studiously avoids encouraging the twins by betraying any interest in them, wanders to the window and looks out to sea with her thoughts far away. The parlormaid, instead of withdrawing, shuts the door and waits at it.

MRS CLANDON. Well, children? How is the toothache, Dolly?

DOLLY. Cured, thank Heaven. Ive had it out. [*She sits down on the step of the operating chair*].

Mrs Clandon takes the writing-table chair.

PHILIP [*striking in gravely from the hearth*] And the dentist, a first rate professional man of the highest standing, is coming to lunch with us.

MRS CLANDON [*looking round apprehensively at the servant*] Phil!

THE PARLORMAID. Beg pardon, maam. I'm waiting for Mr Valentine. I have a message for him.

DOLLY. Who from?

MRS CLANDON [*shocked*] Dolly!

Dolly catches her lips suppressively with her finger tips.

THE PARLORMAID. Only the landlord, maam.

Valentine, in a blue serge suit, with a straw hat in his hand, comes back in high spirits, out of breath with the haste he has made. Gloria turns from the window and studies him with chilling attention.

PHILIP. Let me introduce you, Mr Valentine. My mother, Mrs Lanfrey Clandon. [*Mrs Clandon bows. Valentine bows, self-possessed and quite equal to the occasion.*] My sister Gloria. [*Gloria bows with cold dignity and sits down on the sofa*].

Valentine falls abjectly in love at first sight. He fingers his hat nervously, and makes her a sneaking bow.

MRS CLANDON. I understand that we are to have the pleasure of seeing you at luncheon today, Mr Valentine.

VALENTINE. Thank you – er – if you dont mind – I mean if you will be so kind – [*to the parlormaid, testily*] What is it?

THE PARLORMAID. The landlord, sir, wishes to speak to you before you go out.

VALENTINE. Oh, tell him I have four patients here. [*The Clandons look surprised, except Phil, who is imperturbable*]. If he wouldnt mind waiting just two minutes, I – I'll slip down and see him for a moment. [*Throwing himself confidentially on her sense of position*] Say I'm busy, but that I want to see him.

THE PARLORMAID [*reassuringly*] Yes, sir. [*She goes*].

MRS CLANDON [*on the point of rising*] We are detaining you, I am afraid.

VALENTINE. Not at all, not at all. Your presence here will be the greatest help to me. The fact is, I owe six weeks rent; and Ive had no patients until today. My interview with my landlord will be considerably smoothed by the apparent boom in my business.

DOLLY [*vexed*] Oh, how tiresome of you to let it all out! And weve just been pretending that you were a respectable professional man in a first rate position.

MRS CLANDON [*horrified*] Oh Dolly! Dolly! My dearest: how can you be so rude? [*To Valentine*] Will you excuse these barbarian children of mine, Mr Valentine?

VALENTINE. Dont mention it: I'm used to them. Would it be too much to ask you to wait five minutes while I get rid of my landlord downstairs?

DOLLY. Dont be long. We're hungry.

MRS CLANDON [*again remonstrating*] Dolly, dear!

VALENTINE [*to Dolly*] All right. [*To Mrs Clandon*] Thank you: I shant be long. [*He steals a look at Gloria as he turns to go. She is looking gravely at him. He falls into confusion*]. I – er – er – yes – thank you [*he succeeds at last in blundering himself out of the room; but the exhibition is a pitiful one*].

PHILIP. Did you observe? [*Pointing to Gloria*] Love at first sight. Another scalp for your collection, Gloria. Number fifteen.

MRS CLANDON. Sh – sh pray, Phil. He may have heard you.

PHILIP. Not he. [*Bracing himself for a scene*] And now look here, mamma. [*He takes the stool from the bench; and seats himself majestically in the middle of the room, copying Valentine's recent demonstration. Dolly, feeling that her position on the step of the operating chair is unworthy the dignity of the occasion, rises, looking important and uncompromising. She crosses to the window, and stands with her back to the end of the writing-table, her hands behind her and on the table. Mrs Clandon looks at them, wondering what is coming. Gloria becomes attentive. Phil straightens his back;*]

places his knuckles symmetrically on his knees; and opens his case].
Dolly and I have been talking over things a good deal
lately; and I dont think, judging from my knowledge of
human nature – we dont think that you [*speaking very
pointedly, with the words detached*] quite. Appreciate. The
fact –

DOLLY [*seating herself on the end of the table with a spring*] That
weve grown up.

MRS CLANDON. Indeed? In what way have I given you any
reason to complain?

PHILIP. Well, there are certain matters upon which we are
beginning to feel that you might take us a little more into
your confidence.

MRS CLANDON [*rising, with all the placidity of her age suddenly
breaking up into a curious hard excitement, dignified but dogged,
ladylike but implacable: the manner of the Old Guard*] Phil: take
care. What have I always taught you? There are two sorts
of family life, Phil; and your experience of human nature
only extends, so far, to one of them. [*Rhetorically*] The sort
you know is based on mutual respect, on recognition of the
right of every member of the household to independence
and privacy [*her emphasis on 'privacy' is intense*] in their personal concerns. And because you have always enjoyed that,
it seems such a matter of course to you that you dont value
it. But [*with biting acrimony*] there is another sort of family
life: a life in which husbands open their wives' letters, and
call on them to account for every farthing of their expendi-
ture and every moment of their time; in which women do
the same to their children; in which no room is private and
no hour sacred; in which duty, obedience, affection, home,
morality and religion are detestable tyrannies, and life is
a vulgar round of punishments and lies, coercion and rebel-
lion, jealousy, suspicion, recrimination – Oh! I cannot
describe it to you: fortunately for you, you know nothing
about it. [*She sits down, panting*].

DOLLY [*inaccessible to rhetoric*] See Twentieth Century Parents,
chapter on Liberty, passim.

MRS CLANDON [*touching her shoulder affectionately, softened even by a gibe from her*] My dear Dolly : if you only knew how glad I am that it is nothing but a joke to you, though it is such bitter earnest to me. [*More resolutely, turning to Phil*] Phil : I never ask you questions about your private concerns. You are not going to question me, are you?

PHILIP. I think it due to ourselves to say that the question we wanted to ask is as much our business as yours.

DOLLY. Besides, it cant be good to keep a lot of questions bottled up inside you. You did it, mamma; but see how awfully it's broken out again in me.

MRS CLANDON. I see you want to ask your question. Ask it.

DOLLY AND PHILIP [*beginning simultaneously*] Who – [*They stop*].

PHILIP. Now look here, Dolly : am I going to conduct this business or are you?

DOLLY. You.

PHILIP. Then hold your mouth. [*Dolly does so, literally*]. The question is a simple one. When the ivory snatcher –

MRS CLANDON [*remonstrating*] Phil!

PHILIP. Dentist is an ugly word. The man of ivory and gold asked us whether we were the children of Mr Densmore Clandon of Newbury Hall. In pursuance of the precepts in your treatise on Twentieth Century Conduct, and your repeated personal exhortations to us to curtail the number of unnecessary lies we tell, we replied truthfully that we didnt know.

DOLLY. Neither did we.

PHILIP. Sh ! The result was that the gum architect made considerable difficulties about accepting our invitation to lunch, although I doubt if he has had anything but tea and bread and butter for a fortnight past. Now my knowledge of human nature leads me to believe that we had a father, and that you probably know who he was.

MRS CLANDON [*her agitation returning*] Stop, Phil. Your father is nothing to you, nor to me. [*Vehemently*] That is enough. *The twins are silenced, but not satisfied. Their faces fall. But*

Gloria, who has been following the altercation attentively, suddenly intervenes.

GLORIA [*advancing*] Mother: we have a right to know.

MRS CLANDON [*rising and facing her*] Gloria! 'We'! Who is 'we'?

GLORIA [*steadfastly*] We three. [*Her tone is unmistakable: she is pitting her strength against her mother's for the first time. The twins instantly go over to the enemy*].

MRS CLANDON [*wounded*] In your mouth 'we' used to mean you and I, Gloria.

PHILIP [*rising decisively and putting away the stool*] We're hurting you: let's drop it. We didnt think youd mind. *I* dont want to know.

DOLLY [*coming off the table*] I'm sure *I* dont. Oh, dont look like that, mamma. [*She looks angrily at Gloria and flings her arms round her mother's neck*].

MRS CLANDON. Thank you, my dear. Thanks, Phil. [*She detaches Dolly gently and sits down again*].

GLORIA [*inexorably*] We have a right to know, mother.

MRS CLANDON [*indignantly*] Ah! You insist.

GLORIA. Do you intend that we shall never know?

DOLLY. Oh Gloria, dont. It's barbarous.

GLORIA [*with quiet scorn*] What is the use of being weak? You see what has happened with this gentleman here, mother. The same thing has happened to me.

MRS CLANDON ⎫   ⎧ What do you mean?
DOLLY   ⎬ [*all together*] ⎨ Oh, tell us!
PHILIP   ⎭   ⎩ What happened to you?

GLORIA. Oh, nothing of any consequence. [*She turns away from them and strolls up to the easy chair at the fireplace, where she sits down, almost with her back to them. As they wait expectantly, she adds, over her shoulder, with studied indifference*] On board the steamer, the first officer did me the honor to propose to me.

DOLLY. No: it was to me.

MRS CLANDON. The first officer! Are you serious, Gloria? What did you say to him? [*Correcting herself*] Excuse me: I have no right to ask that.

GLORIA. The answer is pretty obvious. A woman who does not know who her father was cannot accept such an offer.

MRS CLANDON. Surely you did not want to accept it!

GLORIA [*turning a little and raising her voice*] No; but suppose I had wanted to!

PHILIP. Did that difficulty strike you, Dolly?

DOLLY. No. I accepted him.

GLORIA ⎫   ⎧ Accepted him!
MRS CLANDON ⎬ [*all crying out together*] ⎨ Dolly!
PHILIP ⎭   ⎩ Oh, I say!

DOLLY [*naïvely*] He did look such a fool!

MRS CLANDON. But why did you do such a thing, Dolly?

DOLLY. For fun, I suppose. He had to measure my finger for a ring. Youd have done the same thing yourself.

MRS CLANDON. No, Dolly, I would not. As a matter of fact the first officer did propose to me; and I told him to keep that sort of thing for women who were young enough to be amused by it. He appears to have acted on my advice. [*She rises and goes to the hearth*]. Gloria: I am sorry you think me weak; but I cannot tell you what you want. You are all too young.

PHILIP. This is rather a startling departure from Twentieth Century principles.

DOLLY [*quoting*] 'Answer all your children's questions, and answer them truthfully, as soon as they are old enough to ask them.' See Twentieth Century Motherhood –

PHILIP. Page one.

DOLLY. Chapter one.

PHILIP. Sentence one.

MRS CLANDON. My dears: I do not mean that you are too young to know. I mean that you are too young to be taken into my confidence. You are very bright children, all of you; but you are still very inexperienced and consequently sometimes very unsympathetic. There are experiences of mine that I cannot bear to speak of except to those who have gone through what I have gone through. I hope you will never be qualified for such confidences.

PHILIP. Another grievance, Dolly!

DOLLY. We're not sympathetic.

GLORIA [*leaning forward in her chair and looking earnestly up at her mother*] Mother: I did not mean to be unsympathetic.

MRS CLANDON [*affectionately*] Of course not, dear. I quite understand!

GLORIA [*rising*] But, mother –

MRS CLANDON [*drawing back a little*] Yes?

GLORIA [*obstinately*] It is nonsense to tell us that our father is nothing to us.

MRS CLANDON [*provoked to sudden resolution*] Do you remember your father?

GLORIA [*meditatively, as if the recollection were a tender one*] I am not quite sure. I think so.

MRS CLANDON [*grimly*] You are not sure?

GLORIA. No.

MRS CLANDON [*with quiet force*] Gloria: if I had ever struck you [*Gloria recoils: Phil and Dolly are disagreeably shocked: all three stare at her, revolted, as she continues mercilessly*] – struck you purposely, deliberately, with the intention of hurting you, with a whip bought for the purpose! would you remember that, do you think? [*Gloria utters an exclamation of indignant repulsion*]. That would have been your last recollection of your father, Gloria, if I had not taken you away from him. I have kept him out of your life: keep him now out of mine by never mentioning him to me again.

Gloria, with a shudder, covers her face with her hands until, hearing someone at the door, she recomposes herself. Mrs Clandon sits down on the sofa. Valentine returns.

VALENTINE. I hope Ive not kept you waiting. That landlord of mine is really an extraordinary old character.

DOLLY [*eagerly*] Oh, tell us. How long has he given you to pay?

MRS CLANDON [*distracted by her child's manners*] Dolly, Dolly, Dolly dear! You must not ask questions.

DOLLY [*demurely*] So sorry. Youll tell us, wont you, Mr Valentine.

VALENTINE. He doesnt want his rent at all. He's broken his tooth on a Brazil nut; and he wants me to look at it and to lunch with him afterwards.

DOLLY. Then have him up and pull his tooth out at once; and we'll bring him to lunch too. Tell the maid to fetch him along. [*She runs to the bell and rings it vigorously. Then, with a sudden doubt, she turns to Valentine and adds*] I suppose he's respectable? r e a l l y respectable?

VALENTINE. Perfectly. Not like me.

DOLLY. Honest Injun?

> *Mrs Clandon gasps faintly; but her powers of remonstrance are exhausted.*

VALENTINE. Honest Injun!

DOLLY. Then off with you and bring him up.

VALENTINE [*looking dubiously at Mrs Clandon*] I dare say he'd be delighted if – er –?

MRS CLANDON [*rising and looking at her watch*] I shall be happy to see your friend at lunch if you can persuade him to come; but I cant wait to see him now: I have an appointment at the hotel at a quarter to one with an old friend whom I have not seen since I left England eighteen years ago. Will you excuse me?

VALENTINE. Certainly, Mrs Clandon.

GLORIA. Shall I come?

MRS CLANDON. No, dear. I want to be alone. [*She goes out, evidently still a good deal troubled*].

> *Valentine opens the door for her and follows her.*

PHILIP [*significantly to Dolly*] Hmhm!

DOLLY [*significantly to Phil*] Ahah!

> *The parlormaid answers the bell.*

DOLLY. Shew the old gentleman up.

THE PARLORMAID [*puzzled*] Madam?

DOLLY. The old gentleman with the toothache.

PHILIP. The landlord.

THE PARLORMAID. Mr Crampton, sir?

PHILIP. Is his name Crampton?

DOLLY [*to Phil*] Sounds rheumaticky, doesnt it?

PHILIP. Chalkstones, probably.

DOLLY. Shew Mr Crampstones up.

THE PARLORMAID [*going out*] Mr Crampton, miss.

DOLLY [*repeating it to herself like a lesson*] Crampton, Crampton, Crampton, Crampton, Crampton. [*She sits down studiously at the writing-table*] I must get that name right, or
Heaven knows what I shall call him.

GLORIA. Phil: can you believe such a horrible thing as that
about our father? what mother said just now.

PHILIP. Oh, there are lots of people of that kind. Old
Chamico used to thrash his wife and daughters with a cart
whip.

DOLLY [*contemptuously*] Yes, a Portuguese!

PHILIP. When you come to men who are brutes, there is
much in common between the Portuguese and the English
variety. Doll. Trust my knowledge of human nature. [*He
resumes his position on the hearth-rug with an elderly and responsible air*].

GLORIA [*with angered remorse*] I dont think we shall ever play
again at our old game of guessing what our father was to
be like. Dolly: are you sorry for your father? the father
with lots of money!

DOLLY. Oh come! What about your father? the lonely old
man with the tender aching heart! He's pretty well burst
up, I think.

PHILIP. There can be no doubt that the governor is an
exploded superstition. [*Valentine is heard talking to somebody
outside the door*]. But hark! he comes.

GLORIA [*nervously*] Who?

DOLLY. Chalkstones.

PHILIP. Sh! Attention! [*They put on their best manners. Phil
adds in a lower voice to Gloria*] If he's good enough for the
lunch, I'll nod to Dolly; and if she nods to you, invite him
straight away.

*Valentine comes back with his landlord. Mr Fergus Crampton is
a man of about sixty, with an atrociously obstinate ill tempered grasp-
ing mouth, and a dogmatic voice. There is no sign of straitened*

*means or commercial diffidence about him: he is well dressed, and
would be classed at a guess as a prosperous master-manufacturer in
a business inherited from an old family in the aristocracy of trade.
His navy blue coat is not of the usual fashionable pattern. It is not
exactly a pilot's coat; but it is cut that way, double breasted, and
with stout buttons and broad lappels: a coat for a shipyard rather
than a counting house. He has taken a fancy to Valentine, who cares
nothing for his crossness of grain, and treats him with a disrespectful humanity for which he is secretly grateful.*

VALENTINE. May I introduce? This is Mr Crampton: Miss
Dorothy Clandon, Mr Philip Clandon, Miss Clandon.
[*Crampton stands nervously bowing. They all bow*]. Sit down,
Mr Crampton.

DOLLY [*pointing to the operating chair*] That is the most comfortable chair, Mr Ch – crampton.

CRAMPTON. Thank you; but wont this young lady – [*indicating Gloria, who is close to the chair*]?

GLORIA. Thank you, Mr Crampton: we are just going.

VALENTINE [*bustling him across to the chair with good-humored
peremptoriness*] Sit down, sit down. Youre tired.

CRAMPTON. Well, perhaps, as I am considerably the oldest
person present, I – [*he finishes the sentence by sitting down a
little rheumatically in the operating chair. Meanwhile Phil, having
studied him critically during his passage across the room, nods to
Dolly; and Dolly nods to Gloria*].

GLORIA. Mr Crampton: we understand that we are pre-
venting Mr Valentine from lunching with you by taking
him away ourselves. My mother would be very glad indeed if you would come too.

CRAMPTON [*gratefully, after looking at her earnestly for a moment*]
Thank you. I will come with pleasure.

GLORIA ⎫   ⎧ Thank you very much – er –
DOLLY ⎬ [*politely* ⎨ So glad – er –
PHILIP ⎭ *murmuring*] ⎩ Delighted, I'm sure – er –

*The conversation drops. Gloria and Dolly look at one another;
then at Valentine and Phil. Valentine and Phil, unequal to the occasion, look away from them at one another, and are instantly so dis-*

concerted by catching one another's eye, that they look back again and
catch the eyes of Gloria and Dolly. Thus, catching one another all
round, they all look at nothing and are quite at a loss. Crampton looks
at them, waiting for them to begin. The silence becomes unbearable.

DOLLY [*suddenly, to keep things going*] How old are you, Mr
Crampton?

GLORIA [*hastily*] I am afraid|we must be going, Mr Valentine.
It is understood, then, that we meet at half past one. [*She
makes for the door. Phil goes with her. Valentine retreats to the
bell*].

VALENTINE. Half past one. [*He rings the bell*]. Many thanks.
[*He follows Gloria and Phil to the door, and goes out with them*].

DOLLY [*who has meanwhile stolen across to Crampton*] Make him
give you gas. It's five shillings extra; but it's worth it.

CRAMPTON [*amused*] Very well. [*Looking more earnestly at
her*] So you want to know my age, do you? I'm fifty-seven.

DOLLY [*with conviction*] You look it.

CRAMPTON [*grimly*] I dare say I do.

DOLLY. What are you looking at me so hard for? Anything
wrong? [*She feels whether her hat is right*].

CRAMPTON. Youre like somebody.

DOLLY. Who?

CRAMPTON. Well, you have a curious look of my mother.

DOLLY [*incredulously*] Your mother!!! Quite sure you dont
mean your daughter?

CRAMPTON [*suddenly blackening with hate*] Yes: I'm quite sure
I dont mean my daughter.

DOLLY [*sympathetically*] Tooth bad?

CRAMPTON. No, no: nothing. A twinge of memory, Miss
Clandon, not of toothache.

DOLLY. Have it out. 'Pluck from the memory a rooted sorrow.' With gas, five shillings extra.

CRAMPTON [*vindictively*] No, not a sorrow. An injury that
was done me once: thats all. I dont forget injuries: and I
dont want to forget them. [*His features settle into an implacable frown*].

DOLLY [*looking critically at him*] I dont think we shall like you when you are brooding over your injuries.

PHILIP [*who has entered the room unobserved, and stolen behind her*] My sister means well, Mr Crampton; but she is indiscreet. Now Dolly: outside! [*He takes her towards the door*].

DOLLY [*in a perfectly audible undertone*] He says he's only fifty-seven and he thinks me the image of his mother and he hates his daughter and – [*She is interrupted by the return of Valentine*].

VALENTINE. Miss Clandon has gone on.

PHILIP. Dont forget half past one.

DOLLY. Mind you leave Mr Crampton enough teeth to eat with. [*They go out*].

Valentine comes to his cabinet, and opens it.

CRAMPTON. Thats a spoiled child, Mr Valentine. Thats one of your modern products. When I was her age, I had many a good hiding fresh in my memory to teach me manners.

VALENTINE [*taking up his dental mirror and probe*] What did you think of her sister?

CRAMPTON. You liked her better, eh?

VALENTINE [*rhapsodically*] She struck me as being – [*He checks himself, and adds, prosaically*] However, thats not business. [*He assumes his professional tone*]. Open, please. [*Crampton opens his mouth. Valentine puts the mirror in, and examines his teeth*]. Hm! Youve smashed that one. What a pity to spoil such a splendid set of teeth! Why do you crack nuts with them? [*He withdraws the mirror, and comes forward to converse with his patient*].

CRAMPTON. Ive always cracked nuts with them: what else are they for? [*Dogmatically*] The proper way to keep teeth good is to give them plenty of use on bones and nuts, and wash them every day with soap: plain yellow soap.

VALENTINE. Soap! Why soap?

CRAMPTON. I began using it as a boy because I was made to; and Ive used it ever since. And Ive never had toothache in my life.

VALENTINE. Dont you find it rather nasty?

CRAMPTON. I found that most things that were good for me

were nasty. But I was taught to put up with them, and made to put up with them. I'm used to it now: in fact I like the taste when the soap is really good.

VALENTINE [*making a wry face in spite of himself*] You seem to have been very carefully educated, Mr Crampton.

CRAMPTON [*grimly*] I wasnt spoiled, at all events.

VALENTINE [*smiling a little to himself*] Are you quite sure?

CRAMPTON [*crustily*] What d'y' mean?

VALENTINE. Well, your teeth are good, I admit. But Ive seen just as good in very self-indulgent mouths. [*He goes to the cabinet and changes the probe for another one*].

CRAMPTON. It's not the effect on the teeth: it's the effect on the character.

VALENTINE [*placably*] Oh, the character! I see. [*He recommences operations*]. A little wider, please. Hm! Why do you bite so hard? youve broken the tooth worse than you broke the Brazil nut. It will have to come out: it's past saving. [*He withdraws the probe and again comes to the side of the chair to converse*]. Dont be alarmed: you shant feel anything. I'll give you gas.

CRAMPTON. Rubbish, man: I want none of your gas. Out with it! People were taught to bear necessary pain in my day.

VALENTINE. Oh, if you like being hurt, all right. I'll hurt you as much as you like, without any extra charge for the beneficial effect on your character.

CRAMPTON [*rising and glaring at him*] Young man: you owe me six weeks rent.

VALENTINE. I do.

CRAMPTON. Can you pay me?

VALENTINE. No.

CRAMPTON [*satisfied with his advantage*] I thought not. [*He sits down again*]. How soon d'y' think youll be able to pay me if you have no better manners than to make game of your patients?

VALENTINE. My good sir: my patients havnt all formed their characters on kitchen soap.

CRAMPTON [*suddenly gripping him by the arm as he turns away again to the cabinet*] So much the worse for them! I tell you you dont understand my character. If I could spare all my teeth, I'd make you pull them out one after another to shew you what a properly hardened man can go through with when he's made up his mind to it. [*He nods at Valentine to emphasize this declaration, and releases him*].

VALENTINE [*his careless pleasantry quite unruffled*] And you want to be more hardened, do you?

CRAMPTON. Yes.

VALENTINE [*strolling away to the bell*] Well, youre quite hard enough for me already – as a landlord. [*Crampton receives this with a growl of grim humor. Valentine rings the bell, and remarks in a cheerful casual way, whilst waiting for it to be answered*] Why did you never get married, Mr Crampton? A wife and children would have taken some of the hardness out of you.

CRAMPTON [*with unexpected ferocity*] What the devil is that to you?

The parlormaid appears at the door.

VALENTINE [*politely*] Some warm water, please. [*She retires; and Valentine comes back to the cabinet, not at all put out by Crampton's rudeness, and carries on the conversation whilst he selects a forceps and places it ready to his hand with a gag and a tumbler*]. You were asking me what the devil that was to me. Well, I have an idea of getting married myself.

CRAMPTON [*with grumbling irony*] Naturally, sir, naturally. When a young man has come to his last farthing, and is within twenty four hours of having his furniture distrained upon by his landlord, he marries. Ive noticed that before. Well, marry; and be miserable.

VALENTINE. Oh come! what do you know about it?

CRAMPTON. I'm not a bachelor.

VALENTINE. Then there is a Mrs Crampton?

CRAMPTON [*wincing with a pang of resentment*] Yes: damn her!

VALENTINE [*unperturbed*] Hm! A father, too, perhaps, as well as a husband, Mr Crampton?

CRAMPTON. Three children.

VALENTINE [*politely*] Damn them? eh?

CRAMPTON [*jealously*] No, sir: the children are as much mine as hers.

The parlormaid brings in a jug of hot water.

VALENTINE. Thank you. [*She gives him the jug and goes out. He brings it to the cabinet, continuing in the same idle strain*] I really should like to know your family, Mr Crampton. [*He pours some hot water into the tumbler*].

CRAMPTON. Sorry I cant introduce you, sir. I'm happy to say that I dont know where they are, and dont care, so long as they keep out of my way. [*Valentine, with a hitch of his eyebrows and shoulders, drops the forceps with a clink into the hot water*]. You neednt warm that thing to use on me. I'm not afraid of the cold steel. [*Valentine stoops to arrange the gas pump and cylinder beside the chair*]. Whats that heavy thing?

VALENTINE. Oh, never mind. Something to put my foot on, to get the necessary purchase for a good pull. [*Crampton looks alarmed in spite of himself. Valentine stands upright and places the glass with the forceps ready to his hand, chatting on with provoking indifference*]. And so you advise me not to get married, Mr Crampton? [*He puts his foot on the lever by which the chair is raised and lowered*].

CRAMPTON [*irritably*] I advise you to get my tooth out and have done reminding me of my wife. Come along, man. [*He grips the arms of the chair and braces himself*].

VALENTINE. What do you bet that I dont get that tooth out without your feeling it?

CRAMPTON. Your six weeks rent, young man. Dont you gammon me.

VALENTINE [*jumping at the bet and sending him aloft vigorously*] Done! Are you ready?

Crampton, who has lost his grip of the chair in his alarm at its sudden ascent, folds his arms; sits stiffly upright; and prepares for the worst. Valentine suddenly lets down the back of the chair to an obtuse angle.

CRAMPTON [*clutching at the arms of the chair as he falls back*] P!

take care, man! I'm quite helpless in this po –

VALENTINE [*deftly stopping him with the gag, and snatching up the mouthpiece of the gas machine*] Youll be more helpless presently.

He presses the mouthpiece over Crampton's mouth and nose, leaning over his chest so as to hold his head and shoulders well down on the chair. Crampton makes an inarticulate sound in the mouthpiece and tries to lay hands on Valentine, whom he supposes to be in front of him. After a moment his arms wave aimlessly, then subside and drop. He is quite insensible. Valentine throws aside the mouthpiece quickly; picks the forceps adroitly from the glass; and –.

ACT II

*On the terrace at the Marine Hotel. It is a square flagged platform,
glaring in the sun, and fenced on the seaward edge by a parapet. The
head waiter, busy laying napkins on a luncheon table with his back to
the sea, has the hotel on his right, and on his left, in the corner nearest
the sea, a flight of steps leading down to the beach. When he looks
down the terrace in front of him he sees, a little to his left, a middle
aged gentleman sitting on a chair of iron laths at a little iron table
with a bowl of lump sugar on it, reading an ultra-Conservative newspaper, with his umbrella up to defend him from the sun, which, in
August and at less than an hour after noon, is toasting his protended
insteps. At the hotel side of the terrace, there is a garden seat of the
ordinary esplanade pattern. Access to the hotel for visitors is by an entrance in the middle of its façade. Nearer the parapet there lurks a way
to the kitchen, masked by a little trellis porch. The table at which the
waiter is occupied is a long one, set across the terrace with covers and
chairs for five, two at each side and one at the end next the hotel.
Against the parapet another table is prepared as a buffet to serve from.*

*The waiter is a remarkable person in his way. A silky old man,
white haired and delicate looking, but so cheerful and contented that
in his encouraging presence ambition stands rebuked as vulgarity, and
imagination as treason to the abounding sufficiency and interest of the
actual. He has a certain expression peculiar to men who are pre-
eminent in their callings, and who, whilst aware of the vanity of success, are untouched by envy.*

*The gentleman at the iron table is not dressed for the seaside. He
wears his London frock coat and gloves; and his tall silk hat is on the
table beside the sugarbowl. The excellent condition and quality of these
garments and the gold-rimmed folding spectacles through which he is
reading, testify to his respectability. He is about fifty, clean-shaven and
close-cropped, with the corners of his mouth turned down purposely, as
if he suspected them of wanting to turn up, and was determined not to
let them have their way. He keeps his brow resolutely wide open, as if,
again, he had resolved in his youth to be truthful, magnanimous, and
incorruptible, but had never succeeded in making that habit of mind
automatic and unconscious. Still, he is by no means to be laughed at.*

237

There is no sign of stupidity or infirmity of will about him: on the contrary, he would pass anywhere at sight as a man of more than average professional capacity and responsibility. Just at present he is enjoying the weather and the sea too much to be out of patience; but he has exhausted all the news in his paper, and is at present reduced to the advertisements, which are not sufficiently succulent to induce him to persevere with them.

THE GENTLEMAN [*yawning and giving up the paper as a bad job*] Waiter!

WAITER. Sir? [*coming to him*].

THE GENTLEMAN. Are you quite sure Mrs Clandon is coming back before lunch?

WAITER. Quite sure, sir. She expects you at a quarter to one, sir. [*The gentleman, soothed at once by the waiter's voice, looks at him with a lazy smile. It is a quiet voice, with a gentle melody in it that gives sympathetic interest to his most commonplace remark; and he speaks with the sweetest propriety, neither dropping his aitches nor misplacing them, nor committing any other vulgarism. He looks at his watch as he continues*] Not that yet, sir, is it? 12.43, sir. Only two minutes more to wait, sir. Nice morning, sir!

THE GENTLEMAN. Yes: very fresh after London.

WAITER. Yes, sir: so all our visitors say, sir. Very nice family, Mrs Clandon's, sir.

THE GENTLEMAN. You like them, do you?

WAITER. Yes, sir. They have a free way with them that is very taking, sir, very taking indeed: especially the young lady and gentleman.

THE GENTLEMAN. Miss Dorothea and Mr Philip, I suppose.

WAITER. Yes, sir. The young lady, in giving an order, or the like of that, will say, 'Remember, William: we came to this hotel on your account, having heard what a perfect waiter you are.' The young gentleman will tell me that I remind him strongly of his father [*the gentleman starts at this*] and that he expects me to act by him as such. [*With a soothing sunny cadence*] Oh very pleasant sir, very affable and pleasant indeed!

THE GENTLEMAN. You like his father! [*He laughs at the notion*].

WAITER. Oh, sir, we must not take what they say too seriously. Of course, sir, if it were true, the young lady would have seen the resemblance too, sir.

THE GENTLEMAN. Did she?

WAITER. No, sir. She thought me like the bust of Shakespear in Stratford Church, sir. That is why she calls me William, sir. My real name is Walter, sir. [*He turns to go back to the table, and sees Mrs Clandon coming up to the terrace from the beach by the steps*]. Here is Mrs Clandon, sir. [*To Mrs Clandon in an unobtrusively confidential tone*] Gentleman for you, maam.

MRS CLANDON. We shall have two more gentlemen at lunch, William.

WAITER. Right, maam. Thank you, maam. [*He withdraws into the hotel*].

Mrs Clandon comes forward looking for her visitor, but passes over the gentleman without any sign of recognition.

THE GENTLEMAN [*peering at her quaintly from under the umbrella*] Dont you know me?

MRS CLANDON [*incredulously, looking hard at him*] Are you Finch M'Comas?

M'COMAS. Cant you guess? [*He shuts the umbrella; puts it aside; and jocularly plants himself with his hands on his hips to be inspected*].

MRS CLANDON. I believe you are. [*She gives him her hand. The shake that ensues is that of old friends after a long separation*]. Wheres your beard?

M'COMAS [*humorously solemn*] Would you employ a solicitor with a beard?

MRS CLANDON [*pointing to the silk hat on the table*] Is that your hat?

M'COMAS. Would you employ a solicitor with a sombrero?

MRS CLANDON. I have thought of you all these eighteen years with the beard and the sombrero. [*She sits down on the garden seat. M'Comas takes his chair again*] Do you go to the meetings of the Dialectical Society still?

M'COMAS [*gravely*] I do not frequent meetings now.

MRS CLANDON. Finch: I see what has happened. You have become respectable.

M'COMAS. Havent you?

MRS CLANDON. Not a bit.

M'COMAS. You hold to our old opinions still?

MRS CLANDON. As firmly as ever.

M'COMAS. Bless me! And you are still ready to make speeches in public, in spite of your sex [*Mrs Clandon nods*]; to insist on a married woman's right to her own separate property [*she nods again*]; to champion Darwin's view of the origin of species and John Stuart Mill's Essay on Liberty [*nod*]; to read Huxley, Tyndall, and George Eliot [*three nods*]; and to demand University degrees, the opening of the professions, and the parliamentary franchise for women as well as men.

MRS CLANDON [*resolutely*] Yes: I have not gone back one inch; and I have educated Gloria to take up my work when I must leave it. That is what has brought me back to England. I felt I had no right to bury her alive in Madeira: my St Helena, Finch. I suppose she will be howled at as I was; but she is prepared for that.

M'COMAS. Howled at! My dear good lady: there is nothing in any of those views nowadays to prevent her marrying an archbishop. You reproached me just now for having become respectable. You were wrong; I hold to our old opinions as strongly as ever. I dont go to church; and I dont pretend I do. I call myself what I am: a Philosophic Radical standing for liberty and the rights of the individual, as I learnt to do from my master Herbert Spencer. Am I howled at? No: I'm indulged as an old fogey. I'm out of everything, because I ve refused to bow the knee to Socialism.

MRS CLANDON [*shocked*] Socialism!

M'COMAS. Yes: Socialism. Thats what Miss Gloria will be up to her ears in before the end of the month if you let her loose here.

MRS CLANDON [*emphatically*] But I can prove to her that Socialism is a fallacy.

M'COMAS [*touchingly*] It is by proving that, Mrs Clandon, that I have lost all my young disciples. Be careful what you do: let her go her own way. [*With some bitterness*] We're old fashioned: the world thinks it has left us behind. There is only one place in all England where your opinions would still pass as advanced.

MRS CLANDON [*scornfully unconvinced*] The Church, perhaps?

M'COMAS. No: the theatre. And now to business! Why have you made me come down here?

MRS CLANDON. Well, partly because I wanted to see you –

M'COMAS [*with good-humored irony*] Thanks.

MRS CLANDON. – and partly because I want you to explain everything to the children. They know nothing: and now that we have come back to England it is impossible to leave them in ignorance any longer. [*Agitated*] Finch: I cannot bring myself to tell them. I –

    She is interrupted by the twins and Gloria. Dolly comes tearing up the steps, racing Phil, who combines terrific speed with an unhurried propriety of bearing which, however, costs him the race, as Dolly reaches her mother first and almost upsets the garden seat by the precipitancy of her embrace.

DOLLY [*breathless*] It's all right, mamma. The dentist is coming; and he's bringing his old man.

MRS CLANDON. Dolly, dear: dont you see Mr M'Comas? [*M'Comas rises, smiling*].

DOLLY [*her face falling with the most disparagingly obvious disappointment*] This! Where are the flowing locks?

PHILIP [*seconding her warmly*] Where the beard? the cloak? the poetic exterior?

DOLLY. Oh, Mr M'Comas, youve gone and spoiled yourself. Why didnt you wait til we'd seen you?

M'COMAS [*taken aback, but rallying his humor to meet the emergency*] Because eighteen years is too long for a solicitor to go without having his hair cut.

GLORIA [*at the other side of M'Comas*] How do you do, Mr M'Comas? [*He turns; and she takes his hand and presses it, with a frank straight look into his eyes*]. We are glad to meet you at last.

M'COMAS. Miss Gloria, I presume? [*Gloria smiles assent; releases his hand after a final pressure; and retires behind the garden seat, leaning over the back beside Mrs Clandon*]. And this young gentleman?

PHILIP. I was christened in a comparatively prosaic mood. My name is –

DOLLY [*completing his sentence for him declamatorily*] 'Norval. On the Grampian hills' –

PHILIP [*declaiming gravely*] 'My father feeds his flock, a frugal swain' –

MRS CLANDON [*remonstrating*] Dear, dear children: dont be silly. Everything is so new to them here, Finch, that they are in the wildest spirits. They think every Englishman they meet is a joke.

DOLLY. Well, so he is: it's not our fault.

PHILIP. My knowledge of human nature is fairly extensive, Mr M'Comas; but I find it impossible to take the inhabitants of this island seriously.

M'COMAS. I presume, sir, you are Master Philip [*offering his hand*].

PHILIP [*taking M'Comas's hand and looking solemnly at him*] I was Master Philip: was so for many years; just as you were once Master Finch. [*He gives the hand a single shake and drops it; then turns away, exclaiming meditatively*] How strange it is to look back on our boyhood!

DOLLY [*to Mrs Clandon*] Has Finch had a drink?

MRS CLANDON [*remonstrating*] Dearest: Mr M'Comas will lunch with us.

DOLLY. Have you ordered for seven? Dont forget the old gentleman.

MRS CLANDON. I have not forgotten him, dear. What is his name?

DOLLY. Chalkstones. He'll be here at half past one. [*To M'Comas*] Are we like what you expected?

MRS CLANDON [*earnestly, even a little peremptorily*] Dolly: Mr

M'Comas has something more serious than that to tell you. Children: I have asked my old friend to answer the question you asked this morning. He is your father's friend as well as mine; and he will tell you the story of my married life more fairly than I could. Gloria: are you satisfied?

GLORIA [*gravely attentive*] Mr M'Comas is very kind.

M'COMAS [*nervously*] Not at all, my dear young lady: not at all. At the same time, this is rather sudden. I was hardly prepared – er –

DOLLY [*suspiciously*] Oh, we dont want anything prepared.

PHILIP [*exhorting him*] Tell us the truth.

DOLLY [*emphatically*] Bald headed.

M'COMAS [*nettled*] I hope you intend to take what I have to say seriously.

PHILIP [*with profound gravity*] I hope it will deserve it, Mr M'Comas. My knowledge of human nature teaches me not to expect too much.

MRS CLANDON [*remonstrating*] Phil –

PHILIP. Yes, mother: all right. I beg your pardon, Mr M'Comas: dont mind us.

DOLLY [*in conciliation*] We mean well.

PHILIP. Shut up, both.

Dolly holds her lips. M'Comas takes a chair from the luncheon table; places it between the little table and the garden seat, with Dolly on his right and Phil on his left; and settles himself in it with the air of a man about to begin a long communication. The Clandons watch him expectantly.

M'COMAS. Ahem! Your father –

DOLLY. How old is he?

PHILIP. Sh!

MRS CLANDON [*softly*] Dear Dolly: dont let us interrupt Mr M'Comas.

M'COMAS [*emphatically*] Thank you, Mrs Clandon. Thank you. [*To Dolly*] You father is fifty-seven.

DOLLY [*with a bound, startled and excited*] Fifty-seven!! Where does he live?

MRS CLANDON [*remonstrating*] Dolly! Dolly!

M‘COMAS [*stopping her*] Let me answer that, Mrs Clandon. The answer will surprise you considerably. He lives in this town.

Mrs Clandon rises, intensely angry, but sits down again, speechless: Gloria watching her perplexedly.

DOLLY [*with conviction*] I knew it. Phil: Chalkstones is our father!

M‘COMAS. Chalkstones!

DOLLY. Oh, Crampstones, or whatever it is. He said I was like his mother. I knew he must mean his daughter.

PHILIP [*very seriously*] Mr M‘Comas: I desire to consider your feelings in every possible way; but I warn you that if you stretch the long arm of coincidence to the length of telling me that Mr Crampton of this town is my father, I shall decline to entertain the information for a moment.

M‘COMAS. And pray why?

PHILIP. Because I have seen the gentleman; and he is entirely unfit to be my father, or Dolly's father, or Gloria's father, or my mother's husband.

M‘COMAS. Oh, indeed! Well, sir, let me tell you that whether you like it or not, he is your father, and your sisters' father, and Mrs Clandon's husband. Now! What have you to say to that?

DOLLY [*whimpering*] You neednt be so cross. Crampton isnt your father.

PHILIP. Mr M‘Comas: your conduct is heartless. Here you find a family enjoying the unspeakable peace and freedom of being orphans. We have never seen the face of a relative: never known a claim except the claim of freely chosen friendship. And now you wish to thrust into the most intimate relationship with us a man whom we dont know –

DOLLY [*vehemently*] An awful old man [*Reproachfully*] And you began as if you had quite a nice father for us!

M‘COMAS [*angrily*] How do you know that he is not nice? And what right have you to choose your own father? [*Raising his voice*] Let me tell you, Miss Clandon, that you are too young to –

DOLLY [*interrupting him suddenly and eagerly*] Stop: I forgot!
  Has he any money?

M'COMAS. He has a great deal of money.

DOLLY [*delighted*] Oh, what did I always say, Phil?

PHILIP. Dolly: we have perhaps been condemning the old
  man too hastily. Proceed, Mr M'Comas.

M'COMAS. I shall not proceed, sir. I am too hurt, too
  shocked, to proceed.

MRS CLANDON [*struggling with her temper*] Finch: do you
  realize what is happening? Do you understand that my
  children have invited that man to lunch, and that he will
  be here in a few moments?

M'COMAS [*completely upset*] What! Do you mean? am I to
  understand? is it –

PHILIP [*impressively*] Steady, Finch. Think it out slowly and
  carefully. He's coming: coming to lunch.

GLORIA. Which of us is to tell him the truth? Have you
  thought of that?

MRS CLANDON. Finch: you must tell him.

DOLLY. Oh, Finch is no good at telling things. Look at the
  mess he has made of telling us.

M'COMAS. I have not been allowed to speak. I protest
  against this.

DOLLY [*taking his arm coaxingly*] Dear Finch: dont be cross.

MRS CLANDON. Gloria: let us go in. He may arrive at any
  moment.

GLORIA [*proudly*] Do not stir, mother. *I* shall not stir. We
  must not run away.

MRS CLANDON. My dear: we cannot sit down to lunch just
  as we are. We shall come back again. We must have no
  bravado. [*Gloria winces, and goes into the hotel without a
  word*]. Come, Dolly. [*As she goes to the hotel door, the waiter
  comes out with a tray of plates, etc. for two additional covers*].

WAITER. Gentlemen come yet, maam?

MRS CLANDON. Two more to come still, thank you. They
  will be here immediately. [*She goes into the hotel*].

  The waiter takes his tray to the service table.

PHILIP. I have an idea. Mr M'Comas: this communication should be made, should it not, by a man of infinite tact?

M'COMAS. It will require tact, certainly.

PHILIP. Good! Dolly: whose tact were you noticing only this morning?

DOLLY [*seizing the idea with rapture*] Oh yes, I declare!

PHILIP. The very man! [*Calling*] William!

WAITER. Coming, sir.

M'COMAS [*horrified*] The waiter! Stop! stop! I will not permit this. I –

WAITER [*presenting himself between Phil and M'Comas*] Yes, sir. *M'Comas's complexion fades into stone grey: all movement and expression desert his eyes. He sits down stupefied.*

PHILIP. William: you remember my request to you to regard me as your son?

WAITER [*with respectful indulgence*] Yes, sir. Anything you please, sir.

PHILIP. William: at the very outset of your career as my father, a rival has appeared on the scene.

WAITER. Your real father, sir? Well, that was to be expected, sooner or later, sir, wasnt it? [*Turning with a happy smile to M'Comas*] Is it you, sir?

M'COMAS [*renerved by indignation*] Certainly not. My children know how to behave themselves.

PHILIP. No, William: this gentleman was very nearly my father: he wooed my mother, but wooed her in vain.

M'COMAS [*outraged*] Well, of all the –

PHILIP. Sh! Consequently, he is only our solicitor. Do you know one Crampton, of the town?

WAITER. Cock-eyed Crampton, sir, of the Crooked Billet, is it?

PHILIP. I dont know. Finch: does he keep a public house?

M'COMAS [*rising, scandalized*] No, no, no. Your father, sir, is a well known yacht builder, an eminent man here.

WAITER [*impressed*] Oh! Beg pardon, sir, I'm sure. A son of Mr Crampton's! Dear me!

PHILIP. Mr Crampton is coming to lunch with us.

WAITER [*puzzled*] Yes, sir. [*Diplomatically*] Dont usually lunch with his family, perhaps, sir?

PHILIP [*impressively*] William: he does not know that we a r e his family. He has not seen us for eighteen years. He wont know us. [*To emphasize the communication, Phil seats himself on the iron table with a spring, and looks at the waiter with his lips compressed and his legs swinging*].

DOLLY. We want you to break the news to him, William.

WAITER. But I should think he'd guess when he sees your mother, miss.

Phil's legs become motionless. He contemplates the waiter raptly.

DOLLY [*dazzled*] I never thought of that.

PHILIP. Nor I. [*Coming off the table and turning reproachfully on M'Comas*] Nor you!

DOLLY. And you a solicitor!

PHILIP. Finch: your professional incompetence is appalling. William: your sagacity puts us all to shame.

DOLLY. You really a r e like Shakespear, William.

WAITER. Not at all, sir. Dont mention it, miss. Most happy, I'm sure, sir. [*He goes back modestly to the luncheon table and lays the two additional covers, one at the end next the steps, and the other so as to make a third on the side furthest from the balustrade*].

PHILIP [*abruptly seizing M'Comas's arm and leading him towards the hotel*] Finch: come and wash your hands.

M'COMAS. I am thoroughly vexed and hurt, Mr Clandon –

PHILIP [*interrupting him*] You will get used to us. Come, Dolly. [*M'Comas shakes him off and marches into the hotel. Phil follows with unruffled composure*].

DOLLY [*turning for a moment on the steps as she follows them*] Keep your wits about you, William. There will be fireworks.

WAITER. Right miss. You may depend on me, miss. [*She goes into the hotel*].

Valentine comes lightly up the steps from the beach, followed doggedly by Crampton. Valentine carries a walking stick. Crampton, either because he is old and chilly, or with some idea of extenuating the unfashionableness of his reefer jacket, wears a light overcoat. He stops at the chair left by M'Comas in the middle of the terrace, and steadies himself for a moment by placing his hand on the back of it.

CRAMPTON. Those steps make me giddy. [*He passes his hand over his forehead*]. I have not got over that infernal gas yet.

He goes to the iron chair, so that he can lean his elbows on the little table to prop his head as he sits. He soon recovers, and begins to unbutton his overcoat. Meanwhile Valentine interviews the waiter.

VALENTINE. Waiter!

WAITER [*coming forward between them*] Yes, sir.

VALENTINE. Mrs Lanfrey Clandon.

WAITER [*with a sweet smile of welcome*] Yes, sir. We're expecting you, sir. That is your table, sir. Mrs Clandon will be down presently, sir. The young lady and gentleman were just taking about your friend, sir.

VALENTINE. Indeed!

WAITER [*smoothly melodious*] Yes, sir. Great flow of spirits, sir. A vein of pleasantry, as you might say, sir. [*Quickly, to Crampton, who has risen to get the overcoat off*] Beg pardon, sir; but if youll allow me [*helping him to get the overcoat off, and taking it from him*]. Thank you, sir. [*Crampton sits down again; and the waiter resumes the broken melody*]. The young gentleman's latest is that youre his father, sir.

CRAMPTON. What!

WAITER. Only his joke, sir, his favorite joke. Yesterday, *I* was to be his father. Today, as soon as he knew you were coming, sir, he tried to put it up on me that you were his father; his long lost father! Not seen you for eighteen years, he said.

CRAMPTON [*startled*] Eighteen years!

WAITER. Yes, sir. [*With gentle archness*] But I was up to his tricks, sir. I saw the idea coming into his head as he stood there, thinking what new joke he'd have with me. Yes, sir: thats the sort he is: very pleasant, ve – ry offhand and affable indeed, sir. [*Again changing his tempo to say to Valentine, who is putting his stick down against the corner of the garden seat*]

If youll allow me, sir? [*He takes Valentine's stick*]. Thank you, sir. [*Valentine strolls up to the luncheon table and looks at the menu. The waiter turns to Crampton and continues his lay*]. Even the solicitor took up the joke, although he was in a manner of speaking in my confidence about the young gentleman, sir. Yes, sir, I assure you, sir. You would never imagine what respectable professional gentlemen from London will do on an outing, when the sea air takes them, sir.

CRAMPTON. Oh, theres a solicitor with them, is there?

WAITER. The family solicitor, sir: yes, sir. Name of M'Comas, sir. [*He goes towards the hotel entrance with the coat and stick, happily unconscious of the bomblike effect the name has produced on Crampton*].

CRAMPTON [*rising in angry alarm*] M'Comas! [*Calling to Valentine*] Valentine! [*Again, fiercely*] Valentine!! [*Valentine turns*]. This is a plant, a conspiracy. This is my family! my children! my infernal wife.

VALENTINE [*coolly*] Oh indeed! Interesting meeting! [*He resumes his study of the menu*].

CRAMPTON. Meeting! Not for me. Let me out of this. [*Calling across to the waiter*] Give me that coat.

WAITER. Yes, sir. [*He comes back; puts Valentine's stick carefully down against the luncheon table; and delicately shakes the coat out and holds it for Crampton to put on*]. I seem to have done the young gentleman an injustice, sir, havnt I, sir?

CRAMPTON. Rrrh! [*He stops on the point of putting his arms into the sleeves, and turns on Valentine with sudden suspicion*]. Valentine: you are in this. You made this plot. You –

VALENTINE [*decisively*] Bosh! [*He throws the menu down and goes round the table to look out unconcernedly over the parapet*].

CRAMPTON [*angrily*] What d'ye –

M'Comas, followed by Phil and Dolly, comes out, but recoils on seeing Crampton.

WAITER [*softly interrupting Crampton*] Steady, sir. Here they come, sir. [*He takes up Valentine's stick and makes for the hotel, throwing the coat across his arm*].

M'Comas turns the corners of his mouth resolutely down and

249

crosses to Crampton, who draws back and glares, with his hands behind him. M'Comas, with his brow opener than ever, confronts him in the majesty of a spotless conscience.

WAITER [*aside, as he passes Phil on his way out*] Ive broke it to him, sir.

PHILIP. Invaluable William! [*He passes on to the table*].

DOLLY [*aside to the waiter*] How did he take it?

WAITER [*aside to her*] Startled at first, miss; but resigned: very resigned indeed, miss. [*He takes the stick and coat into the hotel*].

M'COMAS [*having stared Crampton out of countenance*] So here you are, Mr Crampton.

CRAMPTON. Yes, here: caught in a trap: a mean trap. Are those my children?

PHILIP [*with deadly politeness*] Is this our father, Mr M'Comas?

M'COMAS [*stoutly*] He is.

DOLLY [*conventionally*] Pleased to meet you again. [*She wanders idly round the table, exchanging a grimace with Valentine on the way*].

PHILIP. Allow me to discharge my first duty as host by ordering your wine. [*He takes the wine list from the table. His polite attention, and Dolly's unconcerned indifference, leave Crampton on the footing of a casual acquaintance picked up that morning at the dentist's. The consciousness of it goes through the father with so keen a pang that he trembles all over; his brow becomes wet; and he stares dumbly at his son, who, just sensible enough of his own callousness to intensely enjoy the humor and adroitness of it, proceeds pleasantly*] Finch: some crusted old port for you, as a respectable family solicitor, eh?

M'COMAS [*firmly*] Apollinaris only. Nothing heating. [*He walks away to the side of the terrace, like a man putting temptation behind him*].

PHILIP. Valentine –?

VALENTINE. Would Lager be considered vulgar?

PHILIP. Probably. We'll order some. [*Turning to Crampton with cheerful politeness*] And now, Mr Crampton, what can we do for you?

CRAMPTON. What d'ye mean, boy?

PHILIP. Boy! [*Very solemnly*] Whose fault is it that I am a boy?

Crampton snatches the wine list rudely from him and irresolutely pretends to read it. Philip abandons it to him with perfect politeness.

DOLLY [*looking over Crampton's right shoulder*]. The whisky's on the last page but one.

CRAMPTON. Let me alone, child.

DOLLY. Child! No, no: you may call me Dolly if you like; but you mustnt call me child. [*She slips her arm through Phil's; and the two stand looking at Crampton as if he were some eccentric stranger*].

CRAMPTON [*mopping his brow in rage and agony, and yet relieved even by their playing with him*] M'Comas: we are – ha! – going to have a pleasant meal.

M'COMAS [*resolutely cheerful*] There is no reason why it should not be pleasant.

PHILIP. Finch's face is a feast in itself.

Mrs Clandon and Gloria come from the hotel. Mrs Clandon advances with courageous self-possession and marked dignity of manner. She stops at the foot of the steps to address Valentine, who is in her path. Gloria also stops, looking at Crampton with a certain repulsion.

MRS CLANDON. Glad to see you again, Mr Valentine. [*He smiles. She passes on and confronts Crampton, intending to address him with complete composure; but his aspect shakes her. She stops suddenly and says anxiously, with a touch of remorse*] Fergus: you are greatly changed.

CRAMPTON [*grimly*] I daresay. A man does change in eighteen years.

MRS CLANDON [*troubled*] I – I did not mean that. I hope your health is good.

CRAMPTON. Thank you. No: it's not my health. It's my happiness: thats the change you meant, I think. [*Breaking out suddenly*] Look at her, M'Comas! Look at her; and [*with a half laugh, half sob*] look at me!

PHILIP. Sh! [*Pointing to the hotel entrance, where the waiter has just appeared*] Order before William!

DOLLY [*touching Crampton's arm warningly*] Ahem!

> *The waiter goes to the service table and beckons to the kitchen entrance, whence issue a young waiter with soup plates, and a cook, in white apron and cap, with the soup tureen. The young waiter remains and serves: the cook goes out, and reappears from time to time bringing in the courses. He carves, but does not serve. The waiter comes to the end of the luncheon table next the steps.*

MRS CLANDON [*as they assemble at the table*] I think you have all met one another already today. Oh no: excuse me. [*Introducing*] Mr Valentine: Mr M'Comas. [*She goes to the end of the table nearest the hotel*]. Fergus: will you take the head of the table, please.

CRAMPTON. Ha! [*Bitterly*] The head of the table!

WAITER [*holding the chair for him with inoffensive encouragement*] This end, sir. [*Crampton submits, and takes his seat*]. Thank you, sir.

MRS CLANDON. Mr Valentine: will you take that side [*indicating the side next the parapet*] with Gloria? [*Valentine and Gloria take their places, Gloria next Crampton and Valentine next Mrs Clandon*]. Finch: I must put you on this side, between Dolly and Phil. You must protect yourself as best you can.

> *The three take the remaining side of the table, Dolly next her mother, Phil next his father. Soup is served.*

WAITER [*to Crampton*] Thick or clear, sir?

CRAMPTON [*To Mrs Clandon*] Does nobody ask a blessing in this household?

PHILIP [*interposing smartly*] Let us first settle what we are about to receive. William!

WAITER. Yes, sir. [*He glides swiftly round the table to Phil's left elbow. On his way he whispers to the younger waiter*] Thick.

PHILIP. Two small Lagers for the children as usual, William; and one large for this gentleman [*indicating Valentine*]. Large Apollinaris for Mr M'Comas.

WAITER. Yes, sir.

DOLLY. Have a six of Irish in it, Finch?

M'COMAS [*scandalized*] No. No, thank you.

PHILIP. Number 413 for my mother and Miss Gloria as

before; and – [*turning inquiringly to Crampton*] Eh?

CRAMPTON [*scowling and about to reply offensively*] I –

WAITER [*striking in mellifluously*] All right, sir. We know what Mr Crampton likes here, sir. [*He goes into the hotel*].

PHILIP [*looking gravely at his father*] You frequent bars. Bad habit!

The cook, followed by a waiter with hot plates, brings in the fish from the kitchen to the service table, and begins slicing it.

CRAMPTON. You have learnt your lesson from your mother, I see.

MRS CLANDON. Phil: will you please remember that your jokes are apt to irritate people who are not accustomed to us, and that your father is our guest today.

CRAMPTON [*bitterly*] Yes: a guest at the head of my own table. [*The soup plates are removed*].

DOLLY [*sympathetically*] It's embarrassing, isnt it? It's just as bad for us, you know.

PHILIP. Sh! Dolly: we are both wanting in tact. [*To Crampton*] We mean well, Mr Crampton; but we are not yet strong in the filial line. [*The waiter returns from the hotel with the drinks*]. William: come and restore good feeling.

WAITER [*cheerfully*] Yes, sir. Certainly, sir. Small Lager for you sir. [*To Crampton*] Seltzer and Irish, sir. [*To M'Comas*] Apollinaris, sir. [*To Dolly*] Small Lager, miss. [*To Mrs Clandon, pouring out wine*] 413, madam. [*To Valentine*] Large Lager for you, sir. [*To Gloria*] 413, miss.

DOLLY [*drinking*] To the family!

PHILIP [*drinking*] Hearth and Home!

Fish is served.

M'COMAS. We are getting on very nicely after all.

DOLLY [*critically*] After all! After all what, Finch?

CRAMPTON [*sarcastically*] He means that you are getting on very nicely in spite of the presence of your father. Do I take your point rightly, Mr M'Comas?

M'COMAS [*disconcerted*] No, no. I only said 'after all' to round off the sentence. I – er – er – er –

WAITER [*tactfully*] Turbot, sir?

M‘COMAS [*intensely grateful for the interruption*] Thank you, waiter: thank you.

WAITER [*sotto voce*] Dont mention it, sir. [*He returns to the service table*].

CRAMPTON [*to Phil*] Have you thought of choosing a profession yet?

PHILIP. I am keeping my mind open on that subject. William!

WAITER. Yes, sir.

PHILIP. How long do you think it would take me to learn to be a really smart waiter?

WAITER. Cant be learnt, sir. It's in the character, sir. [*Confidentially to Valentine, who is looking about for something*] Bread for the lady, sir? yes, sir. [*He serves bread to Gloria, and resumes, at his former pitch*] Very few are born to it, sir.

PHILIP. You dont happen to have such a thing as a son, yourself, have you?

WAITER. Yes, sir: oh yes, sir. [*To Gloria, again dropping his voice*] A little more fish, miss? you wont care for the joint in the middle of the day.

GLORIA. No, thank you.

The fish plates are removed, and the next course served.

DOLLY. Is your son a waiter too, William?

WAITER [*serving Gloria with fowl*] Oh no, miss: he's too impetuous. He's at the Bar.

M‘COMAS [*patronizingly*] A potman, eh?

WAITER [*with a touch of melancholy, as if recalling a disappointment softened by time*] No, sir: the other bar. Your profession, sir. A Q.C., sir.

M‘COMAS [*embarrassed*] I'm sure I beg your pardon.

WAITER. Not at all, sir. Very natural mistake, I'm sure, sir. Ive often wished he was a potman, sir. Would have been off my hands ever so much sooner, sir. [*Aside to Valentine, who is again in difficulties*] Salt at your elbow, sir. [*Resuming*] Yes, sir: had to support him until he was thirty-seven, sir. But doing well now, sir: very satisfactory indeed, sir. Nothing less than fifty guineas, sir.

M'COMAS. Democracy, Crampton! Modern democracy!

WAITER [*calmly*] No, sir, not democracy: only education, sir. Scholarships, sir. Cambridge Local, sir. Sidney Sussex College, sir. [*Dolly plucks his sleeve and whispers as he bends down*]. Stone ginger, miss? Right, miss. [*To M'Comas*] Very good thing for him, sir: he never had any turn for real work, sir. [*He goes into the hotel, leaving the company somewhat overwhelmed by his son's eminence*].

VALENTINE. Which of us dare give that man an order again!

DOLLY. I hope he wont mind my sending him for ginger-beer.

CRAMPTON [*doggedly*] While he's a waiter it's his business to wait. If you had treated him as a waiter ought to be treated, he'd have held his tongue.

DOLLY. What a loss that would have been! Perhaps he'll give us an introduction to his son and get us into London society.

The waiter reappears with the ginger-beer.

CRAMPTON [*growling contemptuously*] London society! London society! Youre not fit for any society, child.

DOLLY [*losing her temper*] Now look here, Mr Crampton. If you think –

WAITER [*softly, at her elbow*] Stone ginger, miss.

DOLLY [*taken aback, recovers her good humor after a long breath, and says sweetly*] Thank you, dear William. You were just in time. [*She drinks*].

M'COMAS. If I may be allowed to change the subject, Miss Clandon, what is the established religion in Madeira?

GLORIA. I suppose the Portuguese religion. I never inquired.

DOLLY. The servants come in Lent and kneel down before you and confess all the things theyve done; and you have to pretend to forgive them. Do they do that in England, William?

WAITER. Not usually, miss. They may in some parts; but it has not come under my notice, miss. [*Catching Mrs Clandon's eye as the young waiter offers her the salad bowl*] You like it without

dressing, maam; yes, maam, I have some for you. [*To his
young colleague, motioning him to serve Gloria*] This side, Jo.
[*He takes a special portion of salad from the service table and puts
it beside Mrs Clandon's plate. In doing so he observes that Dolly
is making a wry face*]. Only a bit of watercress, miss, got in
by mistake [*he takes her salad away*]. Thank you, miss. [*To
the young waiter, admonishing him to serve Dolly afresh*] Jo.
[*Resuming*] Mostly members of the Church of England, miss.

DOLLY. Members of the Church of England? Whats the
subscription?

CRAMPTON [*rising violently amid general consternation*] You
see how my children have been brought up, M‘Comas.
You see it: you hear it. I call all of you to witness – [*He
becomes inarticulate, and is about to strike his fist recklessly on the
table when the waiter considerately takes away his plate*].

MRS CLANDON [*firmly*] Sit down, Fergus. There is no
occasion at all for this outburst. You must remember that
Dolly is just like a foreigner here. Pray sit down.

CRAMPTON [*subsiding unwillingly*] I doubt whether I ought
to sit here and countenance all this. I doubt it.

WAITER. Cheese, sir? or would you like a cold sweet?

CRAMPTON [*taken aback*] What? Oh! Cheese, cheese.

DOLLY. Bring a box of cigarets, William.

WAITER. All ready, miss. [*He takes a box of cigarets from the
service table and places them before Dolly, who selects one and prepares to smoke. He then returns to his table for the matches*].

CRAMPTON [*staring aghast at Dolly*] Does she smoke?

DOLLY [*out of patience*] Really, Mr Crampton, I'm afraid
I'm spoiling your lunch. I'll go and have my cigaret on
the beach. [*She leaves the table with petulant suddenness and
goes to the steps. The waiter strikes a match and adroitly lights
her cigaret*]. Thank you, dear William. [*She vanishes down
the steps*].

CRAMPTON [*furiously*] Margaret: call that girl back. Call
her back, I say.

M‘COMAS [*trying to make peace*] Come, Crampton: never
mind. She's her father's daughter: thats all.

MRS CLANDON [*with deep resentment*] I hope not, Finch. [*She rises: they all rise a little*]. Mr Valentine: will you excuse me? I am afraid Dolly is hurt and put out by what has passed. I must go to her.

CRAMPTON. To take her part against me, you mean.

MRS CLANDON [*ignoring him*] Gloria: will you take my place whilst I am away, dear. [*She crosses to the steps and goes down to the beach*].

Crampton's expression is one of bitter hatred. The rest watch her in embarrassed silence, feeling the incident to be a very painful one. The waiter discreetly shepherds his assistant along with him into the hotel by the kitchen entrance, leaving the luncheon party to themselves.

CRAMPTON [*throwing himself back in his chair*] Theres a mother for you, M'Comas! Theres a mother for you!

GLORIA [*steadfastly*] Yes: a good mother.

CRAMPTON. And a bad father? Thats what you mean, eh?

VALENTINE [*rising indignantly and addressing Gloria*] Miss Clandon: I –

CRAMPTON [*turning on him*] That girl's name is Crampton, Mr Valentine, not Clandon. Do you wish to join them in insulting me?

VALENTINE [*ignoring him*] I'm overwhelmed, Miss Clandon. It's all my fault: I brought him here: I'm responsible for him. And I'm ashamed of him.

CRAMPTON. What d'y' mean?

GLORIA [*rising coldly*] No harm has been done, Mr Valentine. We have all been a little childish, I am afraid. Our party has been a failure: let us break it up and have done with it. [*She puts her chair aside and turns to the steps, adding, with slighting composure, as she passes Crampton*] Goodbye, father.

She descends the steps with cold disgusted indifference. They all look after her, and so do not notice the return of the waiter from the hotel, laden with Crampton's coat, Valentine's stick, a couple of shawls and parasols, and some camp stools, which he deposits on the bench.

CRAMPTON [*to himself, staring after Gloria with a ghastly expression*] Father! Father!! [*He strikes his fist violently on the table*]. Now —

WAITER [*offering the coat*] This is yours, sir, I think, sir. [*Crampton glares at him, then snatches it rudely and comes down the terrace towards the garden seat, struggling with the coat in his angry efforts to put it on. M'Comas rises and goes to his assistance: then takes his hat and umbrella from the little iron table, and turns towards the steps. Meanwhile the waiter, after thanking Crampton with unruffled sweetness for taking the coat, picks up the other articles and offers the parasols to Phil*]. The ladies' sunshades, sir. Nasty glare off the sea today, sir: very trying to the complexion, sir. I shall carry down the camp stools myself, sir.

PHILIP. You are old, Father William; but you are the most thoughtful of men. No: keep the sunshades and give me the camp stools [*taking them*].

WAITER [*with flattering gratitude*] Thank you, sir.

PHILIP. Finch: share with me [*giving him a couple*]. Come along. [*They go down the steps together*].

VALENTINE [*to the waiter*] Leave me something to bring down. One of these [*offering to take a sunshade*].

WAITER [*discreetly*] Thats the younger lady's, sir. [*Valentine lets it go*]. Thank you, sir. If youll allow me, sir, I think you had better take this. [*He puts down his burden on Crampton's chair, and produces from the tail pocket of his dress coat a book with a lady's handkerchief between the leaves to mark the page*]. The elder young lady is reading it at present. [*Valentine takes it eagerly*]. Thank you, sir. The Subjection of Women, sir, you see. [*He takes up the burden again*]. Heavier reading than you and I would care for at the seaside, sir. [*He goes down the steps*].

VALENTINE [*coming rather excitedly to Crampton*] Now look here, Crampton: are you at all ashamed of yourself?

CRAMPTON [*pugnaciously*] Ashamed of myself! What for?

VALENTINE. For behaving like a bear. What will your daughter think of me for having brought you here?

CRAMPTON. I was not thinking of what my daughter was thinking of you.

VALENTINE. No, you were thinking of yourself. Youre a perfect egomaniac.

CRAMPTON [*heartrent*] She told you what I am: a father: a father robbed of his children. What are the hearts of this generation like? Am I to come here after all these years? to see what my children are for the first time! to hear their voices! and carry it all off like a fashionable visitor; drop in to lunch; be Mr Crampton? Mister Crampton! What right have they to talk to me like that? I'm their father: do they deny that? I'm a man, with the feelings of our common humanity: have I no rights, no claims? In all these years who have I had round me? Servants, clerks, business acquaintances. Ive had respect from them: aye, kindness. Would one of them have spoken to me as that girl spoke? Would one of them have laughed at me as that boy was laughing at me all the time? [*Frantically*] My own children! Mister Crampton! My –

VALENTINE. Come, come! theyre only children. She called you father.

CRAMPTON. Yes: 'goodbye, father'. Goodbye! Oh yes: she got at my feelings: with a stab!

VALENTINE [*taking this in very bad part*] Now look here, Crampton: you just let her alone: she's treated you very well. I had a much worse time of it at lunch than you.

CRAMPTON. You!

VALENTINE [*with growing impetuosity*] Yes: I. I sat next her; and I never said a single thing to her the whole time: couldnt think of a blessed word. And not a word did she say to me.

CRAMPTON. Well?

VALENTINE. Well? Well??? [*Tackling him very seriously, and talking faster and faster*] Crampton: do you know whats been the matter with me today? You dont suppose, do you, that I'm in the habit of playing such tricks on my patients as I played on you?

CRAMPTON. I hope not.

VALENTINE. The explanation is that I'm stark mad, or rather that Ive never been in my real senses before. I'm capable of anything: Ive grown up at last: I'm a Man; and it's your daughter thats made a man of me.

CRAMPTON [*incredulously*] Are you in love with my daughter?

VALENTINE [*his words now coming in a perfect torrent*] Love! Nonsense: it's something far above and beyond that. It's life, it's faith, it's strength, certainty, paradise –

CRAMPTON [*interrupting him with acrid contempt*] Rubbish, man! What have you to keep a wife on? You cant marry her.

VALENTINE. Who wants to marry her? I'll kiss her hands; I'll kneel at her feet; I'll live for her; I'll die for her; and thatll be enough for me. Look at her book! See [*He kisses the handkerchief*]. If you offered me all your money for this excuse for going down to the beach and speaking to her again, I'd only laugh at you. [*He rushes buoyantly off to the steps, where he bounces right into the arms of the waiter, who is coming up from the beach. The two save themselves from falling by clutching one another tightly round the waist and whirling one another round*].

WAITER [*delicately*] Steady, sir, steady!

VALENTINE [*shocked at his own violence*] I beg your pardon.

WAITER. Not at all, sir, not at all. Very natural, sir, I'm sure, sir, at your age. The lady has sent me for her book, sir. Might I take the liberty of asking you to let her have it at once, sir.

VALENTINE. With pleasure. And if you will allow me to present you with a professional man's earnings for six weeks – [*offering him Dolly's crown piece*]?

WAITER [*as if the sum were beyond his utmost expectations*] Thank you, sir: much obliged. [*Valentine dashes down the steps*]. Very high-spirited young gentleman, sir: very manly and straight set up.

CRAMPTON [*in grumbling disparagement*] And making his fortune in a hurry, no doubt. *I* know what his six weeks' earnings come to. [*He crosses the terrace to the iron table, and sits down*].

WAITER [*philosophically*] Well, sir, you never can tell. Thats a principle in life with me, sir, if youll excuse my having such a thing, sir. [*Delicately sinking the philosopher in the waiter for a moment*] Perhaps you havnt noticed that you hadnt touched that seltzer and Irish, sir, when the party broke up. [*He takes the tumbler from the luncheon table and sets it before Crampton*]. Yes, sir, you never can tell. There was my son, sir! who ever thought that he would rise to wear a silk gown, sir? And yet, today, sir, nothing less than fifty guineas. What a lesson sir!

CRAMPTON. Well, I hope he is grateful to you, and recognizes what he owes you, as a son should.

WAITER. We get on together very well, very well indeed, sir, considering the difference in our stations. [*Crampton is about to take a drink*]. A small lump of sugar, sir, will take the flatness out of the seltzer without noticeably sweetening the drink, sir. Allow me, sir. [*He drops a lump of sugar into the tumbler*]. But as I say to him, wheres the difference after all? If I must put on a dress coat to shew what I am, sir, he must put on a wig and gown to shew what he is. If my income is mostly tips, and theres a pretence that I dont get them, why, his income is mostly fees, sir; and I understand theres a pretence that he dont get them! If he likes society, and his profession brings him into contact with all ranks, so does mine too, sir. If it's a little against a barrister to have a waiter for his father, sir, it's a little against a waiter to have a barrister for a son: many people consider it a great liberty, sir, I assure you, sir. Can I get you anything else, sir?

CRAMPTON. No, thank you. [*With bitter humility*] I suppose theres no objection to my sitting here for a while: I cant disturb the party on the beach here.

WAITER [*with emotion*] Very kind of you, sir, to put it as if it was not a compliment and an honour to us, Mr Crampton, very kind indeed. The more you are at home here, sir, the better for us.

CRAMPTON [*in poignant irony*] Home!

WAITER [*reflectively*] Well, yes, sir: thats a way of looking at it too, sir. I have always said that the great advantage of a hotel is that it's a refuge from home life, sir.

CRAMPTON. I missed that advantage today, I think.

WAITER. You did, sir: you did. Dear me! It's the unexpected that always happens, isnt it? [*Shaking his head*] You never can tell, sir: you never can tell. [*He goes into the hotel*].

CRAMPTON [*his eyes shining hardly as he props his drawn miserable face on his hands*] Home Home!! [*Hearing someone approaching he hastily sits bolt upright. It is Gloria, who has come up the steps alone, with her sunshade and her book in her hands. He looks defiantly at her, with the brutal obstinacy of his mouth and the wistfulness of his eyes contradicting each other pathetically. She comes to the corner of the garden seat and stands with her back to it, leaning against the end of it, and looking down at him as if wondering at his weakness: too curious about him to be cold, but supremely indifferent to their kinship. He greets her with a growl*]. Well?

GLORIA. I want to speak to you for a moment.

CRAMPTON [*looking steadily at her*] Indeed? Thats surprising. You meet your father after eighteen years; and you actually want to speak to him for a moment! Thats touching: isnt it?

GLORIA. All that is what seems to me so nonsensical, so uncalled for. What do you expect us to feel for you? to do for you? What is it you want? Why are you less civil to us than other people are? You are evidently not very fond of us: why should you be? But surely we can meet without quarrelling.

CRAMPTON [*a dreadful grey shade passing over his face*] Do you realize that I am your father?

GLORIA. Perfectly.

CRAMPTON. Do you know what is due to me as your father?

GLORIA. For instance –?

CRAMPTON [*rising as if to combat a monster*] For instance! For instance!! For instance, duty, affection, respect, obedience –

262

GLORIA [*quitting her careless leaning attitude and confronting him promptly and proudly*] I obey nothing but my sense of what is right. I respect nothing that is not noble. That is my duty. [*She adds, less firmly*] As to affection, it is not within my control. I am not sure that I quite know what affection means. [*She turns away with an evident distaste for that part of the subject, and goes to the luncheon table for a comfortable chair, putting down her book and sunshade*].

CRAMPTON [*following her with his eyes*] Do you really mean what you are saying?

GLORIA [*turning on him quickly and severely*] Excuse me: that is an uncivil question. I am speaking seriously to you; and I expect you to take me seriously. [*She takes one of the luncheon chairs; turns it away from the table; and sits down a little wearily, saying*] Can you not discuss this matter coolly and rationally?

CRAMPTON. Coolly and rationally! No I cant. Do you understand that? I cant.

GLORIA [*emphatically*] No. That I cannot understand. I have no sympathy with –

CRAMPTON [*shrinking nervously*] Stop! Dont say anything more yet: you dont know what youre doing. Do you want to drive me mad? [*She frowns, finding such petulance intolerable. He adds hastily*] No: I'm not angry: indeed I'm not. Wait, wait: give me a little time to think. [*He stands for a moment, screwing and clinching his brows and hands in his perplexity; then takes the end chair from the luncheon table and sits down beside her, saying, with a touching effort to be gentle and patient*] Now I think I have it. At least I'll try.

GLORIA [*firmly*] You see! Everything comes right if we only think it resolutely out.

CRAMPTON [*in sudden dread*] No: dont think. I want you to feel: thats the only thing that can help us. Listen! Do you – but first – I forgot. Whats your name? I mean your pet name. They cant very well call you Sophronia.

GLORIA [*with astonished disgust*] Sophronia! My name is Gloria. I am always called by it.

CRAMPTON [*his temper rising again*] Your name is Sophronia, girl: you were called after your aunt Sophronia, my sister: she gave you your first Bible with your name written in it.

GLORIA. Then my mother gave me a new name.

CRAMPTON [*angrily*] She had no right to do it. I will not allow this.

GLORIA. You had no right to give me your sister's name. I dont know her.

CRAMPTON. Youre talking nonsense. There are bounds to what I will put up with. I will not have it. Do you hear that?

GLORIA [*rising warningly*] Are you resolved to quarrel?

CRAMPTON [*terrified, pleading*] No, no: sit down. Sit down, wont you? [*She looks at him, keeping him in suspense. He forces himself to utter the obnoxious name*]. Gloria. [*She marks her satisfaction with a slight tightening of the lips, and sits down*]. There! You see I only want to shew you that I am your father, my – my dear child. [*The endearment is so plaintively inept that she smiles in spite of herself, and resigns herself to indulge him a little*]. Listen now. What I want to ask you is this. Dont you remember me at all? You were only a tiny child when you were taken away from me; but you took plenty of notice of things. Cant you remember someone whom you loved, or [*shyly*] at least liked in a childish way? Come! someone who let you stay in his study and look at his toy boats, as you thought them? [*He looks anxiously into her face for some response, and continues less hopefully and more urgently*] Someone who let you do as you liked there, and never said a word to you except to tell you that you must sit still and not speak? Someone who was something that no one else was to you – who was your father?

GLORIA [*unmoved*] If you describe things to me, no doubt I shall presently imagine that I remember them. But I really remember nothing.

CRAMPTON [*wistfully*] Has your mother never told you anything about me?

GLORIA. She has never mentioned your name to me. [*He*

groans involuntarily. She looks at him rather contemptuously and continues] Except once; and then she did remind me of something I had forgotten.

CRAMPTON [*looking up hopefully*] What was that?

GLORIA [*mercilessly*] The whip you bought to beat me with.

CRAMPTON [*gnashing his teeth*] Oh! To bring that up against me! To turn you from me! When you need never have known. [*Under a grinding, agonized breath*] Curse her!

GLORIA [*springing up*] You wretch! [*With intense emphasis*] You wretch! You dare curse my mother!

CRAMPTON. Stop; or youll be sorry afterwards. I'm your father.

GLORIA. How I hate the name! How I love the name of Mother! You had better go.

CRAMPTON. I – I'm choking. You want to kill me. Some – I – [*His voice stifles: he is almost in a fit*].

GLORIA [*going up to the balustrade with cool quick resourcefulness, and calling over it to the beach*] Mr Valentine!

VALENTINE [*answering from below*] Yes.

GLORIA. Come here for a moment, please. Mr Crampton wants you. [*She returns to the table and pours out a glass of water*].

CRAMPTON [*recovering his speech*] No: let me alone. I dont want him. I'm all right, I tell you. I need neither his help nor yours. [*He raises and pulls himself together*]. As you say, I had better go. [*He puts on his hat*]. Is that your last word?

GLORIA. I hope so.

He looks stubbornly at her for a moment; nods grimly, as if he agreed to that; and goes into the hotel. She looks at him with equal steadiness until he disappears, when, with a gesture of relief, she turns to Valentine, who comes running up the steps.

VALENTINE [*panting*] Whats the matter? [*Looking round*] Wheres Crampton?

GLORIA. Gone. [*Valentine's face lights up with sudden joy, dread, and mischief as he realizes that he is alone with Gloria. She continues indifferently*] I thought he was ill; but he recovered himself. He wouldnt wait for you. I am sorry. [*She goes for her book and parasol*].

VALENTINE. So much the better. He gets on my nerves after a while. [*Pretending to forget himself*] How could that man have so beautiful a daughter!

GLORIA [*taken aback for a moment; then answering him with polite but intentional contempt*] That seems to be an attempt at what is called a pretty speech. Let me say at once, Mr Valentine, that pretty speeches make very sickly conversation. Pray let us be friends, if we are to be friends, in a sensible and wholesome way. I have no intention of getting married; and unless you are content to accept that state of things, we had much better not cultivate each other's acquaintance.

VALENTINE [*cautiously*] I see. May I ask just this one question? Is your objection an objection to marriage as an institution, or merely an objection to marrying me personally?

GLORIA. I do not know you well enough, Mr Valentine, to have an opinion on the subject of your personal merits. [*She turns away from him with infinite indifference, and sits down with her book on the garden seat*]. I do not think the conditions of marriage at present are such as any self-respecting woman can accept.

VALENTINE [*instantly changing his tone for one of cordial sincerity, as if he frankly accepted her terms and was delighted and reassured by her principles*] Oh, then thats a point of sympathy between us already. I quite agree with you: the conditions are most unfair. [*He takes off his hat and throws it gaily on the iron table*]. No: what I want is to get rid of all that nonsense. [*He sits down beside her, so naturally that she does not think of objecting, and proceeds, with enthusiasm*] Dont you think it a horrible thing that a man and a woman can hardly know one another without being supposed to have designs of that kind? As if there were no other interests! no other subjects of conversation! As if women were capable of nothing better!

GLORIA [*interested*] Ah, now you are beginning to talk humanly and sensibly, Mr Valentine.

VALENTINE [*with a gleam in his eye at the success of his hunter's guile*] Of course! two intelligent people like us! Isnt it pleasant, in this stupid convention-ridden world, to meet with someone on the same plane? someone with an unprejudiced enlightened mind?

GLORIA [*earnestly*] I hope to meet many such people in England.

VALENTINE [*dubiously*] Hm! there are a good many people here: nearly forty millions. Theyre not all consumptive members of the highly educated classes like the people in Madeira.

GLORIA [*now full of her subject*] Oh, everybody is stupid and prejudiced in Madeira; weak sentimental creatures. I hate weakness; and I hate sentiment.

VALENTINE. Thats what makes you so inspiring.

GLORIA [*with a slight laugh*] Am I inspiring?

VALENTINE. Yes. Strength's infectious.

GLORIA. Weakness is, I know.

VALENTINE [*with conviction*] You r e strong. Do you know that you changed the world for me this morning? I was in the dumps, thinking of my unpaid rent, frightened about the future. When you came in, I was dazzled. [*Her brow clouds a little. He goes on quickly*] That was silly, of course; but really and truly something happened to me. Explain it how you will, my blood got – [*he hesitates, trying to think of a sufficiently unimpassioned word*] – oxygenated: my muscles braced; my mind cleared; my courage rose. Thats odd, isnt it? considering that I am not at all a sentimental man.

GLORIA [*uneasily, rising*] Let us go back to the beach.

VALENTINE [*darkly: looking up at her*] What! you feel it too?

GLORIA. Feel what?

VALENTINE. Dread.

GLORIA. Dread?

VALENTINE. As if something were going to happen. It came over me suddenly just before you proposed that we should run away to the others.

GLORIA [*amazed*] Thats strange: very strange I had the same presentiment.

VALENTINE [*solemnly*] How extraordinary. [*Rising*] Well:
shall we run away?

GLORIA. Run away! Oh no: that would be childish. [*She
sits down again. He resumes his seat beside her, and watches her
with a gravely sympathetic air. She is thoughtful and a little
troubled as she adds*] I wonder what is the scientific explanation of those fancies that cross us occasionally!

VALENTINE. Ah, I wonder! It's a curiously helpless sensation: isnt it?

GLORIA [*rebelling against the word*] Helpless?

VALENTINE. Yes, helpless. As if Nature, after letting us
belong to ourselves and do what we judged right and
reasonable for all these years, were suddenly lifting her
great hand to take us – her two little children – by the
scruffs of our little necks, and use us, in spite of ourselves,
for her own purposes, in her own way.

GLORIA. Isnt that rather fanciful?

VALENTINE [*with a new and startling transition to a tone of utter
recklessness*] I dont know. I dont care. [*Bursting out reproachfully*] Oh, Miss Clandon, Miss Clandon: how could you?

GLORIA. What have I done?

VALENTINE. Thrown this enchantment on me. I'm
honestly trying to be sensible and scientific and everything
that you wish me to be. But – but – oh, dont you see what
you have set to work in my imagination?

GLORIA. I hope you are not going to be so foolish – so
vulgar – as to say love.

VALENTINE. No, no, no, no. Not love: we know better
than that. Let's call it chemistry. You cant deny that there
is such a thing as chemical action, chemical affinity,
chemical combination: the most irresistible of all natural
forces. Well, youre attracting me irresistibly. Chemically.

GLORIA [*contemptuously*] Nonsense!

VALENTINE. Of course it's nonsense, you stupid girl. [*Gloria
recoils in outraged surprise*]. Yes, stupid girl: thats a scientific
fact, anyhow. Youre a prig: a feminine prig: thats what
you are. [*Rising*] Now I suppose youve done with me for

ever. [*He goes to the iron table and takes up his hat*].

GLORIA [*with elaborate calm, sitting up like a High-school mistress posing to be photographed*] That shews how very little you understand my real character. I am not in the least offended. [*He pauses and puts his hat down again*]. I am always willing to be told my own defects, Mr Valentine, by my friends, even when they are as absurdly mistaken about me as you are. I have many faults – very serious faults – of character and temper; but if there is one thing that I am not, it is what you call a prig. [*She closes her lips trimly and looks steadily and challengingly at him as she sits more collectedly than ever*].

VALENTINE [*returning to the end of the garden seat to confront her more emphatically*] Oh yes, you are. My reason tells me so: my knowledge tells me so: my experience tells me so.

GLORIA. Excuse my reminding you that your reason and your knowledge and your experience are not infallible. At least I hope not.

VALENTINE. I must believe them. Unless you wish me to believe my eyes, my heart, my instincts, my imagination, which are all telling me the most monstrous lies about you.

GLORIA [*the collectedness beginning to relax*] Lies!

VALENTINE [*obstinately*] Yes, lies. [*He sits down again beside her*] Do you expect me to believe that you are the most beautiful woman in the world?

GLORIA. That is ridiculous, and rather personal.

VALENTINE. Of course it's ridiculous. Well, thats what my eyes tell me. [*Gloria makes a movement of contemptuous protest*]. No: I'm not flattering. I tell you I dont believe it. [*She is ashamed to find that this does not quite please her either*]. Do you think that if you were to turn away in disgust from my weakness, I should sit down here and cry like a child?

GLORIA [*beginning to find that she must speak shortly and pointedly to keep her voice steady*] Why should you, pray?

VALENTINE. Of course not: I'm not such an idiot. And yet my heart tells me I should: my fool of a heart. But I'll argue with my heart and bring it to reason. If I loved you a thousand times, I'll force myself to look the truth steadily in the face. After all, it's easy to be sensible: the facts are the facts. Whats this place? it's not heaven: it's the Marine Hotel. Whats the time? it's not eternity: it's about half past one in the afternoon. What am I? a dentist: a five shilling dentist!

GLORIA. And I am a feminine prig.

VALENTINE [*passionately*] No, no: I cant face that: I must have one illusion left: the illusion about you. I love you. [*He turns towards her as if the impulse to touch her were ungovernable: she rises and stands on her guard wrathfully. He springs up impatiently and retreats a step*]. Oh, what a fool I am! an idiot! You dont understand: I might as well talk to the stones on the beach. [*He turns away, discouraged*].

GLORIA [*reassured by his withdrawal, and a little remorseful*] I am sorry. I do not mean to be unsympathetic, Mr Valentine; but what can I say?

VALENTINE [*returning to her with all his recklessness of manner replaced by an engaging and chivalrous respect*] You can say nothing, Miss Clandon. I beg your pardon: it was my own fault, or rather my own bad luck. You see, it all depended on your naturally liking me. [*She is about to speak: he stops her deprecatingly*] Oh, I know you mustnt tell me whether you like me or not; but –

GLORIA [*her principles up in arms at once*] Must not! Why not? I am a free woman: why should I not tell you?

VALENTINE [*pleading in terror, and retreating*] Dont. I'm afraid to hear.

GLORIA [*no longer scornful*] You need not be afraid. I think you are sentimental, and a little foolish; but I like you.

VALENTINE [*dropping into the nearest chair as if crushed*] Then it's all over. [*He becomes the picture of despair*].

GLORIA [*puzzled, approaching him*] But why?

VALENTINE. Because liking is not enough. Now that I think down into it seriously, I dont know whether I like you or not.

GLORIA [*looking down at him with wondering concern*] I'm sorry.

VALENTINE [*in an agony of restrained passion*] Oh, dont pity me. Your voice is tearing my heart to pieces. Let me alone, Gloria. You go down into the very depths of me, troubling and stirring me. I cant struggle with it. I cant tell you –

GLORIA [*breaking down suddenly*] Oh, stop telling me what you feel: I cant bear it.

VALENTINE [*springing up triumphantly, the agonized voice now solid, ringing, and jubilant*] Ah, it's come at last: my moment of courage. [*He seizes her hands: she looks at him in terror*]. Our moment of courage! [*He draws her to him; kisses her with impetuous strength; and laughs boyishly*]. Now youve done it, Gloria. It's all over: we're in love with one another. [*She can only gasp at him*]. But what a dragon you were! And how hideously afraid I was!

PHILIP'S VOICE [*calling from the beach*] Valentine!

DOLLY'S VOICE. Mr Valentine!

VALENTINE. Goodbye. Forgive me. [*He rapidly kisses her hands and runs away to the steps, where he meets Mrs Clandon ascending*].

    Gloria, quite lost, can only stare after him.

MRS CLANDON. The children want you, Mr Valentine. [*She looks anxiously around*]. Is he gone?

VALENTINE [*puzzled*] He? [*Recollecting*] Oh, Crampton. Gone this long time, Mrs Clandon. [*He runs off buoyantly down the steps*].

GLORIA [*sinking upon the bench*] Mother!

MRS CLANDON [*hurrying to her in alarm*] What is it, dear?

GLORIA [*with heartfelt appealing reproach*] Why didnt you educate me properly?

MRS CLANDON [*amazed*] My child: I did my best.

GLORIA. Oh, you taught me nothing: nothing.

MRS CLANDON. What is the matter with you?

GLORIA [*with the most intense expression*] Only shame! shame!! shame!!! [*Blushing unendurably, she covers her face with her hands and turns away from her mother*].

ACT III

The Clandons' sitting room in the hotel. An expensive apartment on the ground floor, with a French window leading to the garden. In the centre of the room is a substantial table, surrounded by chairs, and draped with a maroon cloth on which opulently bound hotel and railway guides are displayed. A visitor entering through the window and coming down to this central table would have the fireplace on his left, and a writing table against the wall on his right, next the door, which is further down. He would, if his taste lay that way, admire the wall decoration of Lincrusta Walton in plum color and bronze lacquer, with dado and cornice; the ormolu consoles in the corners; the vases on pillar pedestals of veined marble with bases of polished black wood, one on each side of the window; the ornamented cabinet next the vase on the side nearest the fireplace, its centre compartment closed by an inlaid door, and its corners rounded off with curved panes of glass protecting shelves of cheap blue and white pottery; the bamboo tea table, with folding shelves, in the corresponding space on the other side of the window; the photogravures after Burton and Stacy Marks; the saddlebag ottoman in line with the door but on the other side of the room; the two comfortable seats of the same pattern on the hearth-rug; and finally, on turning round and looking up, the massive brass pole above the window, sustaining a pair of maroon rep curtains with decorated borders of staid green. Altogether, a room well arranged to flatter the middle-class occupant's sense of gentility, and reconcile him to a charge of a pound a day for its use.

Mrs Clandon sits at the writing table, correcting proofs. Gloria is standing at the window, looking out in a tormented revery.

The clock on the mantelpiece strikes five with a sickly clink, the bell being unable to bear up against the black marble cenotaph in which it is immured.

MRS CLANDON. Five! I dont think we need wait any longer for the children. They are sure to get tea somewhere.
GLORIA [*wearily*] Shall I ring?
MRS CLANDON. Do, my dear. [*Gloria goes to the hearth and rings*]. I have finished these proofs at last, thank goodness!

GLORIA [*strolling listlessly across the room and coming behind her mother's chair*] What proofs?

MRS CLANDON. The new edition of Twentieth Century Women.

GLORIA [*with a bitter smile*] Theres a chapter missing.

MRS CLANDON [*beginning to hunt among her proofs*] Is there? Surely not.

GLORIA. I mean an unwritten one. Perhaps I shall write it for you – when I know the end of it. [*She goes back to the window*].

MRS CLANDON. Gloria! More enigmas!

GLORIA. Oh no. The same enigma.

MRS CLANDON [*puzzled and rather troubled; after watching her for a moment*] My dear?

GLORIA [*returning*] Yes.

MRS CLANDON. You know I never ask questions.

GLORIA [*kneeling beside her chair*] I know, I know. [*She suddenly throws her arm about her mother and embraces her almost passionately*].

MRS CLANDON [*gently, smiling but embarrassed*] My dear: you are getting quite sentimental.

GLORIA [*recoiling*] Ah no, no. Oh, dont say that. Oh! [*She rises and turns away with a gesture as if tearing herself*].

MRS CLANDON [*mildly*] My dear: what is the matter? What – *The waiter enters with the tea-tray.*

WAITER [*balmily*] Was this what you rang for, maam?

MRS CLANDON. Thank you, yes. [*She turns her chair away from the writing table, and sits down again. Gloria crosses to the hearth and sits crouching there with her face averted*].

WAITER [*placing the tray temporarily on the centre table*] I thought so, maam. Curious how the nerves seem to give out in the afternoon without a cup of tea. [*He fetches the tea table and places it in front of Mrs Clandon, conversing meanwhile*]. The young lady and gentleman have just come back, maam: they have been out in a boat, maam. Very pleasant on a fine afternoon like this: very pleasant and invigorating indeed. [*He takes the tray from the centre table and puts it on the tea table*]. Mr M'Comas will not come to tea, maam: he has gone to call upon Mr Crampton. [*He takes a couple of chairs and sets one at each end of the tea table*].

GLORIA [*looking round with an impulse of terror*] And the other gentleman?

WAITER [*reassuringly, as he unconsciously drops for a moment into the measure of 'Ive been roaming,' which he sang when a boy*] Oh, he's coming, miss: he's coming. He has been rowing the boat, miss, and has just run down the road to the chemist's for something to put on the blisters. But he will be here directly, miss: directly. [*Gloria, in ungovernable apprehension, rises and hurries towards the door*].

MRS CLANDON [*half rising*] Glo –

Gloria goes out. Mrs Clandon looks perplexedly at the waiter, whose composure is unruffled.

WAITER [*cheerfully*] Anything more, maam?

MRS CLANDON. Nothing, thank you.

WAITER. Thank you, maam. [*As he withdraws, Phil and Dolly, in the highest spirits, come tearing in. He holds the door open for them: then goes out and closes it*].

DOLLY [*ravenously*] Oh, give me some tea. [*Mrs Clandon pours out a cup for her*]. Weve been out in a boat. Valentine will be here presently.

PHILIP. He is unaccustomed to navigation. Wheres Gloria?

MRS CLANDON [*anxiously, as she pours out his tea*] Phil: there is something the matter with Gloria. Has anything happened? [*Phil and Dolly look at one another and stifle a laugh*]. What is it?

PHILIP [*sitting down on her left*] Romeo –

DOLLY [*sitting down on her right*] – and Juliet.

PHILIP [*taking his cup of tea from Mrs Clandon*] Yes, my dear mother: the old, old story. Dolly: dont take all the milk [*he deftly takes the jug from her*]. Yes: in the spring –

DOLLY. – a young man's fancy –

PHILIP. – lightly turns to – thank you [*to Mrs Clandon, who has passed the biscuits*] – thoughts of love. It also occurs in the autumn. The young man in this case is –

DOLLY. Valentine.

PHILIP. And his fancy has turned to Gloria to the extent of –

DOLLY. – kissing her –

PHILIP. – on the terrace –

DOLLY [*correcting him*] – on the lips, before everybody.

MRS CLANDON [*incredulously*] Phil! Dolly! Are you joking? [*They shake their heads*]. Did she allow it?

PHILIP. We waited to see him struck to earth by the lightning of her scorn; but –

DOLLY. – but he wasnt.

PHILIP. She appeared to like it.

DOLLY. As far as we could judge. [*Stopping Phil, who is about to pour out another cup*] No: youve sworn off two cups.

MRS CLANDON [*much troubled*] Children: you must not be here when Mr Valentine comes. I must speak very seriously to him about this.

PHILIP. To ask him his intentions? What a violation of Twentieth Century principles!

DOLLY. Quite right, mamma: bring him to book. Make the most of the nineteenth century while it lasts.

PHILIP. Sh! Here he is.

VALENTINE [*entering*] Very sorry to be late, Mrs Clandon. [*She takes up the tea-pot*]. No, thank you: I never take any. No doubt Miss Dolly and Phil have explained what happened to me.

PHILIP [*momentously, rising*] Yes, Valentine: we have explained.

DOLLY [*significantly, also rising*] We have explained very thoroughly.

PHILIP. It was our duty. [*Very seriously*] Come, Dolly. [*He offers Dolly his arm, which she takes. They look sadly at him, and go out gravely arm in arm, leaving Valentine staring*].

MRS CLANDON [*rising and leaving the tea table*] Will you sit down, Mr Valentine. I want to speak to you a little, if you will allow me. [*Valentine goes slowly to the ottoman, his conscience presaging a bad quarter of an hour. Mrs Clandon takes Phil's chair, and seats herself with gentle dignity. Valentine sits down*]. I must begin by throwing myself somewhat on your consideration. I am going to speak of a subject of which I know very little: perhaps nothing. I mean love.

VALENTINE. Love!

MRS CLANDON. Yes, love. Oh, you need not look so alarmed as that, Mr Valentine: I am not in love with you.

VALENTINE [*overwhelmed*] Oh, really, Mrs – [*Recovering himself*] I should be only too proud if you were.

MRS CLANDON. Thank you, Mr Valentine. But I am too old to begin.

VALENTINE. Begin! Have you never –?

MRS CLANDON. Never. My case is a very common one, Mr Valentine. I married before I was old enough to know what I was doing. As you have seen for yourself, the result was a bitter disappointment for both my husband and myself. So you see, though I am a married woman, I have never been in love; I have never had a love affair; and, to be quite frank with you Mr Valentine, what I have seen of the love affairs of other people has not led me to regret that deficiency in my experience. [*Valentine, looking very glum, glances sceptically at her, and says nothing. Her color rises a little; and she adds, with restrained anger*] You do not believe me?

VALENTINE [*confused at having his thought read*] Oh, why not? Why not?

MRS CLANDON. Let me tell you, Mr Valentine, that a life devoted to the Cause of Humanity has enthusiasms and passions to offer which far transcend the selfish personal infatuations and sentimentalities of romance. Those are not your enthusiasms and passions, I take it? [*Valentine, quite aware that she despises him for it, answers in the negative with a melancholy shake of his head*]. I thought not. Well, I am equally at a disadvantage in discussing those so-called affairs of the heart in which you appear to be an expert.

VALENTINE [*restlessly*] What are you driving at, Mrs Clandon?

MRS CLANDON. I think you know.

VALENTINE. Gloria?

MRS CLANDON. Yes. Gloria.

VALENTINE [*surrendering*] Well, yes: I'm in love with Gloria. [*Interposing as she is about to speak*] I know what youre going to say: Ive no money.

MRS CLANDON. I care very little about money, Mr Valentine.

VALENTINE. Then youre very different to all the other mothers who have interviewed me.

MRS CLANDON. Ah, now we are coming to it, Mr Valentine. You are an old hand at this. [*He opens his mouth to protest: she cuts him short with some indignation*]. Oh, do you think, little as I understand these matters, that I have not common sense enough to know that a man who could make as much way in one interview with such a woman as my daughter, can hardly be a novice?

VALENTINE. I can assure you –

MRS CLANDON [*stopping him*] I am not blaming you, Mr Valentine. It is Gloria's business to take care of herself, and you have a right to amuse yourself as you please. But –

VALENTINE [*protesting*] Amuse myself! Oh, Mrs Clandon!

MRS CLANDON [*relentlessly*] On your honor, Mr Valentine, are you in earnest?

VALENTINE [*desperately*] On my honor I am in earnest. [*She looks searchingly at him. His sense of humor gets the better of him; and he adds quaintly*] Only, I always have been in earnest; and yet – ! Well, here I am, you see.

MRS CLANDON. This is just what I suspected. [*Severely*] Mr Valentine: you are one of those men who play with women's affections.

VALENTINE. Well, why not, if the Cause of Humanity is the only thing worth being serious about? However, I understand. [*Rising and taking his hat with formal politeness*] You wish me to discontinue my visits.

MRS CLANDON. No: I am sensible enough to be well aware that Gloria's best chance of escape from you now is to become better acquainted with you.

VALENTINE [*unaffectedly alarmed*] Oh, dont say that, Mrs Clandon. You dont think that, do you?

MRS CLANDON. I have great faith, Mr Valentine, in the

sound training Gloria's mind has had since she was a child.

VALENTINE [*amazingly relieved*] O-oh! Oh, thats all right. [*He sits down again and throws his hat flippantly aside with the air of a man who has no longer anything to fear*].

MRS CLANDON [*indignant at his assurance*] What do you mean?

VALENTINE [*turning confidentially to her*] Come! shall I teach you something, Mrs Clandon?

MRS CLANDON [*stiffly*] I am always willing to learn.

VALENTINE. Have you ever studied the subject of gunnery? artillery? cannons and war-ships and so on?

MRS CLANDON. Has gunnery anything to do with Gloria?

VALENTINE. A great deal. By way of illustration. During this whole century, my dear Mrs Clandon, the progress of artillery has been a duel between the maker of cannons and the maker of armor plates to keep the cannon balls out. You build a ship proof against the best gun known: somebody makes a better gun and sinks your ship. You build a heavier ship, proof against that gun: somebody makes a heavier gun and sinks you again. And so on. Well, the duel of sex is just like that.

MRS CLANDON. The duel of sex!

VALENTINE. Yes: youve heard of the duel of sex, havnt you? Oh, I forgot: youve been in Madeira: the expression has come up since your time. Need I explain it?

MRS CLANDON [*contemptuously*] No.

VALENTINE. Of course not. Now what happens in the duel of sex? The old fashioned daughter received an old fashioned education to protect her against the wiles of man. Well, you know the result: the old fashioned man got round her. The old fashioned mother resolved to protect her daughter more effectually – to find some armor too strong for the old fashioned man. So she gave her daughter a scientific education: your plan. That was a corker for the old fashioned man: he thought it unfair, and tried to howl it down as unwomanly and all the rest of it. But that didnt do him any good. So he had to give up his old fashioned plan of attack: you know: going down on his knees and swearing to love, honor, and obey and so on.

MRS CLANDON. Excuse me: that was what the woman swore.

VALENTINE. Was it? Ah, perhaps youre right. Yes: of course it was. Well, what did the man do? Just what the artillery man does: went one better than the woman: educated himself scientifically and beat her at that game just as he had beaten her at the old game. I learnt how to circumvent the Women's Rights woman before I was twenty-three: it's all been found out long ago. You see, my methods are thoroughly modern.

MRS CLANDON [with quiet disgust] No doubt.

VALENTINE. But for that very reason theres one sort of girl against whom they are of no use.

MRS CLANDON. Pray which sort?

VALENTINE. The thoroughly old fashioned girl. If you had brought up Gloria in the old way, it would have taken me eighteen months to get to the point I got to this afternoon in eighteen minutes. Yes, Mrs Clandon: the Higher Education of Women delivered Gloria into my hands; and it was you who taught her to believe in the Higher Education of Women.

MRS CLANDON [rising] Mr Valentine: you are very clever.

VALENTINE [rising also] Oh, Mrs Clandon!

MRS CLANDON. And you have taught me – n o t h i n g. Goodbye.

VALENTINE [horrified] Goodbye! Oh, maynt I see her before I go?

MRS CLANDON. I am afraid she will not return until you have gone, Mr Valentine. She left the room expressly to avoid you.

VALENTINE [thoughtfully] Thats a good sign. Goodbye. [He bows and makes for the door, apparently well satisfied].

MRS CLANDON [alarmed] Why do you think it a good sign?

VALENTINE [turning near the door] Because I am mortally afraid of her; and it looks as if she were mortally afraid of me.

He turns to go and finds himself face to face with Gloria, who has just entered. She looks steadfastly at him. He stares helplessly at her; then round at Mrs Clandon; then at Gloria again, completely at a loss.

GLORIA [*white, and controlling herself with difficulty*] Mother: is what Dolly told me true?

MRS CLANDON. What did she tell you, dear?

GLORIA. That you have been speaking about me to this gentleman?

VALENTINE [*murmuring*] This gentleman! Oh!

MRS CLANDON [*sharply*] Mr Valentine: can you hold your tongue for a moment?

He looks piteously at them; then, with a despairing shrug, goes back to the ottoman and throws his hat on it.

GLORIA [*confronting her mother, with deep reproach*] Mother: what right had you to do it?

MRS CLANDON. I dont think I have said anything I have no right to say, Gloria.

VALENTINE [*confirming her officiously*] Nothing. Nothing whatever. [*The two women look at him crushingly*]. I beg your pardon. [*He sits down ignominiously on the ottoman*].

GLORIA. I cannot believe that anyone has any right even to think about things that concern me only. [*She turns away from them to conceal a painful struggle with her emotion*].

MRS CLANDON. My dear: if I have wounded your pride –

GLORIA [*turning on them for a moment*] My pride! My pride!! Oh, it's gone: I have learnt now that I have no strength to be proud of. [*Turning away again*] But if a woman cannot protect herself, no one can protect her. No one has any right to try: not even her mother. I know I have lost your confidence, just as I have lost this man's respect; – [*She stops to regain command of her voice*].

VALENTINE. This man! Oh!

MRS CLANDON. Pray be silent, sir.

GLORIA [*continuing*] – but I have at least the right to be left alone in my disgrace. I am one of those weak creatures born to be mastered by the first man whose eye is caught by them; and I must fulfil my destiny, I suppose. At least spare me the humiliation of trying to save me. [*She sits down, with her handkerchief to her eyes, at the further end of the table*].

VALENTINE [*jumping up*] Look here –

MRS CLANDON [*severely*] Mr Va –

VALENTINE [*recklessly*] No: I will speak: Ive been silent for nearly thirty seconds. [*He goes resolutely to Gloria*]. Miss Clandon –

GLORIA [*bitterly*] Oh, not Miss Clandon: you have found it quite safe to call me Gloria.

VALENTINE. No I wont: youll throw it in my teeth afterwards and accuse me of disrespect. I say it's a heart-breaking falsehood that I dont respect you. It's true that I didnt respect your old pride: why should I? it was nothing but cowardice. I didnt respect your intellect: Ive a better one myself: it's a masculine speciality. But when the depths stirred! when my moment came! when you made me brave! ah, then! then!! then!!!

GLORIA. Then you respected me, I suppose.

VALENTINE. No I didnt: I adored you. [*She rises quickly and turns her back on him*]. And you can never take that moment away from me. So now I dont care what happens. [*He comes back to the ottoman, addressing a cheerful explanation to nobody in particular*] I'm perfectly aware that I'm talking nonsense. I cant help it. [*To Mrs Clandon*] I love Gloria; and theres an end of it.

MRS CLANDON [*emphatically*] Mr Valentine: you are a most dangerous man. Gloria: come here. [*Gloria, wondering a little at the command, obeys, and stands, with drooping head, on her mother's right hand, Valentine being on the opposite side. Mrs Clandon then begins, with intense scorn*] Ask this man whom you have inspired and made brave, how many women have inspired him before [*Gloria looks up suddenly with a flash of jealous anger and amazement*]; how many times he has laid the trap in which he has caught you; how often he has baited it with the same speeches; how much practice it has taken to make him perfect in his chosen part in life as the Duellist of Sex.

VALENTINE. This isnt fair. Youre abusing my confidence, Mrs Clandon.

MRS CLANDON. Ask him, Gloria.

GLORIA [*in a flush of rage, going over to him with her fists clenched*] Is that true?

VALENTINE. Dont be angry —

GLORIA [*interrupting him implacably*] Is it true? Did you ever say that before? Did you ever feel that before? for another woman?

VALENTINE [*bluntly*] Yes.

Gloria raises her clenched hands.

MRS CLANDON [*horrified, catching her uplifted arm*] Gloria!! My dear! Youre forgetting yourself.

Gloria, with a deep expiration, slowly relaxes her threatening attitude.

VALENTINE. Remember: a man's power of love and admiration is like any other of his powers: he has to throw it away many times before he learns what is really worthy of it.

MRS CLANDON. Another of the old speeches, Gloria. Take care.

VALENTINE [*remonstrating*] Oh!

GLORIA [*to Mrs Clandon, with contemptuous self-possession*] Do you think I need to be warned now? [*To Valentine*] You have tried to make me love you.

VALENTINE. I have.

GLORIA. Well, you have succeeded in making me hate you: passionately.

VALENTINE [*philosophically*] It's surprising how little difference there is between the two. [*Gloria turns indignantly away from him. He continues, to Mrs Clandon*] I know men whose wives love them; and they go on exactly like that.

MRS CLANDON. Excuse me, Mr Valentine; but had you not better go?

GLORIA. You need not send him away on my account, mother. He is nothing to me now; and he will amuse Dolly and Phil. [*She sits down with slighting indifference, at the end of the table nearest the window*].

VALENTINE [*gaily*] Of course: thats the sensible way of looking at it. Come, Mrs Clandon! you cant quarrel with a mere butterfly like me!

MRS CLANDON. I very greatly mistrust you, Mr Valentine. But I do not like to think that your unfortunate levity of disposition is mere shamelessness and worthlessness; –

GLORIA [*to herself, but aloud*] It is shameless; and it is worthless.

MRS CLANDON [*continuing*] – so perhaps we had better send for Phil and Dolly, and allow you to end your visit in the ordinary way.

VALENTINE [*as if she had paid him the highest compliment*] You overwhelm me, Mrs Clandon. Thank you.

   The waiter returns.

WAITER. Mr M'Comas, maam.

MRS CLANDON. Oh, certainly. Bring him in.

WAITER. He wishes to see you in the reception room, maam.

MRS CLANDON. Why not here?

WAITER. Well, if you will excuse my mentioning it, maam, I think Mr M'Comas feels that he would get fairer play if he could speak to you away from the younger members of your family, maam.

MRS CLANDON. Tell him they are not here.

WAITER. They are within sight of the door, maam; and very watchful, for some reason or other.

MRS CLANDON [*going*] Oh, very well: I'll go to him.

WAITER [*holding the door open for her*] Thank you, maam. [*She goes out. He comes back into the room, and meets the eye of Valentine who wants him to go*]. All right, sir. Only the tea-things, sir. [*Taking the tray*] Excuse me, sir. Thank you, sir. [*He goes out*].

VALENTINE [*to Gloria*] Look here. Youll forgive me, sooner or later. Forgive me now.

GLORIA [*rising to level the declaration more intensely at him*] Never! While grass grows or water runs, never! never!! never!!!

VALENTINE [*unabashed*] Well, I dont care. I cant be unhappy about anything. I shall never be unhappy again,
never, never, never, while grass grows or water runs. The
thought of you will always make me wild with joy. [*Some
quick taunt is on her lips: he interposes swiftly*] No: I never said
that before: thats new.

GLORIA. It will not be new when you say it to the next
woman.

VALENTINE. Oh dont, Gloria, dont. [*He kneels at her feet*].

GLORIA. Get up! Get up! How dare you?

*Phil and Dolly, racing, as usual, for first place, burst into the
room. They check themselves on seeing what is passing. Valentine
springs up.*

PHILIP [*discreetly*] I beg your pardon. Come, Dolly. [*He offers
her his arm and turns to go*].

GLORIA [*annoyed*] Mother will be back in a moment, Phil.
[*Severely*] Please wait here for her. [*She turns away to the
window, where she stands looking out with her back to them*].

PHILIP [*significantly*] Oh, indeed. Hmhm!

DOLLY. Ahah!

PHILIP. You seem in excellent spirits, Valentine.

VALENTINE. I am. [*He comes between them*]. Now look here.
You both know whats going on: dont you?

Gloria turns quickly, as if anticipating some fresh outrage.

DOLLY. Perfectly.

VALENTINE. Well, it's all over. Ive been refused. Scorned.
I'm here on sufferance only. You understand? it's all over.
Your sister is in no sense entertaining my addresses, or
condescending to interest herself in me in any way. [*Gloria,
satisfied, turns back contemptuously to the window*]. Is that
clear?

DOLLY. Serve you right. You were in too great a hurry.

PHILIP [*patting him on the shoulder*] Never mind: youd never
have been able to call your soul your own if she'd married
you. You can now begin a new chapter in your life.

DOLLY. Chapter seventeen or thereabouts, I should imagine.

VALENTINE [*much put out by this pleasantry*] No: dont say

things like that. Thats just the sort of thoughtless remark that makes a lot of mischief.

DOLLY. Oh, indeed? Hmhm!

PHILIP. Ahah! [*He goes to the hearth and plants himself there in his best head-of-the-family attitude*].

M'Comas, looking very serious, comes in quickly with Mrs Clandon, whose first anxiety is about Gloria. She looks round to see where she is, and is going to join her at the window when Gloria comes down to meet her with a marked air of trust and affection. Finally Mrs Clandon takes her former seat, and Gloria posts herself behind it. M'Comas, on his way to the ottoman, is hailed by Dolly.

DOLLY. What cheer, Finch?

M'COMAS [*sternly*] Very serious news from your father, Miss Clandon. Very serious news indeed. [*He passes impressively to the ottoman, and sits down*].

Dolly, duly impressed, follows and sits beside him on his right.

VALENTINE. Perhaps I had better go.

M'COMAS. By no means, Mr Valentine. You are deeply concerned in this. [*Valentine takes a chair from the table and sits astride of it, leaning over the back, near the ottoman*]. Mrs Clandon: your husband demands the custody of his two younger children, who are not of age.

MRS CLANDON [*in quick alarm*] To take Dolly from me?

DOLLY [*touched*] But how nice of him! He likes us, mamma.

M'COMAS. I am sorry to have to disabuse you of any such illusion, Miss Dorothea.

DOLLY [*cooing ecstatically*] Dorothee-ee-ee-a! [*Nestling against his shoulder, quite overcome*]. Oh, Finch!

M'COMAS [*nervously, shrinking away*] No, no, no, no!

MRS CLANDON. The deed of separation gives me the custody of the children.

M'COMAS. It also contains a covenant that you are not to approach or molest him in any way.

MRS CLANDON. Well: have I done so?

M'COMAS. Whether the behaviour of your younger children amounts to legal molestation is a question on which it may

be necessary to take counsel's opinion. At all events, Mr
Crampton not only claims to have been molested; but he
believes that he was brought here by a plot in which Mr
Valentine acted as your agent.

VALENTINE. Whats that? Eh?

M'COMAS. He alleges that you drugged him, Mr Valentine.

VALENTINE. So I did.

M'COMAS. But what did you do that for?

DOLLY. Five shillings extra.

M'COMAS [*to Dolly, short-temperedly*] I must really ask you,
Miss Clandon, not to interrupt this very serious conversation with irrelevant interjections. [*Vehemently*] I insist on
having earnest matters earnestly and reverently discussed.
[*This outburst produces an apologetic silence, and puts M'Comas
himself out of countenance. He coughs, and starts afresh, addressing
himself to Gloria*]. Miss Clandon: it is my duty to tell you
that your father has also persuaded himself that Mr
Valentine wishes to marry you –

VALENTINE [*interposing adroitly*] I do.

M'COMAS [*huffily*] In that case, sir, you must not be surprised
to find yourself regarded by the young lady's father as a
fortune hunter.

VALENTINE. So I am. Do you expect my wife to live on
what I earn? tenpence a week!

M'COMAS [*revolted*] I have nothing more to say, sir. I shall
return and tell Mr Crampton that this family is no place
for a father. [*He makes for the door*].

MRS CLANDON [*with quiet authority*] Finch! [*He halts*]. If Mr
Valentine cannot be serious, you can. Sit down. [*M'Comas,
after a brief struggle between his dignity and his friendship,
succumbs, seating himself this time midway between Dolly and
Mrs Clandon*]. You know that all this is a made up case –
that Fergus does not believe in it any more than you do.
Now give me your real advice: your sincere, friendly advice. You know I have always trusted your judgment. I
promise you the children will be quiet.

M'COMAS [*resigning himself*] Well, well! What I want to say is this. In the old arrangement with your husband, Mrs Clandon, you had him at a terrible disadvantage.

MRS CLANDON. How so, pray?

M'COMAS. Well, you were an advanced woman, accustomed to defy public opinion, and with no regard for what the world might say of you.

MRS CLANDON [*proud of it*] Yes: that is true.

Gloria, behind the chair, stoops and kisses her mother's hair, a demonstration which disconcerts her extremely.

M'COMAS. On the other hand, Mrs Clandon, your husband had a great horror of anything getting into the papers. There was his business to be considered, as well as the prejudices of an old fashioned family.

MRS CLANDON. Not to mention his own prejudices.

M'COMAS. Now no doubt he behaved badly, Mrs Clandon.

MRS CLANDON [*scornfully*] No doubt.

M'COMAS. But was it altogether his fault?

MRS CLANDON. Was it mine?

M'COMAS [*hastily*] No. Of course not.

GLORIA [*observing him attentively*] You do not mean that, Mr M'Comas.

M'COMAS. My dear young lady, you pick me up very sharply. But let me just put this to you. When a man makes an unsuitable marriage (nobody's fault, you know, but purely accidental incompatibility of tastes); when he is deprived by that misfortune of the domestic sympathy which, I take it, is what a man marries for; when, in short, his wife is rather worse than no wife at all (through no fault of her own, of course), is it to be wondered at if he makes matters worse at first by blaming her, and even, in his desperation, by occasionally drinking himself into a violent condition or seeking sympathy elsewhere?

MRS CLANDON. I did not blame him: I simply rescued myself and the children from him.

M'COMAS. Yes; but you made hard terms, Mrs Clandon. You had him at your mercy: you brought him to his knees when you threatened to make the matter public by applying to the Courts for a judicial separation. Suppose he had had that power over you, and used it to take your children away from you and bring them up in ignorance of your very name, how would you feel? what would you do? Well, wont you make some allowance for his feelings? in common humanity.

MRS CLANDON. I never discovered his feelings. I discovered his temper, and his – [*she shivers*] the rest of his common humanity.

M'COMAS [*wistfully*] Women can be very hard, Mrs Clandon.

VALENTINE. Thats true.

GLORIA [*angrily*] Be silent. [*He subsides*].

M'COMAS [*rallying all his forces*] Let me make one last appeal. Mrs Clandon: believe me, there are men who have a good deal of feeling, and kind feeling too, which they are not able to express. What you miss in Crampton is that mere veneer of civilization, the art of shewing worthless attentions and paying insincere compliments in a kindly charming way. If you lived in London, where the whole system is one of false good-fellowship, and you may know a man for twenty years without finding out that he hates you like poison, you would soon have your eyes opened. There we do unkind things in a kind way: we say bitter things in a sweet voice: we always give our friends chloroform when we tear them to pieces. But think of the other side of it! Think of the people who do kind things in an unkind way! people whose touch hurts, whose voices jar, whose tempers play them false, who wound and worry the people they love in the very act of trying to conciliate them, and who yet need affection as much as the rest of us. Crampton has an abominable temper, I admit. He has no manners, no tact, no grace. He'll never be able to gain anyone's affection unless they will take his desire for it on trust. Is he to have none? not even pity? from his own flesh and blood?

DOLLY [*quite melted*] Oh how beautiful, Finch! How nice of you!

PHILIP [*with conviction*] Finch: this is eloquence: positive eloquence.

DOLLY. Oh mamma, let us give him another chance. Let us have him to dinner.

MRS CLANDON [*unmoved*] No, Dolly: I hardly got any lunch. My dear Finch: there is not the least use in talking to me about Fergus. You have never been married to him: I have.

M'COMAS [*to Gloria*] Miss Clandon: I have hitherto refrained from appealing to you, because, if what Mr Crampton told me be true, you have been more merciless even than your mother.

GLORIA [*defiantly*] You appeal from her strength to my weakness!

M'COMAS. Not your weakness, Miss Clandon. I appeal from her intellect to your heart.

GLORIA. I have learnt to mistrust my heart. [*With an angry glance at Valentine*] I would tear my heart out and throw it away if I could. My answer to you is my mother's answer.

M'COMAS [*defeated*] Well, I am sorry. Very sorry. I have done my best. [*He rises and prepares to go, deeply dissatisfied*].

MRS CLANDON. But what did you expect, Finch? What do you want us to do?

M'COMAS. The first step for both you and Crampton is to obtain counsel's opinion as to whether he is bound by the deed of separation or not. Now why not obtain this opinion at once, and have a friendly meeting [*her face hardens*] or shall we say a neutral meeting? to settle the difficulty? Here? In this hotel? Tonight? What do you say?

MRS CLANDON. But where is the counsel's opinion to come from?

M'COMAS. It has dropped down on us out of the clouds. On my way back here from Crampton's I met a most eminent Q.C.: a man whom I briefed in the case that made his name for him. He has come down here from Saturday to Monday for the sea air, and to visit a relative of his who lives here.

He has been good enough to say that if I can arrange a meeting of the parties he will come and help us with his opinion. Now do let us seize this chance of a quiet friendly family adjustment. Let me bring my friend here and try to persuade Crampton to come too. Come: consent.

MRS CLANDON [*rather ominously, after a moment's consideration*] Finch: I dont want counsel's opinion, because I intend to be guided by my own opinion. I dont want to meet Fergus again, because I dont like him, and dont believe the meeting will do any good. However [*rising*], you have persuaded the children that he is not quite hopeless. Do as you please.

M'COMAS [*taking her hand and shaking it*] Thank you, Mrs Clandon. Will nine o'clock suit you?

MRS CLANDON. Perfectly. Phil: will you ring, please. [*Phil rings the bell*]. But if I am to be accused of conspiring with Mr Valentine, I think he had better be present.

VALENTINE [*rising*] I quite agree with you. I think it's most important.

M'COMAS. There can be no objection to that, I think. I have the greatest hopes of a happy settlement. Goodbye for the present. [*He goes out, meeting the waiter, who holds the door open for him*].

MRS CLANDON. We expect some visitors at nine, William. Can we have dinner at seven instead of half past?

WAITER [*at the door*] Seven, maam? Certainly, maam. It will be a convenience to us this busy evening, maam. There will be the band and the arranging of the fairy lights and one thing or another, maam.

DOLLY. Fairy lights!

PHILIP. A band! William: what mean you?

WAITER. The fancy ball, miss.

DOLLY AND PHILIP [*simultaneously rushing to him*] Fancy ball!!!

WAITER. Oh yes, sir. Given by the regatta committee for the benefit of the Life-boat, sir. [*To Mrs Clandon*] We often have them, maam: Chinese lanterns in the garden, maam: very bright and pleasant, very gay and innocent indeed.

[*To Phil*] Tickets downstairs at the office, sir, five shillings: ladies half price if accompanied by a gentleman.

PHILIP [*seizing his arm to drag him off*] To the office, William!

DOLLY [*breathlessly, seizing his other arm*] Quick, before theyre all sold. [*They rush him out of the room between them*].

MRS CLANDON [*following them*] But they mustnt go off dancing this evening. They must be here to meet – [*She disappears*].

Gloria stares coolly at Valentine, and then deliberately looks at her watch.

VALENTINE. I understand. Ive stayed too long. I'm going.

GLORIA [*with disdainful punctiliousness*] I owe you some apology, Mr Valentine. I am conscious of having spoken to you somewhat sharply. Perhaps rudely.

VALENTINE. Not at all.

GLORIA. My only excuse is that it is very difficult to give consideration and respect when there is no dignity of character on the other side to command it.

VALENTINE. How is a man to look dignified when he's infatuated?

GLORIA [*angrily*] Dont say those things to me. I forbid you. They are insults.

VALENTINE. No: theyre only follies. I cant help them.

GLORIA. If you were really in love, it would not make you foolish: it would give you dignity! earnestness! even beauty.

VALENTINE. Do you really think it would make me beautiful? [*She turns her back on him with the coldest contempt*]. Ah, you see youre not in earnest. Love cant give any man new gifts. It can only heighten the gifts he was born with.

GLORIA [*sweeping round at him again*] What gifts were you born with, pray.

VALENTINE. Lightness of heart.

GLORIA. And lightness of head, and lightness of faith, and lightness of everything that makes a man.

VALENTINE. Yes, the whole world is like a feather dancing in the light now; and Gloria is the sun. [*She rears her head*

291

haughtily]. Beg pardon: I'm off. Back at nine. Goodbye. [*He runs off gaily, leaving her standing in the middle of the room staring after him*].

GLORIA [*at the top of her voice; suddenly furious with him for leaving her*] Idiot!

ACT IV

The same room. Nine o'clock. Nobody present. The lamps are lighted; but the curtains are not drawn. The window stands wide open; and strings of Chinese lanterns are glowing among the trees outside, with the starry sky beyond. The band is playing dance-music in the garden, drowning the sound of the sea.

The waiter enters, shewing in Crampton and M'Comas. Crampton looks cowed and anxious. He sits down wearily and timidly on the ottoman.

WAITER. The ladies have gone for a turn through the grounds to see the fancy dresses, sir. If you will be so good as to take seats, gentlemen, I shall tell them. [*He is about to go into the garden through the window when M'Comas stops him*].

M'COMAS. Stop a bit. If another gentleman comes, shew him in without any delay: we are expecting him.

WAITER. Right, sir. What name, sir?

M'COMAS. Boon. Mr Boon. He is a stranger to Mrs Clandon; so he may give you a card. If so, the name is spelt B.O.H.U.N. You will not forget.

WAITER [*smiling*] You may depend on me for that, sir. My own name is Boon, sir, though I am best known down here as Balmy Walters, sir. By rights I should spell it with the aitch you, sir; but I think it best not to take that liberty, sir. There is Norman blood in it, sir; and Norman blood is not a recommendation to a waiter.

M'COMAS. Well, well: 'True hearts are more than coronets, and simple faith than Norman blood.'

WAITER. That depends a good deal on one's station in life, sir. If you were a waiter, sir, youd find that simple faith would leave you just as short as Norman blood. I find it best to spell myself B. double-O.N., and keep my wits pretty sharp about me. But I'm taking up your time, sir. Youll excuse me, sir: your own fault for being so affable, sir. I'll tell the ladies youre here, sir. [*He goes out into the garden through the window*].

M'COMAS. Crampton: I can depend on you, cant I?

CRAMPTON. Yes, yes. I'll be quiet. I'll be patient. I'll do my best.

M'COMAS. Remember: Ive not given you away. Ive told them it was all their fault.

CRAMPTON. You told me that it was all my fault.

M'COMAS. I told you the truth.

CRAMPTON [*plaintively*] If they will only be fair to me!

M'COMAS. My dear Crampton, they wont be fair to you: it's not to be expected from them at their age. If youre going to make impossible conditions of this kind, we may as well go back home at once.

CRAMPTON. But surely I have a right –

M'COMAS [*intolerantly*] You wont get your rights. Now, once for all, Crampton, did your promise of good behaviour only mean that you wont complain if theres nothing to complain of? Because, if so – [*He moves as if to go*].

CRAMPTON [*miserably*] No, no: let me alone, cant you? Ive been bullied enough: Ive been tormented enough. I tell you I'll do my best. But if that girl begins to talk to me like that and to look at me like – [*He breaks off and buries his head in his hands*].

M'COMAS [*relenting*] There, there: itll be all right, if you will only bear and forbear. Come: pull yourself together: theres someone coming. [*Crampton, too dejected to care much, hardly changes his attitude. Gloria enters from the garden. M'Comas goes to meet her at the window; so that he can speak to her without being heard by Crampton*]. There he is, Miss Clandon. Be kind to him. I'll leave you with him for a moment. [*He goes into the garden*].

Gloria comes in and strolls coolly down the middle of the room.

CRAMPTON [*looking round in alarm*] Wheres M'Comas?

GLORIA [*listlessly, but not unsympathetically*] Gone out. To leave us together. Delicacy on his part, I suppose. [*She stops beside him and looks quaintly down at him*] Well, father?

CRAMPTON [*submissively*] Well, daughter?

They look at one another with a melancholy sense of humor, though humor is not their strong point.

GLORIA. Shake hands. [*They shake hands*].

CRAMPTON [*holding her hand*] My dear: I'm afraid I spoke very improperly of your mother this afternoon.

GLORIA. Oh, dont apologize. I was very high and mighty myself: but Ive come down since: oh, yes: Ive been brought down. [*She sits down on the floor beside his chair*].

CRAMPTON. What has happened to you, my child?

GLORIA. Oh, never mind. I was playing the part of my mother's daughter then; but I'm not: I'm my father's daughter. [*Looking at him forlornly*] Thats a come down, isnt it?

CRAMPTON [*angry*] What! [*Her expression does not alter. He surrenders*]. Well, yes, my dear: I suppose it is, I suppose it is. I'm afraid I'm sometimes a little irritable; but I know whats right and reasonable all the time, even when I dont act on it. Can you believe that?

GLORIA. Believe it! Why, thats myself: myself all over. *I* know whats right and dignified and strong and noble, just as well as she does; but oh, the things I do! the things I do! the things I let other people do!

CRAMPTON [*a little grudgingly in spite of himself*] As well as she does? You mean your mother?

GLORIA [*quickly*] Yes, mother. [*She turns to him on her knees and seizes his hands*]. Now listen. No treason to her: no word, no thought against her. She is our superior: yours and mine: high heavens above us. Is that agreed?

CRAMPTON. Yes, yes. Just as you please, my dear.

GLORIA [*not satisfied, letting go his hands and drawing back from him*] You dont like her?

CRAMPTON. My child: you havnt been married to her. I have. [*She raises herself slowly to her feet, looking at him with growing coldness*]. She did me a great wrong in marrying me without really caring for me. But after that, the wrong was all on my side, I daresay. [*He offers her his hand again*].

GLORIA [*taking it firmly and warningly*] Take care. Thats my dangerous subject. My feelings – my miserable cowardly womanly feelings – may be on your side; but my conscience is on hers.

CRAMPTON. I'm very well content with that division, my dear. Thank you.

Valentine arrives. Gloria immediately becomes deliberately haughty.

VALENTINE. Excuse me; but it's impossible to find a servant to announce one: even the never failing William seems to be at the ball. I should have gone myself; only I havnt five shillings to buy a ticket. How are you getting on, Crampton? Better, eh?

CRAMPTON. I am myself again, Mr Valentine, no thanks to you.

VALENTINE. Look at this ungrateful parent of yours, Miss Clandon! I saved him from an excruciating pang; and he reviles me!

GLORIA [*coldly*] I am sorry my mother is not here to receive you, Mr Valentine. It is not quite nine o'clock; and the gentleman of whom Mr M'Comas spoke, the lawyer, has not yet come.

VALENTINE. Oh yes he has. Ive met him and talked to him. [*With gay malice*] Youll like him, Miss Clandon: he's the very incarnation of intellect. You can hear his mind working.

GLORIA [*ignoring the jibe*] Where is he?

VALENTINE. Bought a false nose and gone to the fancy ball.

CRAMPTON [*crustily, looking at his watch*] It seems that everybody has gone to this fancy ball instead of keeping to our appointment here.

VALENTINE. Oh, he'll come all right enough: that was half an hour ago. I didnt like to borrow five shillings from him and go in with him; so I joined the mob and looked through the railings until Miss Clandon disappeared into the hotel through the window.

GLORIA. So it has come to this, that you follow me about in public to stare at me.

VALENTINE. Yes: somebody ought to chain me up.

Gloria turns her back on him and goes to the fireplace. He takes the snub very philosophically, and goes to the opposite side of the room. The waiter appears at the window, ushering in Mrs Clandon and M'Comas.

MRS CLANDON. I am so sorry to have kept you all waiting.

A grotesquely majestic stranger, in a domino and false nose with goggles, appears at the window.

WAITER [*to the stranger*] Beg pardon, sir; but this is a private apartment, sir. If you will allow me, sir, I will shew you the American bar and supper rooms, sir. This way, sir.

He goes into the garden, leading the way under the impression that the stranger is following him. The majestic one, however, comes straight into the room to the end of the table, where, with impressive deliberation, he takes off the false nose and then the domino, rolling up the nose in the domino and throwing the bundle on the table like a champion throwing down his glove. He is now seen to be a tall stout man between forty and fifty, clean shaven, with a midnight oil pallor emphasized by stiff black hair, cropped short and oiled, and eyebrows like early Victorian horsehair upholstery. Physically and spiritually a coarsened man: in cunning and logic a ruthlessly sharpened one. His bearing as he enters is sufficiently imposing and disquieting; but when he speaks, his powerful menacing voice, impressively articulated speech, strong inexorable manner, and a terrifying power of intensely critical listening, raise the impression produced by him to absolute tremendousness.

THE STRANGER. My name is Bohun. [*General awe*]. Have I the honor of addressing Mrs Clandon? [*Mrs Clandon bows. Bohun bows*]. Miss Clandon? [*Gloria bows. Bohun bows*]. Mr Clandon?

CRAMPTON [*insisting on his rightful name as angrily as he dares*] My name is Crampton, sir.

BOHUN. Oh, indeed. [*Passing him over without further notice and turning to Valentine*] Are you Mr Clandon?

VALENTINE [*making it a point of honor not to be impressed by him*] Do I look like it? My name is Valentine. I did the drugging.

BOHUN. Ah, quite so. Then Mr Clandon has not yet arrived?

WAITER [*entering anxiously through the window*] Beg pardon, maam; but can you tell me what became of that – [*He recognizes Bohun, and loses all his self-possession. Bohun waits rigidly for him to pull himself together*]. Beg pardon, sir, I'm sure, sir. [*Brokenly*] Was – was it you, sir?

BOHUN [*remorselessly*] It was I.

WAITER [*Unable to restrain his tears*] You in a false nose, Walter! [*He clings to a chair to support himself*]. I beg your pardon, maam. A little giddiness –

BOHUN [*commandingly*] You will excuse him, Mrs Clandon, when I inform you that he is my father.

WAITER [*heartbroken*] Oh no, no, Walter. A waiter for your father on top of a false nose! What will they think of you?

MRS CLANDON. I am delighted to hear it, Mr Bohun. Your father has been an excellent friend to us since we came here.

Bohun bows gravely.

WAITER [*shaking his head*] Oh no, maam. It's very kind of you: very ladylike and affable indeed, maam; but I should feel at a great disadvantage off my own proper footing. Never mind my being the gentleman's father, maam: it is only the accident of birth after all, maam. Youll excuse me, I'm sure, having interrupted your business. [*He begins to make his way along the table, supporting himself from chair to chair, with his eye on the door*].

BOHUN. One moment. [*The waiter stops, with a sinking heart*]. My father was a witness of what passed today, was he not, Mrs Clandon?

MRS CLANDON. Yes, most of it, I think.

BOHUN. In that case we shall want him.

WAITER [*pleading*] I hope it may not be necessary, sir. Busy evening for me, sir, with that ball: very busy evening indeed, sir.

BOHUN [*inexorably*] We shall want you.

MRS CLANDON [*politely*] Sit down, wont you?

WAITER [*earnestly*] Oh, if you please, maam, I really must

draw the line at sitting down. I couldnt let myself be seen doing such a thing, maam: thank you, I am sure, all the same. [*He looks round from face to face wretchedly, with an expression that would melt a heart of stone*].

GLORIA. Dont let us waste time. William only wants to go on taking care of us. I should like a cup of coffee.

WAITER [*brightening perceptibly*] Coffee, miss? [*He gives a little gasp of hope*]. Certainly, miss. Thank you, miss: very timely, miss, very thoughtful and considerate indeed. [*To Mrs Clandon, timidly but expectantly*] Anything for you, maam?

MRS CLANDON. Er – yes: it's so hot, I think we might have a jug of claret cup.

WAITER [*beaming*] Claret cup, maam! Certainly, maam.

GLORIA. Oh well, I'll have claret cup instead of coffee. Put some cucumber in it.

WAITER [*delighted*] Cucumber, miss! yes miss. [*To Bohun*] Anything special for you, sir? You dont like cucumber, sir.

BOHUN. If Mrs Clandon will allow me: syphon: Scotch.

WAITER. Right, sir. [*To Crampton*] Irish for you, sir, I think, sir? [*Crampton assents with a grunt. The waiter looks inquiringly at Valentine*].

VALENTINE. I like cucumber.

WAITER. Right, sir. [*Summing up*] Claret cup, syphon, one Scotch and one Irish?

MRS CLANDON. I think thats right.

WAITER [*himself again*] Right, maam. Directly, maam. Thank you. [*He ambles off through the window, having sounded the whole gamut of human happiness, from despair to ecstasy, in fifty seconds*].

M'COMAS. We can begin now, I suppose.

BOHUN. We had better wait until Mrs Clandon's husband arrives.

CRAMPTON. What d'y' mean? I'm her husband.

BOHUN [*instantly pouncing on the inconsistency between this and his previous statement*] You said just now that your name was Crampton.

CRAMPTON. So it is.

MRS CLANDON ⎤ [all four ⎡ I –
GLORIA   ⎟ speaking ⎟ My –
M'COMAS   ⎥ simul-   ⎟ Mrs –
VALENTINE   ⎦ taneously] ⎣ You –

BOHUN [drowning them in two thunderous words] One moment.
    [Dead silence]. Pray allow me. Sit down, everybody. [They
    obey humbly. Gloria takes the saddle-bag chair on the hearth.
    Valentine slips round to her side of the room and sits on the ottoman
    facing the window, so that he can look at her. Crampton sits on the
    ottoman with his back to Valentine's. Mrs Clandon, who has all
    along kept at the opposite side of the room in order to avoid
    Crampton as much as possible, sits near the door, with M'Comas
    beside her on her left. Bohun places himself magisterially in the
    centre of the group, near the corner of the table on Mrs Clandon's
    side. When they are settled, he fixes Crampton with his eye, and
    begins] In this family, it appears the husband's name is
    Crampton: the wife's, Clandon. Thus we have on the very
    threshold of the case an element of confusion.

VALENTINE [getting up and speaking across to him with one knee
    on the ottoman] But it's perfectly simple –

BOHUN [annihilating him with a vocal thunderbolt] It is. Mrs
    Clandon has adopted another name. That is the obvious
    explanation which you feared I could not find out for
    myself. You mistrust my intelligence, Mr Valentine –
    [stopping him as he is about to protest] no: I dont want you to
    answer that: I want you to think over it when you feel
    your next impulse to interrupt me.

VALENTINE [dazed] This is simply breaking a butterfly on a
    wheel. What does it matter? [He sits down again].

BOHUN. I will tell you what it matters, sir. It matters that if
    this family difference is to be smoothed over as we all hope
    it may be, Mrs Clandon, as a matter of social convenience
    and decency, will have to resume her husband's name
    [Mrs Clandon assumes an expression of the most determined obstin-
    acy] or else Mr Crampton will have to call himself Mr
    Clandon. [Crampton looks indomitably resolved to do nothing of

the sort]. No doubt you think that an easy matter, Mr
Valentine. [*He looks pointedly at Mrs Clandon, then at Crampton*]. I differ from you. [*He throws himself back in his chair,
frowning heavily*].

MᶜCOMAS [*timidly*] I think, Bohun, we had perhaps better
dispose of the important questions first.

BOHUN. MᶜComas: there will be no difficulty about the
important questions. There never is. It is the trifles that
will wreck you at the harbor mouth. [*MᶜComas looks as if
he considered this a paradox*]. You dont agree with me, eh?

MᶜCOMAS [*flatteringly*] If I did –

BOHUN [*interrupting him*] If you did, you would be me,
instead of being what you are.

MᶜCOMAS [*fawning on him*] Of course, Bohun, your speciality –

BOHUN [*again interrupting him*] My speciality is being right
when other people are wrong. If you agreed with me I
should be no use here. [*He nods at him to drive the point home;
then turns suddenly and forcibly on Crampton*]. Now you, Mr
Crampton: what point in this business have you most at
heart?

CRAMPTON [*beginning slowly*] I wish to put all considerations
of self aside in this matter –

BOHUN [*cutting him short*] So do we all, Mr Crampton. [*To
Mrs Clandon*] You wish to put self aside, Mrs Clandon?

MRS CLANDON. Yes: I am not consulting my own feelings in
being here.

BOHUN. So do you, Miss Clandon?

GLORIA. Yes.

BOHUN. I thought so. We all do.

VALENTINE. Except me. My aims are selfish.

BOHUN. Thats because you think an affectation of sincerity
will produce a better effect on Miss Clandon than an
affectation of disinterestedness. [*Valentine, utterly dismantled
and destroyed by this just remark, takes refuge in a feeble speechless
smile. Bohun, satisfied at having now effectually crushed all rebel-
lion, again throws himself back in his chair, with an air of being
prepared to listen tolerantly to their grievances*]. Now, Mr

Crampton, go on. It's understood that self is put aside. Human nature always begins by saying that.

CRAMPTON. But I mean it, sir.

BOHUN. Quite so. Now for your point.

CRAMPTON. Every reasonable person will admit that it's an unselfish one. It's about the children.

BOHUN. Well? What about the children?

CRAMPTON [*with emotion*] They have –

BOHUN [*pouncing forward again*] Stop. Youre going to tell me about your feelings, Mr Crampton. Dont. I sympathize with them; but theyre not my business. Tell us exactly what you want: thats what we have to get at.

CRAMPTON [*uneasily*] It's a very difficult question to answer, Mr Bohun.

BOHUN. Come: I'll help you out. What do you object to in the present circumstances of the children?

CRAMPTON. I object to the way they have been brought up.
Mrs Clandon's brow contracts ominously.

BOHUN. How do you propose to alter that now?

CRAMPTON. I think they ought to dress more quietly.

VALENTINE. Nonsense.

BOHUN [*instantly flinging himself back in his chair, outraged by the interruption*] When you are done, Mr Valentine: when you are quite done.

VALENTINE. Whats wrong with Miss Clandon's dress?

CRAMPTON [*hotly to Valentine*] My opinion is as good as yours.

GLORIA [*warningly*] Father!

CRAMPTON [*subsiding piteously*] I didnt mean you, my dear. [*Pleading earnestly to Bohun*] But the two younger ones! you have not seen them, Mr Bohun; and indeed I think you would agree with me that there is something very noticeable, something almost gay and frivolous in their style of dressing.

MRS CLANDON [*impatiently*] Do you suppose I choose their clothes for them? Really, this is childish.

CRAMPTON [*furious, rising*] Childish!

302

M'COMAS		Crampton, you promised –
VALENTINE	*[all rising and speaking together]*	Ridiculous. They dress charmingly.
GLORIA		Pray let us behave reasonably.

Tumult. Suddenly they hear a warning chime of glasses in the room behind them. They turn guiltily and find that the waiter has just come back from the bar in the garden, and is jingling his tray as he comes softly to the table with it. Dead silence.

WAITER *[to Crampton, setting a tumbler apart on the table]* Irish for you, sir. *[Crampton sits down a little shamefacedly. The waiter sets another tumbler and a syphon apart, saying to Bohun]* Scotch and syphon for you, sir. *[Bohun waves his hand impatiently. The waiter places a large jug and three tumblers in the middle]*. And claret cup. *[All subside into their seats. Peace reigns]*.

MRS CLANDON. I am afraid we interrupted you, Mr Bohun.

BOHUN *[calmly]* You did. *[To the waiter, who is going out]* Just wait a bit.

WAITER. Yes, sir. Certainly, sir. *[He takes his stand behind Bohun's chair]*.

MRS CLANDON *[to the waiter]* You dont mind our detaining you, I hope. Mr Bohun wishes it.

WAITER *[now quite at his ease]* Oh no, maam, not at all, maam. It is a pleasure to me to watch the working of his trained and powerful mind: very stimulating, very entertaining and instructive indeed, maam.

BOHUN *[resuming command of the proceedings]* Now, Mr Crampton: we are waiting for you. Do you give up your objection to the dressing or do you stick to it?

CRAMPTON *[pleading]* Mr Bohun: consider my position for a moment. I havnt got myself alone to consider: theres my sister Sophronia and my brother-in-law and all their circle. They have a great horror of anything that is at all – at all – well –

BOHUN. Out with it. Fast? Loud? Gay?

CRAMPTON. Not in any unprincipled sense, of course; but – but – *[blurting it out desperately]* those two children would shock them. Theyre not fit to mix with their own people. Thats what I complain of.

MRS CLANDON [*with suppressed anger*] Mr Valentine: do you think there is anything fast or loud about Phil and Dolly?

VALENTINE. Certainly not. It's utter bosh. Nothing can be in better taste.

CRAMPTON. Oh yes: of course you say so.

MRS CLANDON. William: you see a great deal of good English society. Are my children overdressed?

WAITER [*reassuringly*[Oh dear no, maam. [*Persuasively*] Oh no, sir, not at all. A little pretty and tasty no doubt, but very choice and classy, very genteel and high toned indeed. Might be the son and daughter of a Dean, sir, I assure you, sir. You have only to look at them, sir, to –

At this moment a harlequin and a columbine, waltzing to the band in the garden, whirl one another into the room. The harlequin's dress is made of lozenges, an inch square, of turquoise blue silk and gold alternately. His bat is gilt and his mask turned up. The columbine's petticoats are the epitome of a harvest field, golden orange and poppy crimson, with a tiny velvet jacket for the poppy stamens. They pass, an exquisite and dazzling apparition, between M'Comas and Bohun, and then back in a circle to the end of the table, where, as the final chord of the waltz is struck, they make a tableau in the middle of the company, the harlequin down on his left knee, and the columbine standing on his right knee, with her arms curved over her head. Unlike their dancing, which is charmingly graceful, their attitudinizing is hardly a success, and threatens to end in a catastrophe.

THE COLUMBINE [*screaming*] Lift me down, somebody: I'm going to fall. Papa: lift me down.

CRAMPTON [*anxiously running to her and taking her hands*] My child!

DOLLY [*jumping down, with his help*] Thanks: so nice of you. [*Phil sits on the edge of the table and pours out some claret cup. Crampton returns to the ottoman in great perplexity*]. Oh, what fun! Oh dear! [*She seats herself with a vault on the front edge of the table, panting*]. Oh, claret cup! [*She drinks*].

BOHUN [*in powerful tones*] This is the younger lady, is it?

DOLLY [*slipping down off the table in alarm at his formidable voice and manner*] Yes, sir. Please, who are you?

MRS CLANDON. This is Mr Bohun, Dolly, who has very kindly come to help us this evening.

DOLLY. Oh, then he comes as a boon and a blessing –

PHILIP. Sh!

CRAMPTON. Mr Bohun – M'Comas: I appeal to you. Is this right? Would you blame my sister's family for objecting to it?

DOLLY [*flushing ominously*] Have you begun again?

CRAMPTON [*propitiating her*] No, no. It's perhaps natural at your age.

DOLLY [*obstinately*] Never mind my age. Is it pretty?

CRAMPTON. Yes, dear, yes. [*He sits down in token of submission*].

DOLLY [*insistently*] Do you like it?

CRAMPTON. My child: how can you expect me to like it or to approve of it?

DOLLY [*determined not to let him off*] How can you think it pretty and not like it?

M'COMAS [*rising, scandalized*] Really I must say –

Bohun, who has listened to Dolly with the highest approval, is down on him instantly.

BOHUN. No: dont interrupt, M'Comas. The young lady's method is right. [*To Dolly, with tremendous emphasis*] Press your questions, Miss Clandon: press your questions.

DOLLY [*turning to Bohun*] Oh dear, you are a regular overwhelmer! Do you always go on like this?

BOHUN [*rising*] Yes. Dont you try to put me out of countenance, young lady: youre too young to do it. [*He takes M'Comas's chair from beside Mrs Clandon's and sets it beside his own*]. Sit down. [*Dolly, fascinated, obeys; and Bohun sits down again. M'Comas, robbed of his seat, takes a chair on the other side between the table and the ottoman*]. Now, Mr Crampton, the facts are before you: both of them. You think youd like to have the two youngest children to live with you. Well, you wouldnt – [*Crampton tries to protest; but Bohun will not have it on any terms*] no you wouldnt: you think you would; but I know better than you. Youd want this young lady here to give up dressing like a stage columbine in the evening and like a fashionable columbine in the morning. Well, she wont: never. She thinks she will; but –

DOLLY [*interrupting him*] No I dont. [*Resolutely*] I'll never give up dressing prettily. Never. As Gloria said to that man in Madeira, never, never, never! while grass grows or water runs.

VALENTINE [*rising in the wildest agitation*] What! What! [*Beginning to speak very fast*] When did she say that? Who did she say that to?

BOHUN [*throwing himself back with massive pitying remonstrance*] Mr Valentine –

VALENTINE [*pepperily*] Dont you interrupt me, sir: this is something really serious. I insist on knowing who Miss Clandon said that to.

DOLLY. Perhaps Phil remembers. Which was it, Phil? number three or number five?

VALENTINE. Number five!!!

PHILIP. Courage, Valentine! It wasnt number five: it was only a tame naval lieutenant who was always on hand: the most patient and harmless of mortals.

GLORIA [*coldly*] What are we discussing now, pray?

VALENTINE [*very red*] Excuse me: I am sorry, I interrupted. I shall intrude no further, Mrs Clandon. [*He bows to Mrs Clandon and marches away into the garden, boiling with suppressed rage*].

DOLLY. Hmhm!

PHILIP. Ahah!

GLORIA. Please go on, Mr Bohun.

DOLLY [*striking in as Bohun, frowning formidably, collects himself for a fresh grapple with the case*] Youre going to bully us, Mr Bohun.

BOHUN. I –

DOLLY [*interrupting him*] Oh yes, you are: you think youre not; but you are. I know by your eyebrows.

306

BOHUN [*capitulating*] Mrs Clandon: these are clever children: clear headed well brought up children. I make that admission deliberately. Can you, in return, point out to me any way of inducing them to hold their tongues?

MRS CLANDON. Dolly dearest – !

PHILIP. Our old failing, Dolly. Silence.

Dolly holds her mouth.

MRS CLANDON. Now, Mr Bohun, before they begin again –

WAITER [*softly*] Be quick, sir: be quick.

DOLLY [*beaming at him*] Dear William!

PHILIP. Sh!

BOHUN [*unexpectedly beginning by hurling a question straight at Dolly*] Have you any intention of getting married?

DOLLY. I! Well, Finch calls me by my Christian name.

M'COMAS [*starting violently*] I will not have this. Mr Bohun: I use the young lady's Christian name naturally as an old friend of her mother's.

DOLLY. Yes, you call me Dolly as an old friend of my mother's. But what about Dorothee-ee-a?

M'Comas rises indignantly.

CRAMPTON [*anxiously, rising to restrain him*] Keep your temper, M'Comas. Dont let us quarrel. Be patient.

M'COMAS. I will not be patient. You are shewing the most wretched weakness of character, Crampton. I say this is monstrous.

DOLLY. Mr Bohun: please bully Finch for us.

BOHUN. I will. M'Comas: youre making yourself ridiculous. Sit down.

M'COMAS. I –

BOHUN [*waving him down imperiously*] No: sit down, sit down. *M'Comas sits down sulkily; and Crampton, much relieved, follows his example.*

DOLLY [*to Bohun, meekly*] Thank you.

BOHUN. Now listen to me, all of you. I give no opinion, M'Comas, as to how far you may or may not have committed yourself in the direction indicated by this young lady. [*M'Comas is about to protest*]. No: dont interrupt me:

if she doesnt marry you she will marry somebody else. That is the solution of the difficulty as to her not bearing her father's name. The other lady intends to get married.

GLORIA [*flushing*] Mr Bohun!

BOHUN. Oh yes you do: you dont know it; but you do.

GLORIA [*rising*] Stop. I warn you, Mr Bohun, not to answer for my intentions.

BOHUN [*rising*] It's no use, Miss Clandon: you cant put me down. I tell you your name will soon be neither Clandon nor Crampton; and I could tell you what it will be if I chose. [*He goes to the table and takes up his domino. They all rise; and Phil goes to the window. Bohun, with a gesture, summons the waiter to help him to robe*]. Mr Crampton: your notion of going to law is all nonsense: your children will be of age before you can get the point decided. [*Allowing the waiter to put the domino on his shoulder*] You can do nothing but make a friendly arrangement. If you want your family more than they want you, youll get the worst of the arrangement: if they want you more than you want them youll get the better of it. [*He shakes the domino into becoming folds and takes up the false nose. Dolly gazes admiringly at him*]. The strength of their position lies in their being very agreeable people personally. The strength of your position lies in your income. [*He claps on the false nose, and is again grotesquely transfigured*].

DOLLY [*running to him*] Oh, now you look quite like a human being. Maynt I have just one dance with you? Can you dance?

Phil, resuming his part of harlequin, waves his bat as if casting a spell on them.

BOHUN [*thunderously*] Yes: you think I cant: but I can. Allow me. [*He seizes her and dances off with her through the window in a most powerful manner, but with studied propriety and grace*].

PHILIP. 'On with the dance: let joy be unconfined.' William.

WAITER. Yes, sir.

PHILIP. Can you procure a couple of dominos and false noses for my father and Mr M'Comas?

M'COMAS. Most certainly not. I protest –

CRAMPTON. Yes, yes. What harm will it do, just for once, M'Comas? Dont let us be spoil-sports.

M'COMAS. Crampton: you are not the man I took you for. [*Pointedly*] Bullies are always cowards. [*He goes disgustedly towards the window*].

CRAMPTON [*following him*] Well, never mind. We must indulge them a little. Can you get us something to wear, waiter?

WAITER. Certainly, sir. [*He precedes them to the window, and stands aside there to let them pass out before him*]. This way, sir. Dominos and noses, sir?

M'COMAS [*angrily, on his way out*] I shall wear my own nose.

WAITER [*suavely*] Oh dear yes, sir: the false one will fit over it quite easily, sir: plenty of room, sir, plenty of room. [*He goes out after M'Comas*].

CRAMPTON [*turning at the window to Phil with an attempt at genial fatherliness*] Come along, my boy. Come along. [*He goes*].

PHILIP [*cheerily, following him*] Coming, dad, coming. [*On the window threshold he stops; looks after Crampton; then turns fantastically with his hat bent into a halo round his head, and says with lowered voice to Mrs Clandon and Gloria*] Did you feel the pathos of that? [*He vanishes*].

MRS CLANDON [*left alone with Gloria*] Why did Mr Valentine go away so suddenly, I wonder?

GLORIA [*petulantly*] I dont know. Yes, I do know. Let us go and see the dancing.

They go towards the window, and are met by Valentine, who comes in from the garden walking quickly, with his face set and sulky.

VALENTINE [*stiffly*] Excuse me. I thought the party had quite broken up.

GLORIA [*nagging*] Then why did you come back?

309

VALENTINE. I came back because I am penniless. I cant get out that way without a five-shilling ticket.

MRS CLANDON. Has anything annoyed you, Mr Valentine?

GLORIA. Never mind him, mother. This is a fresh insult to me: that is all.

MRS CLANDON [*hardly able to realize that Gloria is deliberately provoking an altercation*] Gloria!

VALENTINE. Mrs Clandon: have I said anything insulting? Have I done anything insulting?

GLORIA. You have implied that my past has been like yours. That is the worst of insults.

VALENTINE. I imply nothing of the sort, I declare that my past has been blameless in comparison with yours.

MRS CLANDON [*most indignantly*] Mr Valentine!

VALENTINE. Well, what am I to think when I learn that Miss Clandon has made exactly the same speeches to other men that she has made to me? Five former lovers, with a tame naval lieutenant thrown in! Oh, it's too bad.

MRS CLANDON. But you surely do not believe that these affairs – mere jokes of the children's – were serious, Mr Valentine?

VALENTINE. Not to you. Not to her, perhaps. But I know what the men felt. [*With ludicrously genuine earnestness*] Have you ever thought of the wrecked lives, the unhappy marriages contracted in the recklessness of despair, the suicides, the – the – the –

GLORIA [*interrupting him contemptuously*] Mother: this man is a sentimental idiot. [*She sweeps away to the fireplace*].

MRS CLANDON [*shocked*] Oh, my dearest Gloria, Mr Valentine will think that rude.

VALENTINE. I am not a sentimental idiot. I am cured of sentiment for ever. [*He turns away in dudgeon*].

MRS CLANDON. Mr Valentine: you must excuse us all. Women have to unlearn the false good manners of their slavery before they acquire the genuine good manners of their freedom. Dont think Gloria vulgar [*Gloria turns, astonished*]: she is not really so.

GLORIA. Mother! You apologize for me to him!

MRS CLANDON. My dear: you have some of the faults of youth as well as its qualities; and Mr Valentine seems rather too old fashioned in his ideas about his own sex to like being called an idiot. And now had we not better go and see what Dolly is doing? [*She goes towards the window*].

GLORIA. Do you go, mother. I wish to speak to Mr Valentine alone.

MRS CLANDON [*startled into a remonstrance*] My dear! [*Recollecting herself*] I beg your pardon, Gloria. Certainly, if you wish. [*She goes out*].

VALENTINE. Oh, if your mother were only a widow! She's worth six of you.

GLORIA. That is the first thing I have heard you say that does you honor.

VALENTINE. Stuff! Come: say what you want to say and let me go.

GLORIA. I have only this to say. You dragged me down to your level for a moment this afternoon. Do you think, if that had ever happened before, that I should not have been on my guard? that I should not have known what was coming, and known my own miserable weakness?

VALENTINE [*scolding at her passionately*] Dont talk of it in that way. What do I care for anything in you but your weakness, as you call it? You thought yourself very safe, didnt you, behind your advanced ideas? I amused myself by upsetting them pretty easily.

GLORIA [*insolently, feeling that now she can do as she likes with him*] Indeed!

VALENTINE. But why did I do it? Because I was being tempted to awaken your heart: to stir the depth in you. Why was I tempted? Because Nature was in deadly earnest with me when I was in jest with her. When the great moment came, who was awakened? who was stirred? in whom did the depths break up? In myself – myself. I was transported: you were only offended – shocked. You are just an ordinary young lady, too ordinary to allow tame lieutenants to go as far as I went. Thats all. I shall not trouble you with conventional apologies. Goodbye. [*He makes resolutely for the door*].

GLORIA. Stop. [*He hesitates*]. Oh, will you understand, if I tell you the truth, that I am not making advances to you?

VALENTINE. Pooh! I know what youre going to say. You think youre not ordinary: that I was right: that you really have those depths in your nature. It flatters you to believe it. [*She recoils*]. Well, I grant that you are not ordinary in some ways: you are a clever girl [*Gloria stifles an exclamation of rage, and takes a threatening step towards him*] but youve not been awakened yet. You didnt care: you dont care. It was my tragedy, not yours. Goodbye. [*He turns to the door. She watches him, appalled to see him slipping from her grasp. As he turns the handle, he pauses; then turns again to her, offering his hand*]. Let us part kindly.

GLORIA [*enormously relieved, and immediately turning her back on him deliberately*] Goodbye. I trust you will soon recover from the wound.

VALENTINE [*brightening up as it flashes on him that he is master of the situation after all*] I shall recover: such wounds heal more than they harm. After all, I still have my own Gloria.

GLORIA [*facing him quickly*] What do you mean?

VALENTINE. The Gloria of my imagination.

GLORIA [*proudly*] Keep your own Gloria: the Gloria of your imagination. [*Her emotion begins to break through her pride*]. The real Gloria: the Gloria who was shocked, offended, horrified – oh yes, quite truly – who was driven almost mad with shame by the feeling that all her power over herself had broken down at her first real encounter with – with – [*The color rushes over her face again. She covers it with her left hand, and puts her right on his left arm to support herself*].

VALENTINE. Take care. I'm losing my senses again.[*Summoning all her courage, she takes away her hand from her face and puts it on his right shoulder, turning him towards her and looking him straight in the eyes. He begins to protest agitatedly*]. Gloria: be sensible: it's no use: I havnt a penny in the world.

GLORIA. Cant you earn one? Other people do.

VALENTINE [*half delighted, half frightened*] I never could:
youd be unhappy. My dearest love: I should be the
merest fortune-hunting adventurer if – [*Her grip of his
arms tightens; and she kisses him*]. Oh Lord! [*Breathless*] Oh
I – [*he gasps*] I dont know anything about women: twelve
years experience is not enough. [*In a gust of jealousy she
throws him away from her; and he reels back into a chair like a
leaf before the wind*].

*Dolly dances in, waltzing with the waiter, followed by Mrs
Clandon and Finch, also waltzing, and Phil pirouetting by himself.*

DOLLY [*sinking on the chair at the writing-table*] Oh, I'm out
of breath. How beautifully you waltz, William!

MRS CLANDON [*sinking on the saddle-bag seat on the hearth*] Oh,
how could you make me do such a silly thing, Finch! I
havnt danced since the soirée at South Place twenty years
ago.

GLORIA [*peremptorily to Valentine*] Get up. [*Valentine gets up
abjectly*]. Now let us have no false delicacy. Tell my
mother that we have agreed to marry one another.

*A silence of stupefaction ensues. Valentine, dumb with panic,
looks at them with an obvious impulse to run away.*

DOLLY [*breaking the silence*] Number six!

PHILIP. Sh!

DOLLY [*tumultuously*] Oh, my feelings! I want to kiss somebody; and we bar it in the family. Wheres Finch?

M'COMAS. No, positively.

Crampton appears at the window.

DOLLY [*running to Crampton*] Oh, youre just in time. [*She
kisses him*]. Now [*leading him forward*] bless them.

GLORIA. No. I will have no such thing, even in jest. When
I need a blessing, I shall ask my mother's.

CRAMPTON [*to Gloria, with deep disappointment*] Am I to
understand that you have engaged yourself to this young
gentleman?

GLORIA [*resolutely*] Yes. Do you intend to be our friend or –

DOLLY – or our father?

CRAMPTON. I should like to be both, my child. But surely – ! Mr Valentine: I appeal to your sense of honor.

VALENTINE. Youre quite right. It's perfect madness. If we go out to dance together I shall have to borrow five shillings from her for a ticket. Gloria: dont be rash: youre throwing yourself away. I'd much better clear straight out of this, and never see any of you again. I shant commit suicide; I shant even be unhappy. Itll be a relief to me: I – I'm frightened, I'm positively frightened; and thats the plain truth.

GLORIA [determinedly] You shall not go.

VALENTINE [quailing] No, dearest: of course not. But – oh, will somebody only talk sense for a moment and bring us all to reason! I cant. Wheres Bohun? Bohun's the man. Phil: go and summon Bohun.

PHILIP. From the vasty deep. I go. [He makes his bat quiver in the air and darts away through the window].

WAITER [harmoniously to Valentine] If you will excuse my putting in a word, sir, do not let a matter of five shillings stand between you and your happiness, sir. We shall be only too pleased to put the ticket down to you; and you can settle at your convenience. Very glad to meet you in any way, very happy and pleased indeed, sir.

PHILIP [reappearing] He comes. [He waves his bat over the window].

Bohun comes in, taking off his false nose and throwing it on the table in passing as he comes between Gloria and Valentine.

VALENTINE. The point is, Mr Bohun –

M'COMAS [interrupting from the hearth-rug] Excuse me, sir: the point must be put to him by a solicitor. The question is one of an engagement between these two young people. The lady has some property, and [looking at Crampton] will probably have a good deal more.

CRAMPTON. Possibly. I hope so.

VALENTINE. And the gentleman hasnt a rap.

BOHUN [nailing Valentine to the point instantly] Then insist on a settlement. That shocks your delicacy: most sensible precautions do. But you ask my advice; and I give it to you. Have a settlement.

GLORIA [*proudly*] He shall have a settlement.

VALENTINE. My good sir, I dont want advice for myself. Give her some advice.

BOHUN. She wont take it. When youre married, she wont take yours either – [*turning suddenly on Gloria*] oh no you wont: you think you will; but you wont. He'll set to work and earn his living – [*turning suddenly on Valentine*] oh yes you will: you think you wont; but you will. She'll make you.

CRAMPTON [*only half persuaded*] Then, Mr Bohun, you dont think this match an unwise one?

BOHUN. Yes I do: all matches are unwise. It's unwise to be born; it's unwise to be married; it's unwise to live; and it's wise to die.

WAITER [*insinuating himself between Crampton and Valentine*] Then, if I may respectfully put a word in, sir, so much the worse for wisdom!

PHILIP. Allow me to remark that if Gloria has made up her mind –

DOLLY. The matter's settled; and Valentine's done for. And we're missing all the dances.

VALENTINE [*to Gloria, gallantly making the best of it*] May I have a dance –

BOHUN [*interposing in his grandest diapason*] Excuse me: I claim that privilege as counsel's fee. May I have the honor? thank you. [*He dances away with Gloria, and disappears among the lanterns, leaving Valentine gasping*].

VALENTINE [*recovering his breath*] Dolly: may I – [*offering himself as her partner*]?

DOLLY. Nonsense! [*eluding him and running round the table to the fireplace*]. Finch: my Finch! [*She pounces on M'Comas and makes him dance.*]

M'COMAS [*protesting*] Pray restrain – really – [*He is borne off dancing through the window*].

VALENTINE [*making a last effort*] Mrs Clandon: may I –

PHILIP [*forestalling him*] Come, mother. [*He seizes his mother and whirls her away*].

MRS CLANDON [*remonstrating*] Phil, Phil – [*She shares M'Comas's fate*].

CRAMPTON [*following them with senile glee*] Ho! ho! He! he! he! [*He goes into the garden chuckling*].

VALENTINE [*collapsing on the ottoman and staring at the waiter*] I might as well be a married man already.

WAITER [*contemplating the defeated Duellist of Sex with ineffable benignity*] Cheer up, sir, cheer up. Every man is frightened of marriage when it comes to the point; but it often turns out very comfortable, very enjoyable and happy indeed, sir – from time to time. *I* never was master in my own house, sir: my wife was like your young lady: she was of a commanding and masterful disposition, which my son has inherited. But if I had my life to live twice over, I'd do it again: I'd do it again, I assure you. You never can tell, sir: you never can tell.

MORE ABOUT PENGUINS

Penguinews, which appears every month, contains details of all the new books issued by Penguins as they are published. From time to time it is supplemented by *Penguins in Print*, which is a complete list of all books published by Penguins which are in print. (There are well over three thousand of these.)

A specimen copy of *Penguinews* will be sent to you free on request, and you can become a subscriber for the price of the postage. For a year's issues (including the complete lists) please send 4s. if you live in the United Kingdom, or 8s. if you live elsewhere. Just write to Dept EP, Penguin Books Ltd, Harmondsworth, Middlesex, enclosing a cheque or postal order, and your name will be added to the mailing list.

Some other books published by Penguins are described on the following pages.

Note: *Penguinews* and *Penguins in Print* are not available in the U.S.A. or Canada

DEATH OF A SALESMAN

Arthur Miller

'A salesman is got to dream, boy. It comes with the territory.'
But Willy had the wrong dreams. All, all wrong.

Death of a Salesman was written in six weeks in the spring of
1948, but it had been brewing in Miller's mind for ten years.
Its 742 performances put it among the 50 longest recorded
Broadway runs: it received the Pulitzer Prize for Theatre and
was later filmed. Miller himself defined his aim in the play as
being 'to set forth what happens when a man does not have a
grip on the forces of life'.

Also available

THE CRUCIBLE
A VIEW FROM THE BRIDGE
AFTER THE FALL
THE PRICE

THE PENGUIN SHAW

Bernard Shaw's *The Intelligent Woman's Guide to Socialism, Capitalism, Sovietism, and Fascism* was the first Pelican book to be published, in May 1937, and has recently been reissued. Since then many of his plays have been published as Penguins. All of them are complete with Shaw's original prefaces, which put the argument of the play in strong and witty terms and serve as examples of Shaw's individual and assertive prose style. The following are available:

ANDROCLES AND THE LION
also available in the Shaw alphabet edition

THE APPLE CART

BACK TO METHUSELAH

THE DOCTOR'S DILEMMA

HEARTBREAK HOUSE

MAJOR BARBARA

MAN AND SUPERMAN

THE MILLIONAIRESS

PLAYS PLEASANT*
(*Arms and the Man, Candida, The Man of Destiny,
You Never Can Tell*)

PLAYS UNPLEASANT
(*Widowers' Houses, The Philanderer, Mrs Warren's Profession*)

PYGMALION

SAINT JOAN

SELECTED ONE ACT PLAYS (in 2 vols.)

SEVEN ONE ACT PLAYS
(*available in the U.S.A.*)

THREE PLAYS FOR PURITANS *
(*The Devil's Disciple, Cæsar and Cleopatra,
Captain Brassbound's Conversion*)

* *Published as separate plays in the U.S.A.*